ITALIAN

A ROUGH GUIDE DICTIONARY PHRASEBOOK

Compiled by

LEXUS

Credits

Compiled by Lexus with Michaela Masci
Lexus Series Editor: Sally Davies
Rough Guides Phrase Book Editor: Jonathan Buckley
Rough Guides Series Editor: Mark Ellingham

First edition published in 1995 by Rough Guides Ltd, 62–70
Shorts Gardens, London WC2H 9AB.
Reprinted 1995 and 1996.
Revised in 1999.

Distributed by the Penguin Group.

Penguin Books Ltd, 27 Wrights Lane, London W8 5TZ
Penguin Books USA Inc., 375 Hudson Street, New York 10014, USA
Penguin Books Australia Ltd, 487 Maroondah Highway,
PO Box 257, Ringwood, Victoria 3134, Australia
Penguin Books Canada Ltd, Alcorn Avenue,
Toronto, Ontario, Canada M4V 1E4
Penguin Book (NZ) Ltd, 182–190 Wairau Road,
Auckland 10, New Zealand

Typeset in Bembo and Helvetica to an original design by Henry Iles.
Printed in Spain by Graphy Cems.

British Library Cataloguing in Publication Data
A catalogue for this book is available from the British Library.

ISBN 1-85828-578-X

Help us get it right

Lexus and Rough Guides have made great efforts to be accurate and
informative in this Rough Guide Italian phrasebook. However, if you
feel we have overlooked a useful word or phrase, or have any other
comments to make about the book, please let us know. All contributors
will be acknowledged and the best letters will be rewarded with a free
Rough Guide phrasebook of your choice. Please write to 'Italian
Phrasebook Update', at either Shorts Gardens (London) or Hudson Street
(New York) – for full addresses see opposite. Alternatively you can email us
at mail@roughguides.co.uk

Online information about Rough Guides can be found at our Web site
www.roughguides.com

CONTENTS

Introduction

The Rough Guide Italian dictionary phrasebook is a highly practical introduction to the contemporary language. Laid out in clear A–Z style, it uses key-word referencing to lead you straight to the words and phrases you want – so if you need to book a room, just look up 'room'. The Rough Guide gets straight to the point in every situation, in bars and shops, on trains and buses, and in hotels and banks.

The main part of the Rough Guide is a double dictionary: English-Italian then Italian-English. Before that, there's a page explaining the pronunciation system we've used, then a section called **The Basics**, which sets out the fundamental rules of the language, with plenty of practical examples. You'll also find here other essentials like numbers, dates and telling the time.

Forming the heart of the guide, the **English-Italian** section gives easy-to-use transliterations of the Italian words wherever pronunciation might be a problem, and to get you involved quickly in two-way communication, the Rough Guide includes dialogues featuring typical responses on key topics – such as renting a car and asking directions. Feature boxes fill you in on cultural pitfalls as well as the simple mechanics of how to make a phone call, what to do in an emergency, where to change money, and more. Throughout this section, cross-references enable you to pinpoint key facts and phrases, while asterisked words indicate where further information can be found in the Basics.

In the **Italian-English** dictionary, we've given not just the phrases you're likely to hear, but also all the signs, labels, instructions and other basic words you might come across in print or in public places.

Finally the Rough Guide rounds off with an extensive **Menu Reader**, giving a run-down of food and drink terms that you'll find indispensable whether you're eating out, stopping for a quick drink, or browsing through a local food market.

buon viaggio!
have a good trip!

Basics

Pronunciation

In this phrase book, the Italian has been written in a system of imitated pronunciation so that it can be read as though it were English bearing in mind the notes on pronunciation given below:

ay	as in m**ay**	ow	as in n**ow**
e	as in g**e**t	y	as in **y**es
g	always hard as in **g**oat		

Letters given in bold type indicate the part of the word to be stressed.

When double consonants are given in the pronunciation such as j-j, t-t and so on, both consonants should be pronounced, for example **formaggio** [form**a**j-jo], **biglietto** [beel-y**e**t-to].

Abbreviations

adj	adjective	m	masculine
f	feminine	mpl	masculine plural
fpl	feminine plural		

Notes

In the English-Italian section, when two forms of the verb are given in phrases such as: 'can you ...?' **puoi/può...?**, the first is the familiar form and the second the polite form (see the entry for **you** in the dictionary).

In other cases, when two forms are given as in expressions like: 'a few' **alcuni/alcune**, the first form is masculine and the second feminine (see Basics page 10).

An asterisk (★) next to a word in the English-Italian or Italian-English means that you should refer to the Basics section for further information.

Nouns

Italian nouns have one of two genders – masculine or feminine. Generally, nouns ending in **-o** are masculine:

il traghetto	**lo zaino**
eel trag**et**-to	lo tza-**ee**no
the ferry	the rucksack

Nouns ending in **-a** are usually feminine:

la macchina	**la benzina**
la m**a**k-keena	la bentz**ee**na
the car	petrol

Nouns ending in **-e** can be either masculine or feminine:

il ristorante	la chiave
eel reestor**a**ntay	la k-y**a**vay
the restaurant	the key

A number of nouns ending in **-a** are used to refer to both men and women:

l'autista m / f
lowt**ee**sta
the driver

l'artista m / f
lart**ee**sta
the artist

la guida f
la gw**ee**da
the guide

il / la centralinista
eel / la chentraleen**ee**sta
the switchboard operator

Plural Nouns

Generally, to form the plural of a noun:

singular	plural
-o	-i
-a	-e
-e	-i

il biglietto	**i biglietti**
eel beel-**yet**-to	ee beel-**yet**-tee
the ticket	the tickets

la strada	**le strade**
la str**a**da	lay str**a**day
the road	the roads

il dolce	**i dolci**
eel d**o**lchay	ee d**o**lchee
the dessert	the desserts

The following variations are common:

singular	plural
-ca, -ga,	-che, -ghe,
-co, -go	-chi, -ghi
-io	-i
-cia, -gia	-ce, -ge

il parco	**i parchi**
eel p**a**rko	ee p**a**rkee
the park	the parks

l'albicocca	**le albicocche**
lalbeek**o**k-ka	lay albeek**o**k-kay
the apricot	the apricots

il negozio	**i negozi**
eel neg**o**tz-yo	i neg**o**tzee
the shop	the shops

l'arancia
larancha
the orange

le arance
lay aranchay
the oranges

Nouns ending in **-i**, **-u**, a stressed vowel or a consonant do not change in the plural:

il taxi / i taxi
the taxi / the taxis

lo sport / gli sport
the sport / the sports

il film / i film
the film / the films

il tram / i tram
the tram / the trams

il caffè / i caffè
eel kaf-**fay** / ee kaf-**fay**
the coffee / the coffees

la città / le città
la cheet-**ta** / lay cheet-**ta**
the city / the cities

A few other common nouns don't change their ending in the plural:

il cinema / i cinema
eel ch**ee**nema / ee ch**ee**nema
the cinema / the cinemas

la radio / le radio
la r**a**d-yo / lay r**a**d-yo
the radio / the radios

Further common exceptions to the above rules are:

il braccio
eel br**a**cho
the arm

le braccia
lay br**a**cha
the arms

il ciclista
eel cheekl**ee**sta
the cyclist

i ciclisti
ee cheekl**ee**stee
the cyclists

il dito
eel d**ee**to
the finger

le dita
lay d**ee**ta
the fingers

l'uomo
lw**o**mo
the man

gli uomini
l-yee w**o**meenee
the men

l'uovo

lwovo

the egg

le uova

lay wova

the eggs

Articles

The words for articles ('the' and 'a') in Italian vary according to three elements:

the gender of the noun

the first letter of the noun

whether the noun is singular or plural

Masculine articles:

il, un (the, a)
lo, uno (the, a) before **s** + consonant, before **gn, ps** and **z**
l', un (the, a) before a vowel

il / un treno

eel / oon trayno

the / a train

l'albergo / un albergo

lalbairgo / oon albairgo

the hotel / a hotel

lo / uno scontrino

lo / oono skontreeno

the / a receipt

lo / uno specchio

lo / oono spek-yo

the / a mirror

lo / uno zaino

lo / oono tza-eeno

the / a rucksack

Feminine articles:

la, una (the, a)
l', un' (the, a) before a vowel

la / una stanza

la / oona stantza

the / a room

l'autostrada / un'autostrada

lowtostrada / oonowtostrada

the motorway / a motorway

Plural Articles

Masculine plural articles correspond to the singular as follows:

singular	plural
il, un	i, dei (the, some)
lo, uno	gli, degli (the, some)
l', un	gli, degli (the, some)

i / dei pomodori
ee / day pomod**o**ree
the / some tomatoes

i / dei biglietti
ee / day beel-y**e**t-tee
the / some tickets

gli / degli sbagli
l-yee / d**ay**l-yee sb**a**-yee
the / some mistakes

gli / degli scompartimenti
l-yee / d**ay**l-yee skomparteem**e**ntee
the / some compartments

gli / degli adolescenti
l-yee / d**ay**l-yee adolesh**e**ntee
the / some teenagers

Feminine plural articles correspond to the singular as follows:

singular	plural
la, una	le, delle (the, some)
l', un'	le, delle (the, some)

le / delle stanze
lay / d**e**l-lay st**a**ntzay
the / some rooms

le / delle arance
lay / d**e**l-lay ar**a**nchay
the / some oranges

le / delle automobili
lay / d**e**l-lay owtom**o**beelee
the / some cars

Prepositions

When used with certain prepositions the article changes its form. Some common examples are:

	il	lo	la	i	gli	le
a (at, to)	al	allo	alla	ai	agli	alle
da (from)	dal	dallo	dalla	dai	dagli	dalle
di (of)	del	dello	della	dei	degli	delle
in (in)	nel	nello	nella	nei	negli	nelle
su (on)	sul	sullo	sulla	sui	sugli	sulle

alla stazione
al-la statz-**yo**nay
at / to the station

alle terme
al-lay t**ai**rmay
to the thermal baths

nella casa
n**e**l-la k**a**za
in the house

nei treni
nay tr**ay**nee
in the trains

Adjectives and Adverbs

Adjectives must agree in gender and number with the noun they refer to. In the English-Italian section of this book, all adjectives are given in the masculine singular form. Adjectives ending in **-o** change as follows:

	singular	plural
m	piccolo	piccoli
f	piccola	piccole

Adjectives ending in **-e** change as follows:

	singular	plural
m	grande	grandi
f	grande	grandi

In Italian, adjectives are generally placed after the noun:

un ristorante caro
oon reestorantay karo
an expensive restaurant

i biglietti cari
i beel-yet-tee karee
the expensive tickets

una mostra interessante
oona mostra eentaires-santay
an interesting exhibition

una camera singola
a single room

delle scarpe italiane
del-lay skarpay eetal-yanay
some Italian shoes

Some common adjectives sometimes precede the noun:

bello beautiful
brutto ugly
giovane jovanay young
vecchio vek-yo old
nuovo nwovo new
largo wide

stretto narrow
grande granday big
piccolo small
breve brayvay short
lungo long
antico ancient

l'antico duomo
lanteeko dwomo
the ancient cathedral

una grande fetta di torta
oona granday fet-ta dee torta
a large slice of cake

A few adjectives are invariable (i.e. the ending never changes):

un vestito blu / rosa
oon vesteeto bloo / roza
a blue / pink dress

una camicia blu / rosa
oona kameecha bloo / roza
a blue / pink shirt

Comparatives

The comparative is formed by placing **più** (more) or **meno** (less) before the adjective and **di** (than) after it:

grande
granday
large

più grande
p-yoo granday
larger

rumoroso   meno rumoroso

roomor**o**zo   m**ay**no roomor**o**zo

noisy   less noisy

questo albergo è più / meno caro di quello

kw**e**sto alb**ai**rgo ay p-yoo / m**ay**no k**a**ro dee kw**e**l-lo

this hotel is more / less expensive than that one

è più tranquillo qui

ay p-yoo trankw**ee**l-lo kwee

it's quieter here

Superlatives

Superlatives are formed by placing one of the following before the adjective:

il / la più   the most   il / la meno   the least

i / le più   i / le meno

questo itinerario è il meno pericoloso

kw**e**sto eeteenair**a**r-yo ay eel m**ay**no paireekol**o**zo

this route is the least dangerous

la pizzeria Napoli è la più popolare

la peetzair**ee**-a n**a**polee ay la p-yoo popol**a**ray

the Napoli pizza restaurant is the most popular

piazza San Marco è la piazza più famosa di Venezia

p-y**a**tza san m**a**rko ay la p-y**a**tza p-yoo fam**o**za dee ven**e**tz-ya

St Mark's Square is the most famous square in Venice

'As … as' is translated as follows:

questo ristorante è tanto caro quanto quello

kw**e**sto reestor**a**ntay ay t**a**nto k**a**ro kw**a**nto kw**e**l-lo

this restaurant is as expensive as that one

la città non è interessante come pensavo

la cheet-t**a** non ay eentaires-s**a**ntay k**o**may pens**a**vo

this town is not as interesting as I thought

Note also:

è venuto il più in fretta possibile
ay ven**oo**to eel p-yoo een fr**et**-ta pos-s**ee**beelay
he came as soon as he could

■ The superlative form ending in **-issimo** indicates that something is 'very / extremely ...' without comparing it to something else:

bello	**bellissimo**
beautiful	very beautiful
vecchio	**vecchissimo**
v**ek**-yo	vek-k**ee**s-seemo
old	very old

The following two adjectives have irregular comparatives and superlatives:

buono	**migliore**	**il migliore**	**ottimo**
bw**o**no	meel-y**o**ray	eel meel-y**o**ray	**o**t-teemo
good	better	the best	excellent
cattivo	**peggiore**	**il peggiore**	**pessimo**
kat-t**ee**vo	pej-j**o**ray	eel pej-j**o**ray	p**es**-seemo
bad	worse	the worst	extremely bad

Adverbs

If the adjective ends in **-o**, take the feminine form and add **-mente** to form the adverb:

esatto	**esattamente**
es**at**-to	esat-tam**en**tay
exact	exactly

If the adjective ends in **-e**, add **-mente** to form the adverb:

veloce	**velocemente**
vel**o**chay	velochem**en**tay
fast, quick	quickly

Possessive Adjectives

Possessive adjectives, like other Italian adjectives, agree with the noun in gender and number:

		singular		
		m		**f**
my	il mio	eel m**ee**-o	la mia	la m**ee**-a
your (fam)*	il tuo	t**oo**-o	la tua	t**oo**-a
his / her / its / your (pol)*	il suo	s**oo**-o	la sua	s**oo**-a
our	il nostro	n**o**stro	la nostra	n**o**stra
your (pl)*	il vostro	v**o**stro	la vostra	v**o**stra
their	il loro	l**o**ro	la loro	l**o**ro

		plural		
		m		**f**
my	i miei	ee mee-y**ay**	le mie	lay m**ee**-ay
your (fam)*	i tuoi	too-**oy**	le tue	t**oo**-ay
his / her / its / your (pol)*	i suoi	soo-**oy**	le sue	s**oo**-ay
our	i nostri	n**o**stree	le nostre	n**o**stray
your (pl)*	i vostri	v**o**stree	le vostre	v**o**stray
their	i loro	l**o**ro	le loro	l**o**ro

*see **Personal Pronouns** page 20.

la sua stanza	**il suo biglietto**
la s**oo**-a st**a**ntza	eel s**oo**-o beel-y**et**-to
his / her / your room	his / her / your ticket

i miei soldi	**il vostro appartamento**
ee m**ee**-yay s**o**ldee	eel v**o**stro ap-partam**e**nto
my money	your flat (plural)

If when using **il suo / la sua** etc, it is unclear whether you mean 'his', 'her' or 'your', you can use the following instead:

il biglietto di lui	**il biglietto di lei**
eel beel-y**et**-to dee l**oo**-ee	eel beel-y**et**-to dee lay
his ticket	her ticket

When talking about members of your family, the article is always omitted if the noun is singular:

mio marito è malato	**questi sono i miei genitori**
m**ee**-o mar**ee**to ay mal**a**to	kw**e**stee s**o**no ee m**ee**-yay jeneet**o**ree
my husband is ill	these are my parents

Possessive Pronouns

To translate 'mine', 'yours', 'theirs' etc, use the same forms as in the table of possessive adjectives on page 19:

ho già ordinato il mio antipasto	**ho già ordinato il mio**
o ja ordin**a**to eel m**ee**-o anteep**a**sto	I've already ordered mine
I've already ordered my starter	

Personal Pronouns

Subject Pronouns

io	**ee**-o	I
tu[1]	too	you
Lei[2]	lay	you
lui	l**oo**-ee	he, it
lei[2]	lay	she, it
noi	noy	we
voi[3]	voy	you
loro	l**o**ro	they

[1] **tu** is used when speaking to one person and is the familiar form generally used when speaking to family, friends and children

[2] **Lei** is the polite form of address, which is also the same form as the feminine third person singular **lei**; it takes the third person singular of verbs, see **Verbs** page 24.

3 **voi** is both the familiar and polite form used when speaking to more than one person

In Italian, the subject pronoun is usually omitted:

vorrei la ricevuta
vor-r**ay** la reechev**oo**ta
I'd like a / the receipt

è partito
ay part**ee**to
he has left

although it may be retained for emphasis or to avoid confusion:

sono io!
s**o**no **ee**-o
it's me!

siamo noi!
s-y**a**mo noy
it's us!

io pago i panini, tu le birre
ee-o p**a**go ee pan**ee**nee, too lay b**ee**r-ray
I'll pay for the sandwiches, you pay for the beers

lui è inglese e lei è americana
l**oo**-ee ay eengl**ay**zay ay lay ay amaireek**a**na
he is English and she is American

Object Pronouns

me / mi	may / mee	me
te / ti	tay / tee	you
Lei / la*	lay / la	you
lui / lo*	l**oo**-ee / lo	him, it
lei / la*	lay / la	her, it
noi / ci	noy / chee	us
voi / vi	voy / vee	you
loro / li	l**o**ro / lee	them

* These become **l'** when preceding a vowel or silent **h**:

l'ha vista ieri?
la v**ee**sta y**ai**ree
did he see her yesterday?

Object pronouns generally precede the verb. The first form given in the table above is used for emphasis and with prepositions:

la riconosco	**conosco lei, non lui**
la reekonosko	konosko lay non loo-ee
I recognize her	I know her, not him
questa pizza è per me	**non ti sento**
kwesta peetza ay pair may	non tee sento
this pizza is for me	I can't hear you
dallo a lui	**vengo con Lei**
dal-lo a loo-ee	vengo kon lay
give it to him	I'm coming with you

When used with infinitives, pronouns are added to the end of the infinitive and the final **-e** of the infinitive is dropped:

portare to take

può portarmi all'aeroporto?
pwo portarmee all-airoporto
can you take me to the airport?

If you are using an object pronoun to mean 'to me', 'to you' etc (although 'to' might not always be necessary in English), you generally use the following:

mi	mee	(to) me
ti	tee	(to) you
Le	lay	(to) you
gli	l-yee	(to) him, (to) it
le	lay	(to) her, (to) it
ci	chee	(to) us
vi	vee	(to) you
loro	loro	(to) them

ci porti dell'acqua, per favore
chee portee del-lakwa, pair favoray
please bring us some water

Carla gli ha dato i soldi

k**a**rla l-yee a d**a**to ee s**o**ldee

Carla has given him the money

Note that when followed by

lo, la, l', li and le
mi, ti, ci and vi change to
me, te, ce and ve:

Carla me l'ha dato

k**a**rla may la d**a**to

Carla has given it to me

and gli + lo, la, l', li or le becomes glielo, gliela, gliel', glieli, gliele:

Carla glielo ha dato

k**a**rla l-yee-**e**lo a d**a**to

Carla has given it to him

Some verbs taking a direct object in English take an indirect object in Italian: e.g. **telefonare**, **credere** BUT some verbs taking an indirect object in English take a direct object in Italian: e.g. **ascoltare** to listen to, **aspettare** to wait for, etc:

gli telefono domani	**ascoltami!** (direct object)
l-yee tel**a**yfono dom**a**nee	ask**o**ltamee
I'll phone him tomorrow	listen to me!

Reflexive Pronouns

These are used with reflexive verbs like **lavarsi** 'to wash (oneself), to have a wash':

mi	mee	(used with 'I')
ti	tee	(used with familiar 'you')
si	see	(used with he / she / it and formal 'you')
ci	chee	(used with 'we')
vi	vee	(used with plural 'you')
si		(used with 'they')

chiamarsi to be called

mi chiamo...
mee k-**ya**mo
my name is ..., I am called ...

divertirsi to enjoy oneself

mi sono divertito / divertita*
mee s**o**no deevairt**ee**to / deevairt**ee**ta
I enjoyed myself

ci siamo divertiti / divertite*
chee s-y**a**mo deevairt**ee**tee / deevairt**ee**tay
we enjoyed ourselves

* masculine / feminine plural forms of the past participle (see page 27)

Verbs

There are three verb types, recognizable by their endings – **-are**, **-ere** and **-ire**, for example:

portare to carry   **chiedere** to ask   **partire** to leave

Present Tense

The present tense corresponds to 'I leave' and 'I am leaving' in English. To form the present tense for the three main types of verb, remove the endings **-are**, **-ere** and **-ire** and add the endings as given below:

portare to carry, also to bring, to wear

porto	p**o**rto	I carry
porti	p**o**rtee	you carry
porta	p**o**rta	he / she / it carries, you carry
portiamo	port-y**a**mo	we carry
portate	port**a**tay	you carry
portano	p**o**rtano	they carry

24

chiedere	to ask	
chiedo	k-**yay**do	I ask
chiedi	k-**yay**dee	you ask
chiede	k-**yay**day	he / she / it asks, you ask
chiediamo	k-yayd-**ya**mo	we ask
chiedete	k-yayd**ay**tay	you ask
chiedono	k-**yay**dono	they ask

partire	to leave	
parto	**par**to	I leave
parti	**par**tee	you leave
parte	**par**tay	he / she / it leaves, you leave
partiamo	part-**ya**mo	we leave
partite	part**ee**tay	you leave
partono	**par**tono	they leave

See the section on **Subject Pronouns** page 20 for the use of the different words for 'you'.

Some common verbs are irregular:

avere	to have		essere	to be	
ho	o		sono	s**o**no	
hai	i		sei	say	
ha	a		è	ay	
abbiamo	ab-**ya**mo		siamo	s-**ya**mo	
avete	av**ay**tay		siete	s-**yay**tay	
hanno	**a**n-no		sono	s**o**no	

andare	to go		venire	to come	
vado	**va**do		vengo	**ven**-go	
vai	vi		vieni	v-**yay**nee	
va	va		viene	v-**yay**nay	
andiamo	and-**ya**mo		veniamo	ven-**ya**mo	
andate	and**a**tay		venite	ven**ee**tay	
vanno	**va**n-no		vengono	**ven**-gono	

25

fare to do, to make

faccio	facho
fai	fi
fa	fa
facciamo	fachamo
fate	fatay
fanno	fan-no

dovere to have to

devo	dayvo
devi	dayvee
deve	dayvay
dobbiamo	dob-yamo
dovete	dovaytay
devono	dayvono

sapere to know

so	so
sai	si
sa	sa
sappiamo	sap-yamo
sapete	sapaytay
sanno	san-no

bere to drink

bevo	bayvo
bevi	bayvee
beve	bayvay
beviamo	bev-yamo
bevete	bevaytay
bevono	bayvono

dire to say

dico	deeko
dici	deechee
dice	deechay
diciamo	deechamo
dite	deetay
dicono	deekono

potere to be able

posso	pos-so
puoi	pwoy
può	pwo
possiamo	pos-yamo
potete	potaytay
possono	pos-sono

volere to want

voglio	vol-yo
vuoi	vwoy
vuole	vwolay
vogliamo	vol-yamo
volete	volaytay
vogliono	vol-yono

dare to give

do	do
dai	di
dà	da
diamo	d-yamo
date	datay
danno	dan-no

Past Tense:
Perfect Tense

To describe an action that has taken place in the past, use the present tense of either **avere** or **essere** (see page 25) followed by the past participle of the verb to form the perfect tense. The past participle is formed by taking the stem (i.e. the verb minus the **-are**, **-ere** or **ire** ending) of the infinitive and adding the endings as follows:

portare to carry	**vedere** to see	**partire** to leave
portato carried	**veduto** seen	**partito** left

Most verbs take **avere** in the perfect tense:

l'ha venduto	ha finito
la vend**oo**to	a feen**ee**to
he / she has sold it	he / she has finished

non l'ho vista
non lo v**ee**sta
I haven't seen her

Some verbs take essere, for example, some verbs of motion like **andare** 'to go' and all reflexive verbs like **alzarsi** 'to get up'. When **essere** is used, the past participle agrees according to whether the subject of the sentence is masculine, feminine or plural:

è partito	è partita
ay part**ee**to	ay part**ee**ta
he left	she left

sono andati / andate** a Firenze la settimana scorsa
s**o**no and**a**tee / and**a**tay a feer**e**ntzay la set-teem**a**na sk**o**rsa
they went to Florence last week

ci siamo alzati / alzate** alle sette
chee s-y**a**mo altz**a**tee / altz**a**tay **a**l-lay s**e**t-tay
we got up at seven o'clock

sono andato / andata* all'ufficio postale ieri

sono and**a**to / and**a**ta al-loof**ee**cho post**a**lay y**ai**ree

I went to the post office yesterday

* = feminine singular form

** = feminine plural form

The following common verbs use essere to form the perfect tense:

andare	to go	sono andato / andata
arrivare	to arrive	sono arrivato / arrivata
cadere	to fall	sono caduto / caduta
entrare	to enter	sono entrato / entrata
nascere	to be born	sono nato / nata
partire	to leave	sono partito / partita
passare	to pass	sono passato / passata
ritornare	to return	sono ritornato / ritornata
salire	to go up	sono salito / salita
scendere	to go down	sono sceso / scesa
venire	to come	sono venuto / venuta

Some common verbs have irregular past participles:

aprire	to open	aperto
bere	to drink	bevuto
chiedere	to ask	chiesto
chiudere	to close	chiuso
comprendere	to include	compreso
correre	to run	corso
dire	to say	detto
essere	to be	stato
fare	to do, to make	fatto
leggere	to read	letto
mettere	to put	messo
offrire	to offer	offerto
perdere	to lose, to waste	perso or perduto
prendere	to take	preso

ridere	to laugh	riso
scendere	to go down	sceso
scrivere	to write	scritto
spingere	to push	spinto
togliere	to take off	tolto
vedere	to see	visto or veduto
venire	to come	venuto
vivere	to live	vissuto

Imperfect Tense

This is used to describe an action in the past which was repeated, habitual, or often taking place over a period of time. To form the imperfect, change the verb endings as follows:

portare	portavo	portavo	I carried, I was carrying,
	portavi	portavee	I used to carry etc
	portava	portava	
	portavamo	portavamo	
	portavate	portavatay	
	portavano	portavano	

vedere	vedevo	vedayvo	I saw, I was seeing,
	vedevi	vedayvee	I used to see etc
	vedeva	vedayva	
	vedevamo	vedevamo	
	vedevate	vedevatay	
	vedevano	vedevano	

partire	partivo	parteevo	I left, I was leaving,
	partivi	parteevee	I used to leave
	partiva	parteeva	
	partivamo	parteevamo	
	partivate	parteevatay	
	partivano	parteevano	

quando ero studente, vivevo a Padova

kwando **ai**ro stood**e**ntay, veev**ay**vo a p**a**dova

when I was a student, I used to live in Padua

com'era il tempo in Sicilia?

kom**ai**ra eel t**e**mpo een seech**ee**l-ya

what was the weather like in Sicily?

Essere is irregular in the imperfect tense:

ero	**ai**ro	I was, I used to be etc
eri	**ai**ree	
era	**ai**ra	
eravamo	airav**a**mo	
eravate	airav**a**tay	
erano	**ai**rano	

Future Tense

For verbs ending in **-ere** and **-ire**, the future tense is formed by removing the final **-e** from the infinitive and adding the endings as in the tables below:

chiedere to ask

chiederò	k-yaydair**o**	I will ask etc
chiederai	k-yaydair**i**	
chiederà	k-yaydair**a**	
chiederemo	k-yaydair**ay**mo	
chiederete	k-yaydair**ay**tay	
chiederanno	k-yaydair**a**n-no	

partire to leave

partirò	parteer**o**	I will leave etc
partirai	parteer**i**	
partirà	parteer**a**	
partiremo	parteer**ay**mo	
partirete	parteer**ay**tay	
partiranno	parteer**a**n-no	

With verbs ending in **-are**, the **-a-** in the stem changes to **-e-**:

portare to bring

porterò	portair**o**	I will bring etc
porterai	portair**i**	
porterà	portair**a**	
porteremo	portair**aymo**	
porterete	portair**aytay**	
porteranno	portair**an-no**	

comprerò una bottiglia di vino rosso
komprair**o oo**na bot-t**eel**-ya dee v**ee**no r**o**s-so
I'll buy a bottle of red wine

For some irregular verbs, these same endings are added to a modified verb stem:

andare	to go	andrò	I will go etc
avere	to have	avrò	
bere	to drink	berrò	
dovere	to have to	dovrò	
essere	to be	sarò	
fare	to do, to make	farò	
potere	to be able	potrò	
sapere	to know	saprò	
stare	to stay	starò	
tenere	to hold	terrò	
vedere	to see	vedrò	
venire	to come	verrò	
vivere	to live	vivrò	
volere	to want	vorrò	

sarà necessario?
sar**a** neches-s**a**r-yo
will it be necessary?

Frequently in Italian, the present tense can be used instead of the future to refer to a future action (as is often the case in English):

partiamo domani
part-y**a**mo dom**a**nee
we leave tomorrow

When an action is imminent, Italian often uses the present tense where English uses the future:

vengo subito da te
v**e**ngo s**oo**beeto da tay
I'll come to your place straight away

Sometimes the Italian future tense is used to indicate probability:

sarà vero
sar**a** v**ai**ro
it might be true

Negatives

To make a sentence negative, place **non** in front of the verb or pronoun:

capisco   **non capisco**
kap**ee**sko   non kap**ee**sko
I understand   I don't understand

mi piace il gelato / non mi piace il gelato
mee p-y**a**chay eel jel**a**to / non mee p-y**a**chay eel jel**a**to
I like ice cream / I don't like ice cream

sono stato a Roma / non sono stato a Roma
I have been to Rome / I have not been to Rome
abbiamo mangiato bene / non abbiamo mangiato bene
ab-y**a**mo manj**a**to b**ay**nay
we've eaten well / we've not eaten well

When there is no verb, **non** is used as follows:

non molto	**non troppo**
non m**o**lto	non tr**o**p-po
not much	not too much

non nuovo	**non per me, grazie**
non nw**o**vo	non pair may gr**a**tzee-ay
not new	not for me, thanks

In other expressions, when translating words like 'nothing / anything' or 'nobody / anybody', Italian uses double negatives:

non c'è nessuno	**non ne so niente**
non chay nes-s**oo**no	non nay so n-y**e**ntay
there's nobody there	I don't know anything about it
there isn't anybody there	I know nothing about it

non ne voglio nessuno
non nay v**o**l-yo nes-s**oo**no
I don't want any

Imperative

The imperative mood is used to express a command (such as 'come here!', 'let's go' etc). Generally, the imperative forms are similar to those of the present tense. Remove the **-are**, **-ere** or **-ire** ending of the verb and add the endings as below:

	tu	Lei	noi	voi
portare to bring	porta	porti	portiamo	portate
chiedere to ask	chiedi	chieda	chiediamo	chiedete
partire to leave	parti	parta	partiamo	partite

fate presto!	**prenda un opuscolo, è gratis**
f**a**tay pr**e**sto	pr**ay**nda oon op**oo**skolo ay gr**a**tees
hurry up! (**plural**)	take a leaflet, it's free (**polite**)

Pronouns are generally added to the end of the imperative form (although in some cases they precede the imperative):

aspettami!
aspet-tamee
wait for me! (familiar)

mi aspetti!
mee aspet-tee
wait for me! (polite)

The following commonly used imperatives are irregular:

vieni qui!
vyaynee kwee
come here!
(familiar)

venga qui!
venga kwee
come here!
(polite)

va' a casa!
va a kaza
go home!

dimmi la verità!
deem-mee la vaireeta
tell me the truth!

fa' presto!
fa presto
hurry up!

da' questo a Gigi
da kwesto a jee-jee
give this to Gigi

The negative form of the imperative is obtained by placing **non** before the verb; for the **tu** form, however, the verb changes to the infinitive:

non parlare così in fretta!
non parlaray cosee een fret-ta
don't speak so fast! (familiar)

non parli così in fretta!
non parlee cosee een fret-ta
don't speak so fast! (polite)

non fate rumore!
non fatay roomoray
don't be noisy!
don't make any noise! (plural)

Questions

Often word order remains the same in a question, but the intonation changes – the voice should be raised at the end of the question:

parla inglese?
parla eenglayzay
do you speak English?

Word order can also be inverted to form a question. This is always the case when a question word is used:

quando chiude il museo?
kwando k-yooday eel moozay-o
when does the museum close?

è arrivato il pacco?
ay ar-reevato eel pak-ko
has the parcel arrived?

Dates

Use the numbers on pages 36–37 to express the date, except for the first when the ordinal **il primo** should be used:

il primo settembre [eel preemo set-tembray] the first of September

il tre marzo [eel tray martzo] the third of March

il ventuno giugno [eel ventoono yoon-yo] the twenty-first of June

Time

what time is it? che ore sono? [kay oray sono]
one o'clock l'una [loona]
two o'clock le due [lay doo-ay]
it's one o'clock è l'una [ay loona]
it's two o'clock sono le due [sono lay doo-ay]
it's ten o'clock sono le dieci [sono lay dee-echee]

five past one l'una e cinque [**loo**na ay ch**ee**nkway]
ten past two le due e dieci [lay d**oo**-ay ay dee-**e**chee]
quarter past one l'una e un quarto [**loo**na ay oon kw**a**rto]
quarter past two le due e un quarto [lay d**oo**-ay]
half past ten le dieci e mezza [lay dee-**e**chee ay m**e**dza]
twenty to ten le dieci meno venti [lay dee-**e**chee m**ay**no v**e**ntee]
quarter to two le due meno un quarto [lay d**oo**-ay m**ay**no oon kw**a**rto]
at eight o'clock alle otto
at half past four alle quattro e mezza [**a**l-lay kw**a**t-tro ay m**e**dza]
14.00 le quattordici [lay kwat-t**o**rdeechee]
17.30 le diciassette e trenta [lay deechas-s**e**t-tay ay tr**e**nta]
2 a.m. le due di notte [lay d**oo**-ay dee n**o**t-tay]
2 p.m. le due del pomeriggio [pomer**ee**j-jo]
6 a.m. le sei del mattino [lay say]
6 p.m. le sei di sera [dee s**ai**ra]
noon mezzogiorno [medzoj**o**rno]
midnight mezzanotte [medzan**o**t-tay]

an hour un'ora [**o**ra]
a minute un minuto [meen**oo**to]
a second un secondo [sek**o**ndo]
a quarter of an hour un quarto d'ora [kw**a**rto d**o**ra]
half an hour mezz'ora [med**zo**ra]
three quarters of an hour tre quarti d'ora [tray kw**a**rtee d**o**ra]

Numbers

0	zero [tz**ai**ro]	8	otto [**o**t-to]
1	uno [**oo**no]	9	nove [n**o**-vay]
2	due [d**oo**-ay]	10	dieci [dee-**ay**chee]
3	tre [tray]	11	undici [**oo**n-deechee]
4	quattro [kw**a**t-tro]	12	dodici [d**oh**-deechee]
5	cinque [ch**ee**nkway]	13	tredici [tr**ay**-deechee]
6	sei [say]	14	quattordici [kwat-t**o**r-deechee]
7	sette [s**e**t-tay]		

15	quindici [kween-deechee]
16	sedici [say-deechee]
17	diciassette [deechas-set-tay]
18	diciotto [deechot-to]
19	diciannove [deechan-no-vay]
20	venti [ventee]
21	ventuno [vent-oono]
22	ventidue [ventee-doo-ay]
23	ventitré [ventee-tray]
30	trenta [trenta]
31	trentuno [trentoono]
40	quaranta [kwaranta]
50	cinquanta [cheenkwanta]
60	sessanta [ses-santa]
70	settanta [set-tanta]
80	ottanta [ot-tanta]
90	novanta [novanta]
100	cento [chento]
110	centodieci [chento-dee-aychee]
200	duecento [doo-ay-chento]
300	trecento [tray-chento]
1,000	mille [meelay]
2,000	duemila [doo-ay-meela]
5,000	cinquemila [cheenkway-meela]
5,720	cinquemilasette-centoventi [cheenkway-meela-set-tay-chento-ventee]

10,000	diecimila [dee-echeemeela]
10,550	diecimilacinque-centocinquanta [dee-echeemeela-cheenkway-chento-cheenkwanta]
20,000	ventimila [venteemeela]
50,000	cinquantamila [cheenkwantameela]
100,000	centomila [chentomeela]
1,000,000	un milione [oon meel-yonay]

In Italian, thousands are written with a full stop instead of a comma, e.g. 1.000, 10.000. Decimals are written with a comma, e.g. 3.5 would be 3,5 in Italian.

Ordinals

1st	primo [preemo]
2nd	secondo [sekondo]
3rd	terzo [tairtzo]
4th	quarto [kwarto]
5th	quinto [kweento]
6th	sesto
7th	settimo [set-teemo]
8th	ottavo [ot-tavo]
9th	nono
10th	decimo [daycheemo]

Conversion Tables

1 centimetre = 0.39 inches   1 inch = 2.54 cm

1 metre = 39.37 inches = 1.09 yards   1 foot = 30.48 cm

1 kilometre = 0.62 miles = 5/8 mile   1 yard = 0.91 m

1 mile = 1.61 km

km	1	2	3	4	5	10	20	30	40	50	100
miles	0.6	1.2	1.9	2.5	3.1	6.2	12.4	18.6	24.8	31.0	62.1

miles	1	2	3	4	5	10	20	30	40	50	100
km	1.6	3.2	4.8	6.4	8.0	16.1	32.2	48.3	64.4	80.5	161

1 gram = 0.035 ounces   1 kilo = 1000 g = 2.2 pounds

g	100	250	500	1 oz = 28.35 g
oz	3.5	8.75	17.5	1 lb = 0.45 kg

kg	0.5	1	2	3	4	5	6	7	8	9	10
lb	1.1	2.2	4.4	6.6	8.8	11.0	13.2	15.4	17.6	19.8	22.0

kg	20	30	40	50	60	70	80	90	100
lb	44	66	88	110	132	154	176	198	220

lb	0.5	1	2	3	4	5	6	7	8	9	10	20
kg	0.2	0.5	0.9	1.4	1.8	2.3	2.7	3.2	3.6	4.1	4.5	9.0

1 litre = 1.75 UK pints / 2.13 US pints

1 UK pint = 0.57 l   1 UK gallon = 4.55 l
1 US pint = 0.47 l   1 US gallon = 3.79 l

centigrade / Celsius $C = (F - 32) \times 5/9$

C	-5	0	5	10	15	18	20	25	30	36.8	38
F	23	32	41	50	59	64	68	77	86	98.4	100.4

Fahrenheit $F = (C \times 9/5) + 32$

F	23	32	40	50	60	65	70	80	85	98.4	101
C	-5	0	4	10	16	18	21	27	29	36.8	38.3

English → Italian

A

a, an* uno/una [**oo**no/**oo**na]

about: about 20 circa venti
[**cheer**ka]

 it's about 5 o'clock sono le
cinque circa

 a film about Italy un film
sull'Italia

above di sopra

 above ... sopra a...

abroad all'estero [al-l**e**stairo]

absolutely (I agree) senz'altro
[sentz**al**tro]

accelerator l'acceleratore m
[achelairat**o**ray]

accept accettare [achet-t**a**ray]

accident l'incidente m
[eencheed**ay**ntay]

 there's been an accident c'è
stato un incidente [chay]

accommodation l'alloggio m
[al-l**o**j-jo] see room

accurate accurato [ak-koor**a**to]

ache (verb) fare male [**fa**ray
m**a**lay]

 my back aches mi fa male la
schiena

across: across the road
dall'altra parte della strada
[**par**tay]

adapter il riduttore [reedoot-
t**o**ray]

address l'indirizzo m
[eendeer**ee**tzo]

 what's your address? qual è
il suo indirizzo? [kwal**ay** ay eel
s**oo**-o]

Addresses in Italy are
written as follows: the
number follows the name
of the street, and the code precedes
the town, e.g.

Signor Mario Rossi
via Salaria 96
00199 Roma

In larger towns, you'll find a double
address system for streets, with one
series for business properties and
another for all others. Business
addresses are followed by a letter 'r'
and are marked on the building with
a red number. Because the two
series are independent, no. 20 might
be a long way from no. 20r.

address book la rubrica

admission charge il prezzo
d'ingresso [**pret**zo deengr**e**s-so]

Adriatic il mare Adriatico
[m**a**ray]

adult l'adulto m [ad**oo**lto]

advance: in advance in
anticipo [een ant**ee**cheepo]

aeroplane l'aeroplano m
[a-airopl**a**no]

after dopo

 after you dopo di lei [lay]

 after lunch dopo pranzo

afternoon il pomeriggio
[pomair**ee**j-jo]

 in the afternoon nel
pomeriggio

 this afternoon questo
pomeriggio

English → Italian

Af

aftershave il dopobarba
aftersun cream la crema
  doposole [doposolay]
afterwards dopo
again di nuovo [dee nwovo]
against contro
age l'età f [ayta]
ago: a week ago una
  settimana fa
  an hour ago un'ora fa
agree: I agree sono d'accordo
AIDS l'aids m [a-eeds]
air l'aria f
  by air per via aerea [pair vee-a
  a-airay-a]
air-conditioning l'aria
  condizionata [kondeetz-yonata]
airmail: by airmail per via
  aerea [a-airay-a]
airmail envelope la busta per
  posta aerea [boosta pair]
airport l'aeroporto m
  [a-airoporto]
  to the airport, please
  all'aeroporto, per favore
  [pair favoray]
airport bus l'autobus
  dell'aeroporto m [lowtoboos]
aisle seat il posto vicino al
  corridoio [veecheeno al kor-
  reedo-yo]
alarm clock la sveglia [zvel-ya]
Albania l'Albania f
Albanian (adj) albanese
  [albanayzay]
alcohol l'alcool m [alkol]
alcoholic alcolico [alkoleeko]
all: all the boys tutti i ragazzi
  [toot-tee ee]

all the girls tutte le ragazze
  [toot-tay lay]
all of it tutto [toot-to]
all of them tutti
that's all, thanks è tutto,
  grazie [ay – gratzee-ay]
allergic: I'm allergic to ... sono
  allergico a... [al-lairjeeko]
allowed: is it allowed? è
  permesso? [ay pairmes-so]
all right (I agree) va bene,
  d'accordo [benay]
  I'm all right sto bene
  are you all right? stai/sta
  bene? [sty/sta]
almond la mandorla
almost quasi [kwazee]
alone solo
alphabet l'alfabeto m

a a   j ee-loonga   s es-say
b bee   k kap-pa   t tee
c chee   l el-lay   u oo
d dee   m em-may   v voo
e ay   n en-nay   w voo dop-yo
f ef-fay   o o   x eeks
g jee   p pee   y eepseelon
h ak-ka   q koo   z tzay-ta
i ee   r air-ray

Alps le Alpi
already già [ja]
also anche [ankay]
although anche se [say]
altogether in tutto [een toot-to]
always sempre [sempray]
am*: I am sono
a.m.: at seven a.m. alle sette
  del mattino [al-lay]

amazing (surprising)
sorprendente [sorprend**e**ntay]
(very good) eccezionale
[echetz-yon**a**lay]
ambulance l'ambulanza f
[ambool**a**ntza]
 call an ambulance! chiamate
un'ambulanza! [k-yam**a**tay]

 Dial 113 for an ambulance
and you will be connected
to one of the ambulance
companies (Croce Rossa,
Misericordia, etc).

America l'America f
[am**a**ireeka]
American americano
[amaireek**a**no]
 I'm American (man/woman)
sono americano/americana
among tra, fra
amount la quantità
(money) la somma
amp: a 13 amp fuse un
fusibile da tredici ampere
[fooz**ee**beelay da – amp**a**iray]
amphitheatre l'anfiteatro m
[anfeetay-**a**tro]
ancient antico
and e [ay]
angry arrabbiato [ar-rab-y**a**to]
animal l'animale m
[aneem**a**lay]
ankle la caviglia [kav**ee**l-ya]
anniversary (wedding)
l'anniversario di
matrimonio m
annoy: this man's annoying

me quest'uomo mi sta
importunando [kwestw**o**mo
mee sta eemportoon**a**ndo]
annoying seccante [sek-k**a**ntay]
another un altro, un'altra
[**o**n]
 can we have another room?
potremmo avere un'altra
stanza? [av**a**iray]
 another beer, please ancora
una birra, per favore
antibiotics gli antibiotici
[anteebee-**o**teechee]
antifreeze l'antigelo m
[anteej**e**lo]
antihistamine l'antistaminico
m
antique: is it an antique? è un
pezzo d'antiquariato? [ay oon
p**e**tzo danteekwar-y**a**to]
antique shop il negozio di
antiquariato [neg**o**tz-yo dee]
antiseptic l'antisettico m
**any: have you got any
bread/tomatoes?** avete del
pane/dei pomodori? [av**e**tay
del – /day]
 do you have any change? ha
degli spiccioli? [a d**a**yl-yee
sp**ee**cholee]
 sorry, I don't have any mi
dispiace, non ne ho [mee
deesp-y**a**chay non nay o]
anybody qualcuno [kwalk**oo**no]
 **does anybody speak
English?** c'è qualcuno che
parla inglese? [chay – kay p**a**rla
eengl**a**yzay]
 there wasn't anybody there

non c'era nessuno lì [non chaira nes-soono]
anything qualcosa [kwalkoza]

dialogues

anything else? altro?
nothing else, thanks
nient'altro, grazie
[n-yentaltro]

would you like anything to
drink? vuole qualcosa da
bere? [vwolay kwalkoza da
bairay]
I don't want anything,
thanks non voglio niente,
grazie [non vol-yo n-yentay]

apart from a parte [partay]
apartment l'appartamento m
aperitif l'aperitivo m
[apaireeteevo]
apology le scuse [skoozay]
Apennines gli Appennini
appendicitis l'appendicite f
[ap-pendeecheetay]
appetizer l'antipasto m
apple la mela [mayla]
appointment l'appuntamento
m [ap-poontamento]

dialogue

good morning, how can I
help you? buongiorno,
mi dica
I'd like to make an
appointment vorrei fissare

un appuntamento [vor-ray
fees-saray]
what time would you like?
per che ora? [pair kay]
three o'clock le tre
I'm afraid that's not
possible; is four o'clock all
right? mi dispiace, non è
possibile: va bene alle
quattro? [mee deesp-yachay,
non ay pos-seebeelay: va
baynay]
yes, that will be fine sì, va
bene
the name was ...? il suo
nome, per favore? [soo-o
nomay]

apricot l'albicocca f [albeekok-
ka]
April aprile [apreelay]
are*: we are siamo [s-yamo]
you are siete [s-yaytay]
they are sono
area la zona
area code il prefisso
arm il braccio [bracho]
arrange: will you arrange it for
us? può organizzarlo per
noi? [pwo organeetzarlo pair noy]
arrival l'arrivo m [ar-reevo]
arrive arrivare [ar-reevaray]
when do we arrive? quando
arriviamo? [kwando ar-reev-
yamo]
has my fax arrived yet? è
arrivato il mio fax?
we arrived today siamo
arrivati oggi [s-yamo]

art l'arte **f** [**a**rtay]
art gallery la galleria d'arte [gal-lair**ee**-a]
artist l'art**i**sta **m/f**
as: as big as (così) grande come [koz**ee** gr**a**nday k**o**may]
as soon as possible al più presto possibile [p-yoo – pos-seebeelay]
ashtray il portacenere [portach**e**nairay]
ask chi**e**dere [k-y**ay**dairay]
I didn't ask for this non ho chiesto questo [non o k-y**e**sto kw**e**sto]
could you ask him to ...? può chi**e**dergli di...? [pwo k-y**ay**dairl-yee dee]
asleep: she's asleep dorme [d**o**rmay]
aspirin l'asp**i**rina **f**
asthma l'**a**sma **f**
astonishing stupef**a**cente [stoopay-fach**e**ntay]
at: at the hotel in alb**e**rgo
at the station alla stazi**o**ne
at six o'clock alle s**e**i [**a**l-lay]
at Giovanni's da Giov**a**nni
athletics l'atl**e**tica **f** [atl**ay**teeka]
attractive attra**e**nte [at-tra-**e**ntay]
aubergine la melanz**a**na [melantz**a**na]
August ag**o**sto

Avoid Italy in August, if at all possible. It is very hot and this is the month when all the workplaces close and masses of Italians go on holiday: everything is either closed or very expensive or very crowded.

aunt la z**i**a [tz**ee**-a]
Australia l'Austr**a**lia **f** [owstr**a**l-ya]
Australian austral**i**ano [owstral-y**a**no]
I'm Australian (man/woman) sono austral**i**ano/austral**i**ana
Austria l'**A**ustria **f** [**o**wstree-a]
Austrian austr**i**aco [owstr**ee**-ako]
automatic autom**a**tico [owtom**a**teeko]
(car) l'autom**o**bile con il c**a**mbio autom**a**tico **f** [owtom**o**beelay kon eel k**a**mb-yo]
automatic teller il bancomat®
autumn l'aut**u**nno **m** [owt**oo**n-no]
in the autumn in aut**u**nno
avenue il vi**a**le [vee-**a**lay]
average (not good) medi**o**cre [med-y**o**kray]
(ordinary) ordin**a**rio [ordeenar-yo] on average in m**e**dia [m**a**yd-ya]
awake: is he awake? è sv**e**glio? [ay zv**a**yl-yo]
away: go away! v**a**ttene! [v**a**ttenay]
is it far away? è lont**a**no?
awful terr**i**bile [tair-r**ee**beelay]
axle l'**a**sse **m** [**a**s-say]

B

baby (male/female) il bambino,
la bambina
baby food gli alimenti per
bambini
baby's bottle il biberon
baby-sitter il/la baby-sitter
back (of body) la schiena
[sk-**ay**na]
(back part) la parte posteriore
[p**a**rtay postair-y**o**ray]
at the back dietro [d-y**e**tro]
can I have my money back?
posso riavere i miei soldi?
[ree-av**ai**ray ee mee-y**ay** s**o**ldee]
to come/go back tornare
[torn**a**ray]
backache il mal di schiena
[sk-y**ay**na]
bacon la pancetta [panch**e**t-ta]
bad cattivo [kat-t**ee**vo]
a bad headache un brutto
mal di testa [br**oo**t-to]
badly male [m**a**lay]
bag la borsa
(handbag) la borsetta
(suitcase) la valigia [val**ee**ja]
baggage i bagagli [bag**a**l-yee]
baggage check (US) il
deposito bagagli
baggage claim il ritiro
bagagli
bakery la panetteria [panet-
tair**ee**-a], il panificio
[paneef**ee**cho]
balcony il balcone [balk**o**nay]
a room with a balcony una

stanza con balcone
bald calvo
ball (large) la palla
(small) la pallina
ballet il balletto
banana la banana
band (musical) il gruppo
[gr**oo**p-po]
bandage la fasciatura
[fashat**oo**ra]
Bandaids® i cerotti [chair**o**t-
tee]
bank (money) la banca

Banks are generally open
from Monday to Friday,
but hours vary from bank
to bank and from town to town.
Banks usually open between 8.15
and 8.45 a.m. and close at 1.15 or
1.30 p.m., opening again at 2 or 2.30
p.m. and closing at 4 or 4.30 p.m. In
larger towns, you may find one or
two banks open on Saturday
morning. A passport is required for
all transactions.

bank account il conto in
banca
bar il bar

In Italy, it is usual to have
water and a glass or two
of wine with each meal,
but it is not so usual to go out for a
drink. You'll rarely see drunks in
public, young people don't devote
their nights to getting wasted, and
women especially are frowned upon

if they're seen to be over-indulging.
Bars are less social centres than
functional places, and are all very
similar to each other – brightly-lit
places, with a chrome counter, a
Gaggia coffee machine and a
picture of the local football team on
the wall. You'll come here for
ordinary drinking: a coffee in the
morning, a quick beer, a cup of tea,
but people don't generally idle away
the day or evening in bars. Indeed in
more rural places, it's difficult to find
a bar open much after 9 p.m. Where
it does fit into the general
Mediterranean pattern is that there
are no set licensing hours and
children are always allowed in. In
addition to traditional bars, there are
also **birrerie** (beer cellars) and
imitation British pubs, which are
fashionable among young people. In
bars, you generally have to pay first
at the cash desk then show your
receipt (**scontrino**) at the bar when
ordering. It's cheaper if you stand at
the bar to drink. Bars sell hot drinks,
soft and alcoholic drinks, and also
often sell savoury snacks, cakes and
ice creams.

a bar of chocolate una
tavoletta di cioccolato [chok-
kol**a**to]
barber's il barbiere [barb-
y**a**iray]
basket il cestino [chest**ee**no]
(in shop) il cestello [chestel-lo]
bath il bagno [b**a**n-yo]

can I have a bath? posso fare
un bagno? [f**a**ray]
bathroom il bagno, la stanza
da bagno [st**a**ntza]
with a private bathroom con
bagno
bath towel l'asciugamano da
bagno **m** [ashoogam**a**no]
bathtub la vasca da bagno
battery la batteria [bat-
tair**ee**-a]
bay la baia [b**a**-ya]
be* essere [**e**s-sairay]
beach la spiaggia [spee-**a**j-ja]

 A **spiaggia libera** is free
of charge, but where you
see the sign **stabilimento**
(concession) you will have to pay
rather high charges for the rental of
beach umbrellas, deckchairs, etc.

beach mat la stuoia [stw**o**-ya]
beach umbrella l'ombrellone
m [ombrel-l**o**nay]
beans i fagioli [faj**o**lee]
French beans i fagiolini
[fajol**ee**nee]
broad beans le fave [f**a**vay]
beard la barba
beautiful bello
because perché [pairk**ay**]
because of ... a causa di...
[k**ow**za]
bed il letto
I'm going to bed vado a letto
bed and breakfast camera
con prima colazione [pr**ee**ma
kolatz-y**o**nay]

Prices of hotel rooms do not always include breakfast. Always ask if it is included: '**la colazione è compresa?**' [komprayza]. Contrary to what some hoteliers would have you believe, breakfast is not compulsory.

bedroom la camera da letto
beef il manzo [**mantzo**]
beer la birra [**beer**-ra]
  two beers, please due birre, per favore [**doo**-ay **beer**-ray]

 Beer terms are as follows:
chiara [k-**yara**] amber-coloured, light beer
rossa darker, maltier beer
scura [**skoo**ra] darker than rossa
in bottiglia [een bot-**teel**-ya] in bottles
in lattina in cans
alla spina draught
piccola small (20 cl)
media medium (30 cl)
grande large (40 cl)

before prima di [**preema**]
begin cominciare [komeen**charay**]
  when does it begin? quando comincia? [**kwando** kom**een**cha]
beginner il/la principiante [preencheep-**yantay**]
beginning: at the beginning all'inizio [al-een**eetz**-yo]
behind dietro (a) [d-**yetro**]
  behind me dietro di me

beige beige [**may**]
beige beige
believe credere [**kray**dairay]
bell (church) la campana (doorbell) il campanello
below sotto (a)
belt la cintura [cheen**toor**a]
bend (in road) la curva [**koo**rva]
berth la cuccetta [kooch**et**-ta]
beside: beside the ... accanto a... [ak-**kanto**]
best il migliore [meel-**yoray**]
better meglio [**mayl**-yo]
  are you feeling better? ti senti/si sente meglio? [see **sentay**]
between tra, fra
beyond oltre [**oltray**]
bicycle la bicicletta [beecheek**let**-ta]
big grande [**granday**]
  too big troppo grande
  it's not big enough non è abbastanza grande [ay ab-bas**tantza**]
bike la bici [**beechee**] (motorbike) la moto(cicletta) [motocheek**let**-ta]
bikini il bikini
bill il conto
  could I have the bill, please? il conto, per favore

 If you go out with a group of friends, it is usual to share the bill equally, i.e. **fare alla romana** (to go Dutch). If someone intends to pay for everything, they will say '**pago io**' or '**faccio io**' [facho]. If someone invites other people out, he or she is expected to pay.

bin la pattumiera [pat-toom-y**ai**ra]
bin liners i sacchetti per la pattumiera [sak-k**e**t-tee pair la pat-toom-y**ai**ra]
binding (ski) l'attacco **m**
bird l'uccello **m** [**oo**chel-lo]
biro® la biro
birthday il compleanno [komplay-**a**n-no]
  happy birthday! buon compleanno! [bwon]
biscuit il biscotto
bit: a little bit un po'
  a big bit un grosso pezzo [p**e**tzo]
  a bit of ... un pezzetto di... [petz**e**t-to dee]
  a bit expensive un po' caro
bite (by insect) la puntura [poont**oo**ra]
  (by dog) il morso
bitter amaro
black nero [n**ai**ro]
blanket la coperta [kop**ai**rta]
blast! accidenti! [acheed**e**ntee]
bleach (for toilet) la varechina [varek**ee**na]
bless you! salute! [sal**oo**tay]
blind cieco [chee-**ay**ko]
blinds gli avvolgibili [av-volj**ee**beelay]
blister la vescica [vesh**ee**ka]
blocked (road, pipe) bloccato

(sink) intasato [eentaz**a**to]
block of apartments il caseggiato [kasej-j**a**to]
blond biondo [b-y**o**ndo]
blood il sangue [s**a**ngway]
  high blood pressure la pressione alta [press-y**o**nay]
blouse la camicetta [kameech**e**t-ta]
blow-dry l'asciugatura col fon **f** [ashoogat**oo**ra]
  I'd like a cut and blow-dry vorrei taglio e piega con il fon [vor-r**ay** tal-yo ay p-y**ay**ga]
blue blu [bloo]
  blue eyes gli occhi azzurri [**o**k-kee adz**oo**r-ree]
blusher il fard
boarding house la pensione [pens-y**o**nay]
boarding pass la carta d'imbarco [eemb**a**rko]
boat la barca
  (for passengers) il battello
body il corpo
boil (verb: of water) bollire [bol-l**ee**ray]
  (water, potatoes etc) far bollire
boiled egg l'uovo sodo **m** [w**o**vo]
boiler lo scaldabagno [skaldab**a**n-yo]
bone l'osso **m**
bonnet (of car) il cofano
book il libro
  (verb) prenotare [prenot**a**ray]
  can I book a seat? posso prenotare un posto?

dialogue

I'd like to book a table for two vorrei prenotare un tavolo per due [vor-ray prenotaray – pair doo-ay]
what time would you like it booked for? per che ora lo vuole? [kay – vwolay]
half past seven per le sette e mezza
that's fine va bene [baynay]
and your name? il suo nome, per favore [soo-o nomay]

bookshop/bookstore la libreria [leebrairee-a]
boot (footwear) lo stivale [steevalay]
(of car) il bagagliaio [bagal-ya-yo]
border (of country) il confine [konfeenay]
bored: I'm bored mi sto annoiando [an-noy-ando]
boring noioso [noy-ozo]
born: I was born in Manchester sono nato/nata a Manchester
I was born in 1960 sono nato/nata nel millenovecentosessanta
borrow prendere a prestito [prendairay]
may I borrow ...? posso prendere a prestito...?
both tutti e due [toot-tee ay doo-ay], tutte e due [toot-tay]

bother: sorry to bother you mi scusi il disturbo [skoozee eel deestoorbo]
bottle la bottiglia [bot-teel-ya]
a bottle of house red una bottiglia di (vino) rosso della casa
bottle-opener il cavatappi
bottom (of person) il sedere [sedairay]
at the bottom of ... (hill etc) ai piedi di... [a-ee p-yaydee]
(street, sea etc) in fondo a...
box la scatola
(wooden) la cassetta
box office il botteghino [bot-tegeeno]
boy il ragazzo [ragatzo]
boyfriend il ragazzo
bra il reggiseno [rej-jeesayno]
bracelet il braccialetto [brachaletto]
brake il freno [frayno]
brandy il brandy
bread il pane [panay]
white bread il pane bianco [b-yanko]
brown bread il pane nero [nairo]
wholemeal bread il pane integrale [eentegralay]
break (verb) rompere [rompairay]
I've broken the ... ho rotto il/la... [o rot-to]
I think I've broken my wrist credo di essermi rotto il polso [kraydo dee es-sairmee]
break down (car) rimanere in

panne [reemanairay een pan-nay]
I've broken down sono
rimasto in panne
breakdown il guasto [gwasto]

If you break down dial
116 at the nearest phone
and tell the operator
where you are, the type of car and
your registration number; the Italian
Automobile Club (ACI) (via Marsala
8, 00185 Roma) will send someone
to fix your car, although it's not a
free service. It could be cheaper if
you join the ACI outright.

breakdown service il servizio
riparazioni [sairveetz-yo
reeparatz-yonee]
breakfast la (prima)
colazione [kolatz-yonay]
break-in: I've had a break-in
mi sono entrati i ladri in
casa
breast il seno [sayno], il petto
breathe respirare [respeeraray]
breeze la brezza [bretza]
bridge (over river) il ponte
[pontay]
brief breve [brayvay]
briefcase la cartella
bright (light etc) brillante
[breel-lantay]
bright red rosso acceso
[achayzo]
brilliant (idea, person) brillante
[breel-lantay]
bring portare [portaray]
I'll bring it back later lo

riporterò più tardi
[reeportairo]
Britain la Gran Bretagna
[bretan-ya]
British britannico
brochure l'opuscolo m
[opooskolo]
broken rotto [rot-to]
bronchitis la bronchite
[bronkeetay]
brooch la spilla
broom la scopa
brother il fratello
brother-in-law il cognato
[kon-yato]
brown marrone [mar-ronay]
brown hair i capelli castani
brown eyes gli occhi castani
[ok-kee]
bruise il livido
brush (for hair) la spazzola
[spatzola]
(artist's) il pennello
(for cleaning) la scopa
bucket il secchio [sek-yo]
buffet car il vagone
ristorante [vagonay
reestorantay]
buggy (for child) il passeggino
[pas-sej-jeeno]
building l'edificio m
[edeefeecho]
bulb (light bulb) la lampadina
bumper il paraurti [para-
oortee]
bunk la cuccetta [koochet-ta]
bureau de change l'agenzia
di cambio f [ajentzee-a dee
kamb-yo]

The best rates for exchanging money or traveller's cheques are to be found in banks, rather than in bureaux de change.

burglary il furto [**foor**to]
burn la bruciatura
[broochat**oo**ra]
(verb) bruciare [broocha**ray**]
burnt: this is burnt questo è
bruciato [kw**e**sto ay
brooch**a**to]
burst: a burst pipe una
tubatura scoppiata
[toobat**oo**ra skop-y**a**ta]
bus l'autobus **m**
[**ow**toboos]
what number bus is it to ...?
che numero va a...? [kay
n**oo**mairo]
when is the next bus to ...?
quando parte il prossimo
autobus per...? [kw**a**ndo
part**ay**]
what time is the last bus? a
che ora parte l'ultimo
autobus?
**could you let me know when
we get there?** mi può dire
quando siamo arrivati? [pwo
d**ee**ray kw**a**ndo s-y**a**mo]

Bus tickets generally have to be bought in advance from newsstands, tobacconists or bars and validated in the ticket-stamping machine on the bus. Although most city buses

operate on a flat fare system (however long the journey), sometimes a special ticket is available, enabling you to travel on more than one bus for a specified period. The front and rear doors are usually for boarding and the middle door is the exit. In Rome and Milan underground tickets are also valid for bus travel for up to one hour from the time of issue.

dialogue

does this bus go to ...?
questo autobus va a...?
[kw**e**sto]
no, you need a number ...
no, deve prendere il...
[**day**vay prend**ai**ray]

business gli affari
bus station la stazione degli
autobus [statz-y**o**nay d**ay**l-yee
owtoboos]
bus stop la fermata
dell'autobus [fair**ma**ta]
bust il busto [**boo**sto]
busy (restaurant etc) animato
I'm busy tomorrow domani
ho da fare [o da far**ay**]
but ma
butcher's il macellaio [machel-
la-yo]
butter il burro [**boor**-ro]
button il bottone [bot-t**o**nay]
buy comprare [kompra-ray]
where can I buy ...? dove
vendono...?

by: by bus/car in
autobus/macchina [een]
written by ... scritto da...
by the window vicino al
finestrino [veech**een**o]
by the sea sul mare [sool]
by Thursday per giovedi
[pair]
bye ciao [chow]

C

cabbage il cavolo
cabin (on ship) la cabina
cable car la funivia [fooneevee-
a]
café il caffè [kaf-f**ay**]
see **bar**
cagoule la giacca a vento
[**jak**-ka]
cake la torta
cake shop la pasticceria
[pasteechair**ee**-a]
call (verb) chiamare
[k-yam**a**ray]
(to phone) telefonare
[telefon**a**ray]
what's it called? come si
chiama? [**ko**may see k-y**a**ma]
he/she/it is called ... si
chiama...
please call the doctor
chiamate un medico, per
favore [k-yam**a**tay oon
m**ay**deeko]
**please give me a call at 7.30
a.m. tomorrow** domani
mattina, mi svegli alle sette

e mezza, per favore [mee
zv**ay**l-yee **a**l-lay]
please ask him to call me gli
chieda di chiamarmi, per
favore [l-yee kee-y**ay**da dee]
call back: I'll call back later
(phone back) richiamerò più
tardi [reek-yamair**o** p-yoo]
**call round: I'll call round
tomorrow** passerò domani
camcorder la videocamera
camera la macchina
fotografica [**m**ak-keena]
camera shop il negozio del
fotografo [neg**o**tz-yo del]
camp (verb) campeggiare
[kampej-j**a**ray]
can we camp here?
possiamo accamparci qui?
[pos-y**a**mo ak-kamp**a**rchee kwee]
camping gas il gas liquido
[**lee**kweedo]

 Camping gas canisters
can be bought either from
a **ferramenta** (hardware
store) or from campsite shops; you
can't carry canisters on aeroplanes.

campsite il campeggio
[kamp**ej**-jo]

 Camping is not as popular
in Italy as it is in some
European countries, but
there are plenty of sites, and most of
them are well-equipped. The snag is
that they're expensive, and, once
you've added the cost of a tent and

vehicle, they don't always work out a great deal cheaper than staying in a hotel or hostel. Local tourist offices have details of nearby sites and the Touring Club Italiano publish a comprehensive guide to campsites countrywide, **Campeggi e Villaggi Turistici**. If you don't need something this detailed, you can obtain an abridged version, along with a location map, free of charge from Centro Internazionale Prenotazioni, Federcampeggio, Casella Postale 23, 50041 Calenzano, Firenze (tel. 055/882 391). This is also the place to book places on campsites in advance.

can la lattina
  a can of beer una lattina di birra
can*: can you ...? puoi/può...? [pwoy/pwo]
  can I have ...? posso avere...? [avairay]
  I can't ... (am not able to) non posso...
  (don't know how to) non so...
Canada il Canada
Canadian canadese [kanadayzay]
  I'm Canadian sono canadese
canal il canale [kanalay]
cancel annullare [an-nool-laray]
candies le caramelle [karamel-lay]
candle la candela [kandayla]
canoe la canoa [kano-a]

canoeing la canoa
can opener l'apriscatole m [apreeskatolay]
cap (hat) il berretto [bair-ret-to]
  (of bottle) il tappo
car la macchina [mak-keena], l'auto(mobile) f [owtomobeelay]
  by car in macchina
carafe la caraffa
  a carafe of house white, please una caraffa di (vino) bianco della casa, per favore [kaza]
caravan la roulotte [roolot]
caravan site il campeggio per roulotte [kampej-jo pair]
carburettor il carburatore [karbooratoray]
card (birthday etc) il biglietto [beel-yet-to]
  my (business) card il mio biglietto da visita [veezeeta]
cardigan il cardigan
cardphone il telefono a scheda [telayfono a skayda]
careful attento
  be careful! fa'/faccia attenzione! [facha at-tentz-yonay]
caretaker il portinaio [porteena-yo]
car ferry la nave traghetto [navay]
car hire l'autonoleggio m [owtonolej-jo]
carnival il carnevale [karnevalay]

Fancy dress carnival parties and parades, including the famous Carnevale di Venezia and Carnevale di Viareggio, take place on Shrove Tuesday and the immediately preceding days every year.

car park il parcheggio [parkej-jo]

carpet il tappeto [tap-**pay**to] (wall to wall) la moquette [mo**ket**]

carriage (of train) la carrozza [kar-**rotza**]

carrier bag il sacchetto [sak-**ket**-to]

carrot la carota

carry portare [por**tar**ay]

carry-cot il porte-enfant [port-on**fan**]

carton il tetrapack®, la scatola di cartone

carwash l'autolavaggio m [owtolavaj-jo]

case (suitcase) la valigia [val**ee**ja]

cash il contante [kont**an**tay] (verb) riscuotere [reeskw**o**tairay]

will you cash this cheque for me? mi cambia questo assegno? [kw**e**sto as-s**en**-yo]

cash desk la cassa

cash dispenser il bancomat®

cashier (man/woman) il cassiere [kas-y**air**ay], la cassiera

cassette la cassetta

cassette recorder il registratore a cassette [rejeestrat**o**ray a kas-**set**-tay]

castle il castello

casualty department il pronto soccorso

cat il gatto

catch (verb) prendere [pr**en**dairay]

where do we catch the bus to ...? dove prendiamo l'autobus per...? [d**o**vay prend-y**a**mo]

cathedral la cattedrale [kat-tedr**a**lay], il duomo [dw**o**mo]

Catholic cattolico

cauliflower il cavolfiore [kavolf-y**o**ray]

cave la grotta

ceiling il soffitto

celery il sedano [s**ay**dano]

cellar (for wine) la cantina

cemetery il cimitero [cheemeet**air**o]

Centigrade* centigrado [chent**ee**grado]

centimetre* il centimetro [chent**ee**metro]

central centrale [chentr**a**lay]

central heating il riscaldamento autonomo [owt**o**nomo]

centre il centro [ch**en**tro]

how do we get to the city centre? come si arriva in centro? [k**o**may]

cereal i cereali [chairay-**a**lee]

certainly certamente [chairtam**en**tay]

certainly not certamente no

chair la sedia [**say**d-ya]

chair lift la seggiovia [sej-jo**vee**-a]

change (money) gli spiccioli [**spee**cholee]

(verb: money, trains) cambiare [kamb-ya**ray**]

can I change this for ...? posso cambiarlo con...? [kamb-ya**rlo**]

I don't have any change non ho spiccioli [o]

can you give me change for a 100,000 lire note? mi può cambiare 100.000 (centomila) lire? [mee pwo – **lee**ray]

dialogue

do we have to change (trains)? dobbiamo cambiare? [dob-ya**mo**]

yes, change at Rome/no it's a direct train sì, cambiate a Roma/no, è diretto [kamb-ya**tay** – ay]

changed: to get changed cambiarsi [kamb-ya**rsee**]

chapel la cappella

charge il prezzo [**pre**tzo]

(verb) far pagare [pa**ga**ray]

what is the charge per night? quant'è a notte? [kwan**tay**]

charge card la carta di addebito

see **credit card**

cheap a buon mercato [bwon mair**ka**to]

do you have anything cheaper? ha qualcosa di meno caro? [kwal**ko**za]

check (verb) controllare [kontrol-la**ray**]

(US: noun) l'assegno m [as-**sen**-yo]

see **cheque**

(US: bill) il conto

see **bill**

could you check the ..., please? può controllare..., per favore? [pwo]

checkbook il libretto degli assegni [**day**l-yee as-**sen**-yee]

check-in il check-in

check in (at airport) fare il check-in [**fa**ray]

where do we have to check in? dove dobbiamo fare il check-in? [**do**vay dob-ya**mo**]

cheek la guancia [**gwan**cha]

cheerio! ciao! [chow]

cheers! (toast) alla salute! [sa**loo**tay]

cheese il formaggio [for**maj**-jo]

chemist's la farmacia [farma**chee**-a]

Italian pharmacists are well-qualified to give you advice on minor ailments and to dispense prescriptions; there's generally an all-night pharmacy in bigger towns and cities; they work on a rota system and you'll find the address of the one currently open on the door of any chemist's. It is less expensive to buy toiletries, plasters, cotton wool etc at a supermarket or department store.

cheque l'assegno m [as-sen-yo]
  do you take cheques?
  accettate assegni? [achet-tatay as-sen-yee]
cheque book il libretto degli assegni [dayl-yee]
cheque card la carta assegni
cherry la ciliegia [cheel-yay-ja]
chess gli scacchi [skak-kee]
chest il petto
chewing gum il chewing gum
chicken il pollo
chickenpox la varicella [varee-chel-la]
child (male/female) il bambino, la bambina

 Children are welcome in most public places, and it is normal for whole family groups to take children to restaurants.

child minder la bambinaia [bambeena-ya]
children's pool la piscina per bambini [peesheena pair]
children's portion la porzione per bambini [portz-yonay]
chin il mento
china la porcellana [porchel-lana]

Chinese cinese [cheenayzay]
chips le patatine fritte [patateenay freet-tay]
chocolate il cioccolato [chok-kolato]
  milk chocolate il cioccolato al latte [al lat-tay]
  plain chocolate il cioccolato fondente [fondentay]
  a hot chocolate una cioccolata calda
choose scegliere [shayl-yairay]
Christian name il nome di battesimo [nomay dee bat-tayzeemo]
Christmas il Natale [natalay]
  Christmas Eve la vigilia di Natale [veejeel-ya]
  merry Christmas! Buon Natale! [bwon]
church la chiesa [k-yayza]
cider il sidro
cigar il sigaro
cigarette la sigaretta

 Cigarettes can be bought from **tabaccai** (tobacconists) which can be identified by a white T on a black background. The state monopoly brand, MS, is most widely smoked, but the more expensive imported brands are more popular with young people.

cigarette lighter l'accendino m [achendeeno]

cinema il cinema [cheenema]

Cinemas open at about 2 p.m. and close around midnight. Unless the sign states that a foreign film will be in **lingua originale**, the film will be dubbed. **Vietato ai minori di 14/18 anni** means that the film has a 14/18 certificate.

circle il cerchio [chairk-yo]
(in theatre) la galleria
city la città [cheet-ta]
city centre il centro [chentro]
clean (adj) pulito [pooleeto]
  can you clean these for me?
  me li/le può pulire? [may lee/lay pwo pooleeray]
cleaning solution (for contact lenses) la soluzione per la pulizia delle lenti a contatto [solootz-yonay pair la pooleetzee-a]
cleansing lotion la lozione detergente [lotz-yonay detairjentay]
clear chiaro [k-yaro]
clever intelligente [eentel-leejentay]
cliff la scogliera [skol-yaira]
climbing l'alpinismo **m**
cling film la pellicola trasparente [trasparentay]
clinic la clinica
cloakroom il guardaroba [gwardaroba]
clock l'orologio **m** [orolojo]
close (verb) chiudere [k-yoodairay]

dialogue

what time do you close? a che ora chiudete? [kay – k-yoodaytay]
we close at 8 pm chiudiamo alle otto [k-yood-yamo]
do you close for lunch? chiudete per pranzo?
yes, between 1 and 3.30 pm sì, dall'una alle tre e mezza

closed chiuso [k-yoozo]
cloth (fabric) la stoffa
(for cleaning etc) lo straccio [stracho]
clothes gli abiti
clothes line la corda del bucato
clothes peg la molletta da bucato
cloud la nuvola [noovola]
cloudy nuvoloso [noovolozo]
clutch la frizione [freetz-yonay]
coach (bus) la corriera [kor-yaira], il pullman
(on train) la carrozza [kar-rotza]
coach station la stazione dei pullman [statz-yonay day]
coach trip la gita in pullman [jeeta]
coast la costa
  on the coast sulla costa [sool-la]
coat (long coat) il cappotto
(jacket) la giacca [jak-ka]
coathanger la gruccia

58

[gr**oo**cha]
cockroach lo scarafaggio
[skaraf**aj**-jo]
cocoa il cacao [kak**a**-o]
code (for telephoning) il prefisso
[prayf**ee**s-so]
**what's the (dialling) code for
Florence?** qual è il prefisso
di Firenze? [kwal**ay**]
coffee il caffè [kaf-f**ay**]
two coffees, please due
caffè, per favore

 If you ask for **un caffè**
you will be given an
espresso (strong black
coffee); other types of coffee are:
un caffellatte [kaf-fel-lat-tay]
coffee with lots of milk
un caffè macchiato [mak-yato]
espresso with a dash of milk
un cappuccino frothy, milky coffee
sprinkled with chocolate powder
un caffè lungo [l**oo**ngo] weaker
black coffee
un caffè corretto espresso with a
liqueur or spirit
un caffè decaffeinato [dekaf-fay-
eenato] decaffeinated coffee
un caffè ristretto strong **espresso**
un caffè doppio [d**o**p-yo] double
espresso

coin la moneta [mon**ay**ta]
Coke® la Coca-Cola
cold (adj) freddo
I'm cold ho freddo [o]
I have a cold ho il
raffreddore [raf-fred-d**o**ray]

collapse: he's collapsed ha
avuto un collasso [a av**oo**to]
collar il colletto
collect prendere [pr**e**ndairay]
I've come to collect ... sono
venuto a prendere...
collect call la telefonata a
carico del destinatario
college l'istituto superiore **m**
[eesteet**oo**to soopair-y**o**ray]
colour il colore [kol**o**ray]
**do you have this in other
colours?** ce l'ha in altri
colori? [chay la]
colour film la pellicola a
colori
comb il pettine [p**e**t-teenay]
come venire [ven**ee**ray]

dialogue

where do you come from?
di dov'è? [dee dov**ay**]
I come from Edinburgh
sono di Edimburgo

come back ritornare
[reetorn**a**ray]
I'll come back tomorrow
tornerò domani [tornair**o**]
come in entrare [entr**a**ray]
comfortable comodo
compact disc il compact disc
company (business) la ditta
compartment (on train) lo
scompartimento
compass la bussola [b**oo**s-sola]
complain lamentarsi
complaint il reclamo [rekl**a**mo]

I have a complaint voglio
fare un reclamo [**vol**-yo **far**ay]
completely completamente
[kompleta-**men**tay]
computer il computer
concert il concerto
[konch**air**to]
concussion la commozione
cerebrale [kom-motz-y**o**nay
chairay-br**a**lay]
conditioner (for hair) il
balsamo
condom il preservativo
[prezairvat**ee**vo]
conference la conferenza
[konfair**en**tza]
confirm dare conferma [**da**ray
konf**air**ma]
congratulations!
congratulazioni!
[kongratool**a**tz-y**o**nee]
connecting flight la
coincidenza [ko-eenchee-
dentza]
connection la coincidenza
conscious cosciente
[kosh**en**tay]
constipation la stitichezza
[steeteek**et**za]
consulate il consolato
contact mettersi in contatto
con
contact lenses le lenti a
contatto
contraceptive il
contraccettivo [kontrachet-
teevo]
convenient comodo
that's not convenient non

(mi) va bene [**bay**nay]
cook (verb) cucinare
[koocheen**a**ray]
it's not cooked non è
abbastanza cotto [ay ab-
bast**an**za]
cooker la cucina
[kooch**ee**na]
cookie il biscotto
cooking utensils gli utensili
da cucina [kooch**ee**na]
cool fresco
cork il tappo
corkscrew il cavatappi
corner: on the corner
all'angolo
in the corner nell'angolo
cornflakes i fiocchi di
granturco [f-y**ok**-kee dee
grant**oor**ko]
correct (right) esatto
corridor il corridoio [kor-
reed**o**-yo]
cosmetics i cosmetici
[kosm**e**teechee]
cost costare [kost**a**ray]
how much does it cost?
quanto costa? [**kwan**to]
cot il lettino
cotton il cotone [kot**o**nay]
cotton wool l'ovatta f
couch (sofa) il divano
couchette la cuccetta
[kooch**et**-ta]
cough la tosse [**tos**-say]
cough medicine lo sciroppo
per la tosse [sheer**op**-po pair]
could: could you ...?
potresti/potrebbe...?

[potrayb-bay]

could I have ...? vorrei... [vor-ray]

I couldn't ... (wasn't able to) non ho potuto... [o pot**oo**to]

country il paese [pa-**ay**zay]

(countryside) la campagna [kampan-ya]

couple (two people) la coppia [k**o**p-ya]

a couple of ... un paio di... [p**a**-yo dee]

courgette il zucchino [zook-k**ee**no]

courier la guida turistica [gw**ee**da]

course (main course etc) la port**a**ta

of course naturalmente [natooralm**e**ntay]

of course not no di certo [dee ch**ai**rto]

cousin (male/female) il cugino [kooj**ee**no], la cugina

cow la mucca [m**oo**k-ka]

crab il granchio [gr**a**nk-yo]

cracker il cracker [kr**e**kair]

craft shop il negozio di artigianato [nay-g**o**tz-yo dee arteejan**a**to]

crash l'incidente **m** [eench**ee**dentay]

I've had a crash ho avuto un incidente [o av**oo**to]

crazy pazzo [p**a**tzo]

cream (on milk, in cake) la p**a**nna

(lotion) la crema [kr**ay**ma]

(colour) crema

crèche l'asilo nido **m**

credit card la carta di credito [kr**ay**deeto]

do you take credit cards? prendete carte di credito? [prend**ay**tay k**a**rtay]

 Major credit and charge cards are accepted in many shops, hotels and restaurants and also for cash advances at many banks, but not always at petrol stations. Many outlets also refuse credit cards if they consider the amount too small.

dialogue

can I pay by credit card? posso pagare con una carta di credito? [pag**a**ray]

which card do you want to use? con quale carta vuole pagare? [kw**a**lay – vw**o**lay]

Access/Visa

yes, sir sì, signore [seen-y**o**ray]

what's the number? qual è il numero? [kwal ay eel n**oo**mairo]

and the expiry date? e la data di scadenza? [ay – skad**e**ntza]

crisps le patatine [patat**ee**nay]

crockery il vasellame [vazel-l**a**may]

crossing (by sea) la traversata

[travair-s**a**ta]

crossroads l'incrocio **m**
[eenkr**o**cho]

crowd la folla

crowded affollato

crown (on tooth) la capsula
[k**a**psoola]

cruise la crociera [kroch**ai**ra]

crutches le stampelle
[stamp**e**l-lay]

cry (verb) piangere
[p-y**a**njairay]

cucumber il cetriolo [chetree-**o**lo]

cup la tazza [t**a**tza]

a cup of ..., please una tazza
di..., per favore

cupboard l'armadio **m** [armad-yo]

(in kitchen) la credenza
[kred**e**ntza]

cure la cura [k**oo**ra]

curly riccio [r**ee**cho]

current la corrente [kor-r**e**ntay]

curtains le tende [t**e**nday]

cushion il cuscino
[koosh**ee**no]

custom il costume
[kost**oo**may]

Customs la dogana

cut il taglio [t**a**l-yo]

(verb) tagliare [t**a**l-yaray]

I've cut myself mi sono
tagliato [t**a**l-y**a**to]

cutlery le posate [poz**a**tay]

cycling il ciclismo
[cheekl**ee**smo]

cyclist il ciclista [cheekl**ee**sta]

D

dad il papà

daily ogni giorno [**o**n-yee j**o**rno]

(adj) quotidiano [kwoteed-y**a**no]

damage (verb) danneggiare
[dan-nej-j**a**ray]

damaged danneggiato [dan-nej-j**a**to]

I'm sorry, I've damaged this
mi dispiace, l'ho
danneggiato [mee deesp-y**a**chay lo]

damn! accidenti! [acheed**e**ntee]

damp (adj) umido [**oo**meedo]

dance il ballo

(verb) ballare [bal-l**a**ray]

would you like to dance?
balla?

dangerous pericoloso
[paireekol**o**zo]

Danish danese [dan**ay**zay]

dark (adj: colour) scuro [sk**oo**ro]

(hair) bruno [br**oo**no]

it's getting dark si sta
facendo buio [fach**e**ndo b**oo**-yo]

date*: what's the date today?
che giorno è oggi? [kay j**o**rno ay **o**j-jee]

let's make a date for next
Monday possiamo fissare un
appuntamento per lunedì
prossimo? [pos-y**a**mo fees-s**a**ray oon ap-poontam**e**nto]

dates (fruit) i datteri [dattairee]

daughter la figlia [**feel**-ya]

daughter-in-law la nuora [**nwo**ra]

dawn l'alba f

at dawn all'alba

day il giorno [**jor**no]

the day after il giorno dopo

the day after tomorrow dopodomani

the day before il giorno prima

the day before yesterday l'altroieri m [altro-**ya**iree]

every day ogni giorno [**on**-yee]

all day? tutto il giorno?

in two days' time tra due giorni

have a nice day! buona giornata! [bwona jor**na**ta]

day trip la gita (di un giorno) [**jee**ta dee oon **jor**no]

dead morto

deaf sordo

deal (business) l'affare m [af-**fa**ray]

it's a deal affare fatto

death la morte [**mor**tay]

decaffeinated coffee il caffè decaffeinato [kaf-**fay** dekaf-fee-ay**na**to]

December dicembre [deech**em**bray]

decide decidere [dech**ee**dairay]

we haven't decided yet non abbiamo ancora deciso [ab-**ya**mo – dech**ee**zo]

decision la decisione [decheez-**yo**nay]

deck (on ship) il ponte (di coperta) [**pon**tay dee kop**air**ta]

deckchair la sedia a sdraio [**sayd**-ya a zdra-yo]

deep profondo

definitely certamente [chairtam**en**tay]

definitely not assolutamente no [as-soolootam**en**tay]

degree (qualification) la laurea [**low**ray-a]

delay il ritardo

deliberately volutamente [volootam**en**tay]

delicatessen (shop) la gastronomia

delicious delizioso [deleetz-**yo**zo]

deliver consegnare [konsen-**ya**ray]

delivery (of mail) la consegna [kons**en**-ya]

Denmark la Danimarca

dental floss il filo interdentale [eentaird**en**talay]

dentist il dentista m/f

Citizens of EU countries get free dental treatment by going to the USSL (local health authority) with form E111 (obtainable from post offices before you go). Otherwise, you can go privately to any dentist, but they are very expensive. Dentists in

63

Sicily are not covered by the Italian health service, so the E111 is useless there.

dialogue

it's this one here è questo qui [ay kwesto kwee]
this one? questo?
no that one no, quello [kwel-lo]
here? qui?
yes sì

dentures la dentiera [dent-yaira]
deodorant il deodorante [day-odorantay]
department il reparto
department store il grande magazzino [granday magatzeeno]
departure la partenza [partentza]
departure lounge la sala d'attesa (delle partenze) [at-tayza del-lay partentzay]
depend: it depends dipende [deependay]
it depends on ... dipende da...
deposit (on bottle) la cauzione [kowtz-yonay]
(for reservation) la caparra
(as part payment) l'acconto m

You will be asked to leave a deposit when renting a car or a bicycle, or when

booking a flight. You can also leave a deposit for an item you intend to buy, but for which you are not able to pay immediately.

description la descrizione [deskreetz-yonay]
dessert il dessert [des-sair]
destination la destinazione [desteenatz-yonay]
develop sviluppare [zveeloop-paray]

dialogue

could you develop these films? può sviluppare queste pellicole? [pwo – kwestay pel-leekolay]
yes certainly sì, certo [chairto]
when will they be ready? quando sono pronte? [kwando – prontay]
tomorrow afternoon domani pomeriggio [pomaireej-jo]
how much is the 24-hour service? quanto costa lo sviluppo in giornata? [kwanto – jornata]

diabetic (man/woman) il diabetico [dee-abayteeko], la diabetica
diabetic foods gli alimenti per diabetici [dee-abayteechee]
dial (verb) comporre il

numero (di...) [kompor-ray eel
n**oo**mairo dee]

dialling code il prefisso
telefonico [pref**ee**s-so]

 For direct international
calls from Italy, dial the
country code (given
below), the area code (minus the
first 0), and finally the subscriber
number:

UK: 0044
Australia: 0061
Ireland: 00353
New Zealand: 0064
US & Canada: 001

Calling Italy from abroad, dial 0039
then the full subscriber number,
which now includes what was
formerly the area prefix – eg all
Rome numbers now begin with 06.
Dialling within Italy, you dial the full
number, including the zero,
regardless of where you're calling
from.

diamond il diamante [dee-
am**a**ntay]

diarrhoea la diarrea [dee-ar**ay**-
a]

diary (business etc) l'agenda **f**
[aj**e**nda]
(for personal experiences) il
diario [dee-**a**r-yo]

dictionary il dizionario [deetz-
yon**a**rio]

didn't*
see **not**

die morire [mor**ee**ray]

diesel il gasolio [gaz-**o**l-yo]

diet la dieta [d-y**ay**ta]
I'm on a diet sono a dieta
I have to follow a special diet
devo seguire una dieta
speciale [**day**vo segw**ee**ray –
spech**a**lay]

difference la differenza [deef-
fair**e**ntza]
what's the difference? qual è
la differenza? [kwal**ay**]

different diverso [deev**ai**rso]
this one is different questo è
diverso [kw**e**sto ay]
a different table un altro
tavolo

difficult difficile [deef-
f**ee**cheelay]

difficulty la difficoltà

dinghy il gommone
[gomm**o**nay]

dining room la sala da pranzo
[pr**a**ntzo]

dinner (evening meal) la cena
[ch**ay**na]
to have dinner cenare
[chen**a**ray]

direct (adj) diretto
[deer**e**t-to]
is there a direct train? c'è un
treno diretto? [chay]

direction la direzione [deeretz-
y**o**nay]
which direction is it? in
quale direzione è? [kw**a**lay –
ay]
is it in this direction? è in
questa direzione? [ay een
kw**e**sta]

directory enquiries
informazioni elenco
abbonati [eenformatz-**yo**nee]

The number for directory
enquiries is 12 for Italy,
176 for Europe, 170 for
the rest of the world.

dirt lo sporco
dirty sporco
disabled invalido
**is there access for the
disabled?** c'è un accesso per
gli invalidi? [chay oon ach**e**s-so
pair]
disappear scomparire
[skompar**ee**ray]
it's disappeared è sparito
[ay]
disappointed deluso [del**oo**zo]
disappointing deludente
[del**oo**d**e**ntay]
disaster il disastro
disco la discoteca
discount lo sconto
is there a discount? c'è uno
sconto? [chay]
disease la malattia [malat-**tee**-
a]
disgusting (taste, food)
disgustoso [deesgoost**o**zo]
dish (meal) il piatto [p-**yat**-to]
(bowl) la scodella
dishes i piatti
dishcloth lo strofinaccio per
i piatti [strofeen**a**cho pair]
disinfectant il disinfettante
[deeseenfet-**ta**ntay]

disk (for computer) il dischetto
[deesk**et**-to]
disposable diapers i
pannolini (usa e getta) [**oo**za
ay **je**t-ta]
disposable nappies i
pannolini (usa e getta)
distance la distanza
[deest**a**ntza]
in the distance in lontananza
[lontan**a**ntza]
distilled water l'acqua
distillata **f** [**a**kwa]
district la zona
disturb disturbare
[deestoob**a**ray]
diversion (detour) la
deviazione [dev-yatz-**yo**nay]
diving board il trampolino
divorced divorziato [deevortz-
yato]
dizzy: I feel dizzy mi gira la
testa [mee **jee**ra]
do fare [**fa**ray]
what shall we do? che
facciamo? [kay fach**a**mo]
how do you do it? come si
fa? [**ko**may]
will you do it for me? lo può
fare lei per me? [pwo **fa**ray lay
pair may]

dialogues

how do you do? piacere
[p-yach**a**iray]
nice to meet you molto
lieto [l-**yay**to]
what do you do? (work)

che lavoro fa? [kay]
I'm a teacher, and you?
sono insegnante, e lei?
[eensen-ya**nt**ay, ay lay]
I'm a student sono
studente [stood**e**ntay]
**what are you doing this
evening?** che cosa fa
questa sera? [kay k**o**za fa
kw**e**sta s**ai**ra]
**we're going out for a drink;
do you want to join us?**
andiamo a bere qualcosa:
vuole venire con noi?
[and-y**a**mo a b**ai**ray kwalk**o**za:
vw**o**lay ven**ee**ray kon noi]

do you want cream? con
panna?
I do, but she doesn't per
me sì, ma non per lei
[pair may – lay]

doctor il medico [**may**deeko]
we need a doctor abbiamo
bisogno di un medico [ab-
y**a**mo beez**o**n-yo dee]
please call a doctor può
chiamare un medico, per
fav**o**re? [pwo k-yam**a**ray]

Any chemist's will have a
list of the nearest
doctors; take the form
E111 (obtainable from post offices
before you leave) with you – this
should enable you to get free
treatment and pay for prescriptions
at the local rate. If possible, you

should take it to the USSL (local
health authority) before seeking
treatment, in order to get an
entitlement document.

dialogue

where does it hurt? dove
le fa male? [**do**vay lay fa
m**a**lay]
right here proprio qui
[kwee]
does that hurt more? così
le fa male di più? [lay –
m**a**lay dee p-yoo]
yes sì
take this to a chemist porti
questo in farmacia [kw**e**sto
een farmach**ee**-a]

document il documento
[dokoom**e**nto]
dog il cane [k**a**nay]
doll la bambola
domestic flight il volo
nazionale [natz-yon**a**lay]
donkey l'asino **m**
don't!: don't do that! non
farlo!
see **not**
door (of room) la porta
(of train, car) lo sportello
doorman il portiere [port-
y**ai**ray]
double doppio [**d**op-yo]
double bed il letto a due
piazze [**d**oo-ay p-y**a**tzay]
double room la camera
doppia [**d**op-ya]

doughnut il krapfen
down giù [joo]
  down here quaggiù [kwaj-**joo**]
  put it down over there lo/la
  metta giù lì
  it's down there on the right è
  giù di lì sulla destra
  it's further down the road è
  più avanti su questa strada
  [ay p-yoo – soo kw**esta**]
downhill skiing la discesa
libera [deesh**ay**za l**ee**baira]
downmarket (restaurant etc)
scadente [skad**entay**]
downstairs di sotto
dozen la dozzina [dotz**ee**na]
  half a dozen mezza dozzina
  [m**etza**]
drain lo scarico
draught beer la birra alla
spina [**beer**-ra]
draughty: it's draughty c'è
corrente [chay kor-**rentay**]
drawer il cassetto
drawing il disegno [dees**ayn**-
yo]
dreadful terribile [tair-r**eeb**-
beelay]
dream il sogno [**son**-yo]
dress il vestito
dressed: to get dressed
(oneself) vestirsi
dressing (for cut) la fasciatura
[fasha-**too**ra]
  salad dressing il
  condimento
dressing gown la vestaglia
[vestal-ya]
drink (alcoholic) la bevanda

alcolica
  (non-alcoholic) la bibita
  analcolica
  (verb) bere [**bai**ray]
  a cold drink una bevanda
  fredda
  can I get you a drink? posso
  offrirti qualcosa da bere?
  [kwalk**o**za da b**ai**ray]
  what would you like (to
  drink)? cosa vuoi bere? [k**o**za
  vwoy]
  no thanks, I don't drink no,
  grazie, non bevo alcolici
  [**bay**vo alk**o**leechee]
  I'll just have a drink of water
  posso avere solo un po'
  d'acqua? [av**ai**ray – d**a**kwa]
  see bar
drinking water l'acqua
potabile [**a**kwa pot**a**beelay]
  is this drinking water? è
  potabile quest'acqua? [ay –
  kw**est**]
drive (verb) guidare
[gweed**a**ray]
  can you drive? sa guidare?
  we drove here siamo venuti
  in macchina [s-y**a**mo ven**oo**tee
  een mak-k**ee**na]
  I'll drive you home ti/la
  accompagno a casa in
  macchina [ak-komp**an**-yo]

 It's compulsory to carry
your car documentation,
driving licence and
passport while you're driving, and
you may be required to present

them if stopped by the police – not
an uncommon occurrence. Rules of
the road are straightforward: drive
on the right; at junctions, where
there's any ambiguity, give priority to
vehicles coming from the right;
observe the speed limits – 50kph in
built-up areas, 110kph on country
roads and 130kph on motorways.
The legal limit for alcohol when
driving is infinitesimally small, so
don't drink and drive.

driver (of car) l'autista **m/f**
[owt**ee**sta]
(of bus) il/la conducente
[kondooch**e**ntay]
driving licence la patente
[pat**e**ntay]
drop: just a drop, please (of
drink) solo una goccia [g**o**cha]
drug la medicina
[medeech**ee**na]
drugs (narcotics) la droga
drunk (adj) ubriaco [oobree-
ako]
drunken driving la guida in
stato di ebbrezza [g**wee**da –
eb-br**e**tza]
dry (adj) asciutto [ash**oo**t-to]
(wine) secco
dry-cleaner il lavasecco
duck l'anatra **f**
**due: he was due to arrive
yesterday** doveva arrivare
ieri [dov**ay**va ar-reev**a**ray]
when is the train due? a che
ora dovrebbe arrivare il
treno? [a kay **o**ra dovr**e**b-bay]

dull (pain) sordo
(weather) uggioso [uj-j**o**so]
(boring) noioso [noy-**o**zo]
dummy (baby's) il succhiotto
[sook-y**o**t-to]
during durante [door**a**ntay]
dust la polvere [p**o**lvairay]
dusty polveroso
dustbin la pattumiera [pat-
toom-y**ai**ra]
duty-free (goods) merci
esenti da dazio [m**ai**rchee
es**e**ntee da d**a**tz-yo]
duty-free shop il duty free
duvet il piumone [p-yoo-
m**o**nay]

E

each (every) ciascuno
[chask**oo**no]
how much are they each?
quanto vengono l'uno/una?
[kw**a**nto]
ear l'orecchio **m** [or**e**k-yo]
earache: I have earache ho
mal d'orecchi [o mal dor**e**k-
kee]
early presto
early in the morning di
mattina presto
I called by earlier sono
passato/passata prima
earrings gli orecchini [or**e**k-
eenee]
east l'est **m**
in the east ad est
Easter la Pasqua [p**a**skwa]

easy facile [**fa**cheelay]
eat mangiare [manj**a**ray]
we've already eaten, thanks
abbiamo già mangiato,
grazie [ab-**ya**mo ja manj**a**to]

eating habits
Italians usually have
three meals a day: a light
breakfast, consisting of **espresso** or
caffellatte and biscuits or a
cornetto (croissant) or bread and
jam; a substantial lunch, with a first
course of pasta or rice, with a second
course of meat or fish and
vegetables, followed by fruit, then
coffee; an evening meal which can
start with soup, or may simply
consist of ham, cheese, fish or meat
and vegetables, followed by fruit.
Desserts are usually reserved for
Sunday or feast day lunches. Some
people also have mid-morning
snacks, with coffee, and/or a
merenda (afternoon snack), and an
aperitivo (drink and snack) before
lunch.

eau de toilette l'eau de
toilette **f**
EC la CE [chay]
economy class la classe
turistica [kl**a**s-say]
Edinburgh Edimburgo
egg l'uovo **m** [**wo**vo]
eggplant la melanzana
[melan**za**na]
Eire la Repubblica d'Irlanda
[rep**oo**b-bleeka deerl**a**nda]

either: either ... or ... o... o...
either of them o l'uno/l'una
o l'altro/l'altra
elastic l'elastico **m**
elastic band l'elastico **m**
elbow il gomito
electric elettrico
electrical appliances gli
elettrodomestici [elet-
trodom**e**steechee]

Electrical supply in Italy is
220v, although anything
requiring 240v will work.
Plugs have two or three round pins,
so you will need an adapter.

electric fire la stufa elettrica
[st**oo**fa]
electrician l'elettricista **m**
[elet-treech**ee**sta]
electricity l'elettricità **f** [elet-
treech**ee**ta]
see **voltage**
elevator l'ascensore **m**
[ashens**o**ray]
else: something else
qualcos'altro [kw**a**lk**o**z]
somewhere else da
qualche altra parte [kw**a**lkay –
partay]

dialogue

would you like anything
else? altro?
no, nothing else, thanks
nient'altro, grazie
[n-yent**a**ltro]

embassy l'ambasciata f
[ambash**a**ta]
emergency l'emergenza f
[emair**j**entza]
this is an emergency! è
un'emergenza! [ay]

In an emergency, dial 113
for the **polizia** (police) or
ambulance, 112 for the
Carabinieri (army police), and 115
for **Vigili del Fuoco** (fire brigade);
call **guardia medica** (doctor on call)
for medical emergencies.

emergency exit l'uscita di
sicurezza f [oosh**ee**ta dee
seekoor**e**tza]
empty vuoto [vw**o**to]
end la fine [**fee**nay]
(verb) finire [feen**ee**ray]
at the end of the street in
fondo alla strada
when does it end? quando
finisce? [kw**a**ndo feen**ee**shay]
engaged (toilet, telephone)
occupato [ok-koop**a**to]
(to be married) fidanzato
[feedantz**a**to]
engine (car) il motore
[mot**o**ray]
England l'Inghilterra f
[eengheelt**ai**r-ra]
English inglese [eengl**ay**zay]
I'm English sono inglese
do you speak English? parla
inglese?
enjoy: to enjoy oneself
divertirsi

dialogue

how did you like the film?
ti/le è piaciuto il film?
[lay ay p-yach**oo**to]
I enjoyed it very much; did
you enjoy it? mi è
piaciuto molto; e a
te/lei? [ay a tay/lay]

enjoyable piacevole
[p-yach**ay**volay]
enlargement (of photo)
l'ingrandimento m
enormous enorme
[en**o**rmay]
enough abbastanza [ab-
bast**a**ntza]
there's not enough ... non
c'è abbastanza... [non chay]
it's not big enough non è
grande abbastanza [ay]
that's enough basta
entrance l'entrata f
envelope la busta [**boo**sta]
epileptic epilettico
equipment l'attrezzatura f [at-
tretzat**oo**ra]
error l'errore m [er-r**o**ray]
especially specialmente
[spechalm**e**ntay]
essential essenziale [es-sentz-
y**a**lay]
it is essential that ... è
essenziale che... [ay – kay]
EU l'UE f [oo ay]
euro l'euro m [ay-**oo**ro]
Eurocheque l'eurocheque m
[ay-**oo**rochek]

Eurocheque card la carta
eurocheque
Europe l'Europa f [ay-ooropa]
European europeo [ay-
ooropay-o]
even perfino [pairfeeno]
even if ... anche se... [ankay
say]
evening la sera [saira]
this evening questa sera
[kwesta]
in the evening di sera
evening meal la cena [chayna]
eventually alla fine [feenay]
ever mai [my]

dialogue

have you ever been to
Padua? è mai stato a
Padova? [ay]
yes, I was there two years
ago sì, ci sono stato due
anni fa [chee]

every ogni [on-yee]
every day ogni giorno
everyone ognuno [on-yoono]
everything tutto [toot-to]
everywhere dappertutto [dap-
pairtoot-to]
exactly! esattamente! [esat-
tamentay]
exam l'esame m [esamay]
example l'esempio m [esemp-
yo]
for example per esempio
[pair]
excellent eccellente

[echelentay]
excellent! ottimo!
except eccetto [echet-to]
excess baggage il bagaglio
in eccesso [bagal-yo een eches-
so]
exchange rate il tasso di
cambio [kamb-yo]
exciting emozionante [emotz-
yonantay]
excuse me (to get past)
permesso [pairmes-so]
(to get attention) mi scusi [mee
skoozee]
(to say sorry) chiedo scusa
[k-yaydo skooza]
exhaust (pipe) il tubo di
scappamento [toobo]
exhausted (tired) esausto
[esowsto]
exhibition la mostra
exit l'uscita f [oosheeta]
where's the nearest exit?
dov'è l'uscita più vicina?
[dovay – p-yoo veecheena]
expect aspettare [aspet-taray]
expensive caro
experienced esperto [espairto]
explain spiegare [sp-yegaray]
can you explain that? me lo
puoi/può spiegare? [may lo
pwoy/pwo]
express (mail, train) l'espresso
m
extension (telephone) l'interno
m [eentairno]
extension 221, please
interno duecentoventuno,
per favore

extension lead la prolunga

extra: can we have an extra
one? possiamo averne
uno/una in più? [poss-yamo
avairnay – p-yoo]

do you charge extra for that?
si paga in più per questo?
[pair kwesto]

extraordinary straordinario
[stra-ordeenar-yo]

extremely estremamente
[estrema-mentay]

eye l'occhio m [ok-yo]

will you keep an eye on my
suitcase for me? mi tiene
d'occhio la valigia, per
favore? [mee t-yaynay]

eyebrow pencil la matita per
le sopracciglia [pair lay sopra-
cheel-ya]

eye drops il collirio [kol-leer-
yo]

eyeglasses (US) gli occhiali
[ok-yalee]

eyeliner l'eye-liner m

eye make-up remover lo
struccante per gli occhi
[strook-kantay pair l-yee ok-kee]

eye shadow l'ombretto m

F

face la faccia [facha]

factory la fabbrica

Fahrenheit* Fahrenheit

faint (verb) svenire [sveneeray]

she's fainted è svenuta [ay
svenoota]

I feel faint mi sento venir
meno [mayno]

fair (funfair) il luna park
[loona]

(trade) la fiera [f-yaira]

(adj) giusto [joosto]

fairly abbastanza [ab-
bastantza]

fake il falso

Fall l'autunno m [owtoon-no]

fall (verb) cadere [kadairay]

she's had a fall è caduta [ay
kadoota]

false falso

family la famiglia [fameel-ya]

famous famoso

fan (electrical) il ventilatore
[venteelato-ray]

(hand held) il ventaglio [vental-
yo]

(sports: man/woman) il tifoso, la
tifosa

fan belt la cinghia della
ventola [cheeng-ya]

fantastic fantastico

far lontano

dialogue

is it far from here? è
lontano da qui? [ay –
kwee]

no, not very far no, non è
molto lontano

well how far? quant'è
lontano? [kwantay]

it's about 20 kilometres
circa venti chilometri
[cheerka]

fare il prezzo del biglietto [pretzo del beel-yet-to]
farm la fattoria [fat-toree-a]
fashionable di moda
fast veloce [velochay]
fat (person) grasso
   (on meat) il grasso
father il padre [padray]
father-in-law il suocero [swochairo]
faucet il rubinetto
fault il difetto
   sorry, it was my fault mi dispiace, è stata colpa mia [mee deesp-yachay ay – mee-a]
   it's not my fault non è colpa mia
faulty difettoso [deefet-tozo]
favourite preferito [prefaireeto]
fax il fax
   (verb: person) mandare un fax a [mandaray]
   (document) mandare per fax
February febbraio [feb-bra-yo]
feel sentire [senteeray]
   I feel hot sento caldo
   I feel unwell non mi sento bene [baynay]
   I feel like going for a walk ho voglia di fare una passeggiata [o vol-ya dee faray oona pas-sej-jata]
   how are you feeling? come si sente? [komay see sentay]
   I'm feeling better mi sento meglio [mayl-yo]
felt-tip (pen) il pennarello

fence lo steccato
fender il paraurti [para-oortee]
ferry il traghetto [traget-to]
festival (music, arts) il festival
fetch (andare a) prendere [prendairay]
   I'll fetch him vado a prenderlo [prendairlo]
   will you come and fetch me later? passi/passa a prendermi più tardi? [prendairmee p-yoo]
feverish febbricante [feb-breecheetantay]
few: a few alcuni/alcune [alkoonee/alkoonay]
   a few days alcuni giorni
fiancé il fidanzato [feedantzato]
fiancée la fidanzata
field il campo
fight la lite [leetay]
figs i fichi [feekee]
fill riempire [r-yempeeray]
fill in riempire
   do I have to fill this in? devo riempire questo? [dayvo – kwesto]
fill up fare il pieno [faray eel p-yayno]
   fill it up, please il pieno, per favore
filling (in cake, sandwich) il ripieno [reep-yayno]
   (in tooth) l'otturazione f [ot-tooratz-yonay]
film (movie) il film [feelm]
   (for camera) la pellicola

dialogue

do you have this kind of film? avete questo tipo di pellicola? [avaytay kwesto]
yes; how many exposures? sì, da quante pose? [kwantay pozay]
36 trentasei

film processing lo sviluppo della pellicola [zveeloop-po]
filthy lurido [looreedo]
find (verb) trovare [trovaray]
I can't find it non lo/la trovo
I've found it l'ho trovato/trovata
find out scoprire [skopreeray]
could you find out for me? può informarsi per me? [pwo – pair may]
fine (weather) bello
(punishment) la multa

dialogues

how are you? come sta? [komay]
I'm fine, thanks bene, grazie [baynay gratzee-ay]

is that OK? va bene?
that's fine, thanks va bene, grazie

finger il dito
finish (verb) finire [feeneeray]
I haven't finished yet non ho ancora finito [o]

when does it finish? quando finisce? [kwando feeneeshay]
fire: fire! al fuoco! [fwoko]
can we light a fire here? si possono accendere fuochi qui? [achendairay fwokee kwee]
it's on fire è in fiamme [ay een f-yam-may]
fire alarm l'allarme antincendio m [al-larmay anteenchend-yo]
fire brigade i vigili del fuoco [veejeelee del fwoko]

In the event of a fire, phone 115.

fire escape l'uscita di sicurezza [oosheeta dee seekooretza]
fire extinguisher l'estintore m [esteen-toray]
first primo [preemo]
I was first c'ero prima io [chairo – ee-o]
at first all'inizio [eeneetz-yo]
the first time la prima volta
first on the left la prima a sinistra
first aid il pronto soccorso
first aid kit la cassetta del pronto soccorso
first class (travel etc) in prima classe [klassay]
first floor (UK) il primo piano (US) il piano terra [tair-ra]
first name il nome di battesimo [nomay dee bat-tayseemo]
fish il pesce [peshay]

fishing village il villaggio di pescatori [veel-laj-jo]

fishmonger's la pescheria [peskairee-a]

fit (attack) l'attacco m

it doesn't fit me non mi sta

fitting room il camerino di prova

fix (verb) riparare [reepararay] (arrange) fissare [fees-saray]

can you fix this? può ripararlo? [pwo]

fizzy frizzante [freetzantay]

flag la bandiera [band-yaira]

flannel la pezza di spugna [petza dee spoon-ya]

flash (for camera) il flash

flat (noun: apartment) l'appartamento m (adj) piatto [p-yat-to]

I've got a flat tyre ho una gomma a terra [o – tair-ra]

flavour il sapore [saporay]

flea la pulce [poolchay]

flight il volo

flight number il numero del volo [noomairo]

flippers le pinne [peen-nay]

flood l'inondazione f [eenondatz-yonay]

floor (of room) il pavimento (of building) il piano

on the floor sul pavimento [sool]

Florence Firenze [feerentzay]

Florentine (adj) fiorentino

florist il fioraio [f-yora-yo]

flour la farina

flower il fiore [f-yoray]

flu l'influenza f

fluent: he speaks fluent Italian parla l'italiano correntemente [eetal-yano korrentementay]

fly la mosca (verb) volare [volaray]

fly in arrivare in aereo [arreevaray een a-airay-o]

fly out partire in aereo [parteeray]

fog la nebbia

foggy: it's foggy c'è nebbia [chay]

folk dancing le danze folk [dantzay]

folk music la musica folk [moozeeka]

follow seguire [segweeray]

follow me mi segua [mee say-gwa]

food il cibo [cheebo]

food poisoning l'intossicazione alimentare f [eentos-seekatz-yonay alimentaray]

food shop/store il negozio di generi alimentari [negotz-yo dee jaynairee]

foot* il piede [p-yayday]

on foot a piedi

football il calcio [kalcho] (ball) il pallone [pal-lonay]

football match la partita di calcio

for per [pair], da

do you have something for ...? (headache/diarrhoea etc) avete qualcosa contro...?

76

[a**vay**tay kwalk**o**za]

dialogues

who's the ice cream for?
per chi è il gelato? [pair
kee ay]
that's for me è per me
[may]
and this one? e questa?
[ay kw**e**sta]
that's for her quella è per
lei [kw**e**l-la – lay]

where do I get the bus for
San Pietro? dove si
prende l'autobus per San
Pietro? [d**o**vay see pr**e**nday
l**ow**-toboos pair]
the bus for San Pietro
leaves from Termini Station
l'autobus per San Pietro
parte dalla Stazione
Termini [p**a**rtay – statz-
y**o**nay]

how long have you been
here for? da quanto è
qui? [kw**a**nto ay kwee]
I've been here for two
days, how about you?
sono qui da due giorni, e
lei? [j**o**rnee, ay lay]
I've been here for a week
sono qui da una
settimana

forehead la fronte [fr**o**ntay]
foreign straniero [stran-y**ai**ro]

foreigner (man/woman) lo
straniero [stran-y**ai**ro], la
straniera
forest la foresta
forget dimenticare
[deementeek**a**ray]
I forget non ricordo
I've forgotten ho
dimenticato
fork la forchetta [fork**et**-ta]
(in road) la biforcazione
[beeforkatz-y**o**nay]
form (document) il modulo
[m**o**doolo]
formal (dress) da cerimonia
[chaireem**o**n-ya]
fortnight quindici giorni
[kweend**ee**chee j**o**rnee]
fortunately fortunatamente
[fortoonata-m**e**ntay]
forward: could you forward my
mail? potrebbe inoltrare la
mia corrispondenza? [potreb-
bay eenoltr**a**ray la m**ee**-a kor-
reespond**e**ntza]
forwarding address il nuovo
recapito [nw**o**vo]
foundation cream il
fondotinta
fountain la fontana
foyer (of hotel) l'atrio m
(theatre) il foyer
fracture la frattura [frat-t**oo**ra]
France la Francia [fr**a**ncha]
free libero [l**ee**bairo]
(no charge) gratuito [grat**oo**-
eeto]
is it free (of charge)? è gratis?
freeway l'autostrada f

[owtostra**da**]
see **motorway**
freezer il freezer [fr**ee**tzair]
French francese [franch**ay**zay]
French fries le patatine fritte
[patat**ee**-nay fr**ee**t-tay]
frequent frequente
[frekw**e**ntay]
how frequent is the bus to
Perugia? ogni quanto passa
l'autobus per Perugia? [**on**-
yee kw**a**nto – pair]
fresh fresco
fresh orange juice il succo
d'arancia [**soo**k-ko dar**a**ncha]
Friday venerdì [venaird**ee**]
fridge il frigo
fried fritto
fried egg l'uovo al tegamino
m [w**o**vo]
friend (male/female) l'amico **m**,
l'amica **f**
friendly cordiale [kord-y**a**lay]
from da
when does the next train
from Rome arrive? quando
arriva il prossimo treno da
Roma? [kw**a**ndo]
from Monday to Friday dal
lunedì al venerdì
from next Thursday da
giovedì prossimo

dialogue

where are you from? di
dov'è? [dov**ay**]
I'm from Slough sono di
Slough

front il davanti
in front davanti
in front of the hotel davanti
all'albergo
at the front sul davanti
[s**oo**l]
frost il gelo [**jay**lo]
frozen ghiacciato [g-y**a**chato]
frozen food i cibi surgelati
[**chee**bee soor-jel**a**tee]
fruit la frutta [fr**oo**t-ta]
fruit juice il succo di frutta
[**soo**k-ko dee fr**oo**t-ta]
fry friggere [fr**ee**j-jairay]
frying pan la padella
full pieno [p-y**ay**no]
it's full of ... è pieno/piena
di... [ay]
I'm full sono pieno/piena
full board la pensione
completa [pens-y**o**nay
kompl**ay**ta]
fun: it was fun è stato
divertente [deevairt**e**ntay]
funeral il funerale [foonair**a**lay]
funny (strange) strano
(amusing) buffo [b**oo**f-fo]
furniture i mobili
further più avanti [p-y**oo**]
it's further down the road è
più avanti su questa strada

dialogue

how much further is it to
San Gimignano? quanto
manca a San
Gimignano? [kw**a**nto]
about 5 kilometres circa

78

cinque chilometri
[**cheer**ka – kee**lo**metree]

fuse il fusibile [foo**zee**beelay]
the lights have fused sono
saltate le valvole [salt**a**tay lay
valvolay]
fuse box i fusibili
[foo**zee**beelee]
fuse wire il filo fusibile
[-beelay]
future il futuro [foot**oo**ro]
in future in futuro

G

gallon* il gallone [gal-**lo**nay]
game (cards etc) il gioco [**jo**-ko]
(match) la partita
(meat) la selvaggina [selvaj-**jee**na]
garage (for fuel) il distributore
di benzina [deestreeboot**o**ray
dee bent**zee**na]
(for repairs) l'autofficina f
[owtof-feech**ee**na]
(for parking) l'autorimessa f
[owtoreem**es**-sa]

 Garages are generally
open Monday to Saturday
from 8 a.m. to 7.30 p.m.
and close for lunch between 1 and 3
p.m. Opening times, however, do
vary. Garages take turns to open on
Sundays and if one garage is closed
for a holiday, another should be

open nearby. In the majority of
garages, the pump assistant will fill
the tank for you, and also clean the
windscreen and check the water, oil
and tyres. Very few garages accept
credit cards.

garden il giardino [jard**ee**no]
garlic l'aglio m [**al**-yo]
gas il gas
gas cylinder (camping gas) la
bombola del gas
gas permeable lenses le lenti
semirigide [semee**ree**jeeday]
gasoline (US) la benzina
[bent**zee**na]
see petrol
gas station la stazione di
servizio [statz-**yo**nay dee
sair**vee**tz-yo]
gate il cancello [kanch**el**-lo]
(at airport) l'uscita f [oosh**ee**ta]
gay il gay
gay bar il bar gay
gear la marcia [**mar**cha]
gearbox la scatola del
cambio [**kamb**-yo]
gear lever la leva del cambio
general generale [jenair**a**lay]
Genoa Genova [**jay**nova]
gents (toilet) la toilette (degli
uomini) [twal**et** dayl-yee wo-
meenee]
genuine (antique etc) autentico
[owt**en**teeko]
German (adj) tedesco
German measles la rosolia
Germany la Germania
get (fetch) prendere

[prendairay]

will you get me another one, please? me ne porta un altro/un'altra, per favore? [may nay]

how do I get to ...? come si arriva a...? [komay]

do you know where I can get them? sa dove posso trovarli/trovarle? [dovay – trovarlay]

dialogue

can I get you a drink? posso offrirle qualcosa da bere? [of-freerlay kwalkoza da bairay]

no, I'll get this one, what would you like? no, offro io questa volta, cosa prende? [ee-o kwesta – koza prenday]

a glass of red wine un bicchiere di vino rosso [beek-k-yairay]

get back (return) tornare [tornaray]

get in (arrive) arrivare [ar-reevaray]

get off scendere [shendairay]

where do I get off? dove devo scendere? [dovay dayvo]

get on (to train etc) salire [saleeray]

get out (of car etc) scendere [shendairay]

get up (in the morning) alzarsi

[altzarsee]

gift il regalo

gift shop il negozio di articoli da regalo [negotz-yo]

gin il gin

a gin and tonic, please un gin tonic, per favore

girl la ragazza [ragatza]

girlfriend la ragazza

give dare [daray]

can you give me some change? mi può dare degli spiccioli? [mee pwo – dayl-yee]

I gave it to him l'ho dato a lui [lo – loo-ee]

will you give this to ...? puoi/può dare questo a...? [pwoy/pwo – kwesto]

dialogue

how much do you want for this? quanto vuole per questo? [kwanto vwolay pair kwesto]

100,000 lire 100.000 (centomila) lire [leeray]

I'll give you 80,000 lire gliene do 80.000 (ottantamila) [l-yee-aynee]

give back restituire [resteetweeray]

glad contento

glass (material) il vetro (tumbler) il bicchiere [beek-yairay] (wine glass) il bicchiere da vino

a glass of wine un bicchiere di vino

glasses (spectacles) gli occhiali [ok-yalee]

gloves i guanti [gwantee]

glue la colla

go (verb) andare [andaray]

we'd like to go to the Roman Forum vorremmo andare al Foro Romano [vor-rem-mo]

where are you going? dove stai andando? [dovay sty]

where does this bus go? dove va questo autobus? [dovay va kwesto]

let's go! andiamo! [and-yamo]

she's gone (left) se n'è andata [say nay]

where has he gone? dov'è andato? [dovay]

I went there last week ci sono andato la settimana scorsa [chee]

pizza to go una pizza da portare via [portaray vee-a]

go away andare via [andaray]

go away! vattene! [vat-tenay]

go back (return) tornare [tornaray]

go down (the stairs etc) scendere [shendairay]

go in entrare [entraray]

go out (in the evening) uscire [oosheeray]

do you want to go out tonight? vuoi/vuole uscire stasera? [vwoy/vwolay]

go through attraversare [at-travairsaray]

go up (stairs) salire [saleeray]

goat la capra

goats' cheese il caprino

God Dio [dee-o]

goggles (for skiing) gli occhiali da sci [ok-yalee da shee]

(for swimming) gli occhiali da nuoto [nwoto]

gold l'oro m

golf il golf

golf course il campo di golf

gondola la gondola

gondolier il gondoliere [gondol-yairay]

good buono [bwono]

good! bene! [baynay]

it's no good non va bene

goodbye arrivederci [ar-reevedairchee]

good evening buonasera [bwonasaira]

Good Friday Venerdì Santo [venairdee santo]

Good Friday is not a public holiday in Italy. Shops are open and public transport operates in the usual way. However, some offices might close earlier than usual.

good morning buongiorno [bwonjorno]

good night buonanotte [bwonanot-tay]

goose l'oca f

got: we've got to leave dobbiamo partire [dob-yamo parteeray]

have you got any ...?
avete...? [av**ay**tay]
government il governo
[gov**ai**rno]
gradually gradualmente
[gradoo-al**men**tay]
grammar la grammatica
gram(me) il grammo
granddaughter la nipote
[neep**o**tay]
grandfather il nonno
grandmother la nonna
grandson il nipote [neep**o**tay]
grapefruit il pompelmo
grapefruit juice il succo di
pompelmo [**sook**-ko]
grapes l'uva **f** [**oo**va]
grass l'erba **f** [**air**ba]
grateful grato
gravy il sugo [**soo**go]
great (excellent) fantastico
that's great! magnifico!
a great success un gran
successo [soo**ches**-so]
Great Britain la Gran
Bretagna [bretan-ya]
Greece la Grecia [gr**e**cha]
greedy goloso
Greek (adj) greco
green verde [**vair**day]
green card (car insurance) la
carta verde
greengrocer's il fruttivendolo
[froot-teev**e**ndolo]
grey grigio [**gree**jo]
grill la griglia [gr**eel**-ya]
grilled alla griglia
grocer's il negozio di
alimentari [neg**o**tz-yo]

ground la terra [**tair**-ra]
on the ground per terra [pair]
ground floor il piano terra
[**tair**-ra]
group il gruppo [gr**oo**p-po]
guarantee la garanzia
[garantz**ee**-a]
is it guaranteed? è garantito?
[ay]
guest l'ospite **m/f** [**o**speetay]
guesthouse la pensione [pens-
yonay]
guide la guida [gw**ee**da]
guidebook la guida
guided tour la visita guidata
[**vee**zeeta gweed**a**ta]
guitar la chitarra [keet**ar**-ra]
gum (in mouth) la gengiva [jen-
jeeva]
gun il fucile [fooch**ee**lay]
gym la palestra

H

hair i capelli
hairbrush la spazzola per
capelli [**spatz**ola pair]
haircut il taglio di capelli [**tal**-
yo]
hairdresser (men's) il barbiere
[barb-y**ai**ray]
(women's: man/woman) il
parrucchiere [par-rook-y**ai**ray]
la parrucchiera

Hairdressers are open
from Tuesday to Saturday.
It is always advisable to

book, but you might still have to wait.

hairdryer il fon

hair gel il gel per capelli [jel pair]

hairgrips i fermacapelli

hair spray la lacca per capelli

half la metà

  half an hour mezz'ora [metzora]

  half a litre mezzo litro [metzo]

  about half that una metà di quello [kwel-lo]

half board la mezza pensione [metza pens-yonay]

half bottle mezza bottiglia [bot-teel-ya]

half fare mezzo biglietto [metzo beel-yet-to]

half price metà prezzo [pretzo]

ham il prosciutto [proshoot-to]

Prosciutto crudo is Parma ham, which, as the word **crudo** indicates, is raw meat that has been cured. **Prosciutto cotto** is similar to roast ham, not to reconstituted cooked ham or gammon. Both kinds of prosciutto are sold in **salumeria** in thin slices by the **etto** (100 grams) and are used in sandwiches, starters and a variety of dishes.

hamburger l'hamburger **m** [amboorgair]

hammer il martello

hand la mano

handbag la borsetta

handbrake il freno a mano [frayno]

handkerchief il fazzoletto [fatzolet-to]

handle (on door, suitcase) la maniglia [maneel-ya] (on handbag) il manico

hand luggage il bagaglio a mano [bagal-yo]

hang-gliding il deltaplano

hangover i postumi della sbornia [zborn-ya]

  I've got a hangover soffro per i postumi di una sbornia

happen succedere [soochaydairay]

  what's happening? che succede? [kay soochayday]

  what has happened? che è successo? [ay soochays-so]

happy felice [feleechay]

  I'm not happy about this non ne sono convinto [nay]

harbour il porto

hard duro [dooro] (difficult) difficile [deef-feecheelay]

hard-boiled egg l'uovo sodo **m** [wovo]

hard lenses le lenti rigide [reejeeday]

hardly a mala pena

  hardly ever quasi mai [kwazee my]

hardware shop il negozio di ferramenta [negotz-yo dee fair-ramenta]

hat il cappello
hate (verb) detestare [detestaray]
have* avere [avairay]
  can I have ...? vorrei... [vor-ray]
  do you have ...? hai/ha...? [a-ee/a]
  what'll you have? cosa prendi/prende? [koza prendee/prenday]
  I have to leave now devo andarmene adesso [dayvo andarmenay]
  do I have to ...? devo...?
  can we have some ...? vorremmo un po' di... [vorrem-mo]
hayfever la febbre da fieno [feb-bray da f-yayno]
hazelnuts le nocciole [nocholay]
he* lui [loo-ee]
head la testa
headache il mal di testa
headlights i fari
headphones la cuffia [koof-ya]
health food shop il negozio di cibi naturali [negotz-yo dee cheebee]
healthy sano
hear sentire [senteeray]

dialogue

  can you hear me? mi sente? [sentay]
  I can't hear you, could you repeat that? non la sento, può ripetere? [pwo reepetairay]

hearing aid l'apparecchio acustico m [ap-parek-yo akoosteeko]
heart il cuore [kworay]
heart attack l'infarto m
heat il caldo
heater (in room) il radiatore [rad-yatoray]
  (in car) il riscaldamento
heating il riscaldamento
heavy pesante [pezantay]
heel (of foot) il tallone [tal-lonay]
  (of shoe) il tacco
  could you heel these? può rifare i tacchi a queste scarpe? [pwo reefaray ee tak-kee a kwestay skarpay]
heelbar riparazione scarpe [reeparatz-yonay]
height l'altezza f [altetza]
helicopter l'elicottero m [eleekot-tairo]
hello (in the daytime) buongiorno [bwonjorno]
  (late afternoon, in the evening) buonasera [bwonasaira]
  (answer on phone) pronto
helmet (for motorcycle) il casco
help l'aiuto m [a-yooto]
  (verb) aiutare [a-yootaray]
  help! aiuto!
  can you help me? mi può aiutare? [pwo]
  thank you very much for your help grazie dell'aiuto

[gratzee-ay]

helpful disponibile
[deesponeebeelay]

hepatitis l'epatite f [epateetay]

her*: I haven't seen her non
l'ho vista [lo]

to her a lei [lay], le [lay]

with her con lei, con sé [say]

for her per lei

that's her è lei

that's her towel è il suo
asciugamano [ay eel soo-o]

herbal tea la tisana [teezana]

herbs le erbe [airbay]

here qui [kwee]

here is/are ... ecco...

here you are ecco a te/lei
[tay/lay]

hers*: that's hers quello è suo
[kwel-lo ay soo-o]

hey! ehi! [ay-ee]

hi! (hello) ciao! [chow], salve!
[salvay]

hide (verb) nascondere
[naskondairay]

high alto

highchair il seggiolone [sej-
jolonay]

highway l'autostrada f
[owtostrada]

see motorway

hill la collina

him*: I haven't seen him non
l'ho visto [lo]

to him a lui [loo-ee], gli [l-yee]

with him con lui, con sé
[say]

for him per lui [pair]

that's him è lui [ay]

hip il fianco [f-yanko]

hire noleggiare [nolej-jaray]

for hire a nolo

where can I hire a bike? dove
posso noleggiare una
bicicletta? [dovay]

see also rent

his*: it's his car è la sua
macchina [ay la soo-a]

that's his quello è suo [kwel-
lo ay soo-o]

hit (verb) colpire [kolpeeray]

hitch-hike fare l'autostop
[faray lowtostop]

hobby l'hobby m

hockey l'hockey m

hold (verb) tenere [tenairay]

hole il buco [booko]

holiday la vacanza [vakantza]

on holiday in vacanza

home la casa [kaza]

at home (in my house etc) a
casa

(in my country) in patria

we go home tomorrow
torniamo in patria domani
[torn-yamo]

honest onesto

honey il miele [m-yaylay]

honeymoon la luna di miele
[loona dee]

hood (US) il cofano

hope la speranza [spairantza]

I hope so spero di sì [spairo]

I hope not spero di no

hopefully se tutto va bene
[say toot-to va baynay]

horn (of car) il clacson

horrible orribile [or-reebeelay]

horse il cavallo
horse riding l'equitazione **f**
[ekweetatz-**yo**nay]
hospital l'ospedale **m**
[ospeda**lay**]
hospitality l'ospitalità **f**
thank you for your hospitality
grazie dell'ospitalità

If you are invited to someone's home, take a bunch of flowers (but not carnations or chrysanthemums which are used in cemeteries) or a plant. If you are staying at someone's house, take presents such as whisky, tea, etc.

hot caldo
(spicy) piccante [peek-**kan**tay]
I'm hot ho caldo [o]
it's hot today fa caldo oggi
[**o**j-jee]
hotel l'albergo **m** [al**bair**go]

Hotels are star-rated from one-star to five-star and required to post their prices clearly in each room. Most tourist offices have details of hotel rates in their town or region, and usually these are broadly accurate. Establish the full price of your room before you accept it. In popular resorts and the major cities – Venice, Rome, Florence especially – booking ahead is always advisable.

hotel room la camera

d'albergo
hour l'ora **f**
house la casa [**ka**za]
house wine il vino della casa
hovercraft l'hovercraft **m**
how come [**ko**may]
how many? quanti? [**kwan**tee]
how much? quanto?

dialogues

how are you? come
stai/sta? [**ko**may sty]
fine, thanks, and you?
bene, grazie, e lei? [**bay**nay
– ay lay]

how much is it? quanto
costa? [**kwan**to]
... lire ... lire [**lee**ray]
I'll take it lo/la prendo

humid umido [**oo**meedo]
humour l'umorismo **m**
[oomo**reez**mo]
hungry: I'm hungry ho fame
[o **fa**may]
are you hungry? ha fame? [a]
hurry (verb) sbrigarsi
I'm in a hurry ho fretta [o]
there's no hurry non c'è
fretta [non chay]
hurry up! sbrigati! [zbr**ee**gatee]
hurt far male [**ma**lay]
it really hurts mi fa proprio
male
husband il marito [ma**ree**to]
hydrofoil l'aliscafo **m**
hypermarket l'ipermercato **m**

I

I io [**ee**-o]
ice il ghiaccio [g-**ya**cho]
 with ice con ghiaccio
 no ice, thanks niente
 ghiaccio, grazie [n-**ye**nty]
ice cream il gelato [je**la**to]
ice-cream cone il cono gelato
iced coffee il caffè freddo
 [kaf-f**ay**]
ice lolly il ghiacciolo
 [g-yach**o**lo]
ice rink la pista di pattinaggio
 (sul ghiaccio) [pat-teen**a**j-jo
 sool g-**ya**cho]
ice skates i pattini da
 ghiaccio
idea l'idea f [eed**ay**-a]
idiot l'idiota m/f [eed-**yo**ta]
if se [say]
ignition l'accensione m
 [achens-**yo**nay]
ill malato
 I feel ill mi sento male
 [**ma**lay]
illness la malattia [malat-t**ee**-a]
imitation (leather etc)
 l'imitazione f [eemeetatz-
 yonay]
immediately
 immediatamente [eem-med-
 yata**me**ntay]
important importante
 [eempor**ta**ntay]
 it's very important è molto
 importante [ay]
 it's not important non ha

importanza [non a
 eempor**ta**ntza]
impossible impossibile
 [eempos-s**ee**beelay]
impressive notevole [no**tay**-
 volay]
improve migliorare [meel-
 yor**a**ray]
 I want to improve my Italian
 voglio migliorare il mio
 italiano [**vol**-yo – eel m**ee**-o]
in: it's in the centre è in
 centro [**che**ntro]
 in my car con la mia
 macchina
 in Florence a Firenze
 in two days from now tra due
 giorni
 in five minutes tra cinque
 minuti
 in May a maggio
 in English in inglese [een]
 in Italian in italiano
 is he in? c'è? [chay]
inch* il pollice [**pol**-leechay]
include comprendere
 [kompr**e**ndairay]
 does that include meals?
 sono compresi i pasti?
 [kompr**ay**zee]
 is that included? questo è
 compreso? [kw**e**sto ay]
inconvenient scomodo
incredible incredibile
 [eenkred**ee**beelay]
Indian indiano [eend-**ya**no]
indicator la freccia [**fre**cha]
indigestion l'indigestione f
 [eendeejest-**yo**nay]

indoor pool la piscina coperta [pee-sheena kopairta]

indoors all'interno [eentairno]

inexpensive a buon mercato [bwon mairkato]
see cheap

infection l'infezione f [eenfetz-yonay]

infectious contagioso [kontajozo]

inflammation l'infiammazione f [eenf-yam-matz-yonay]

informal informale [eenformalay]

information l'informazione f [eenformatz-yonay]

do you have any information about ...? ha informazioni su...?

information desk il banco (delle) informazioni [del-lay]

injection l'iniezione f [een-yetz-yonay]

injured ferito [faireeto]
she's been injured è rimasta ferita [ay]

in-laws i suoceri [swochairee]

inner tube (for tyre) la camera d'aria

innocent innocente [een-nochentay]

insect l'insetto m

insect bite la puntura d'insetto [poon-toora]

do you have anything for insect bites? ha qualcosa per le punture d'insetto? [a kwalkoza pair lay poon-tooray]

insect repellent l'insettifugo m [eenset-teefoogo]

inside dentro
inside the hotel nell'albergo
let's sit inside sediamoci dentro [sed-yamochee]

insist insistere [eenseestairay]
I insist insisto

insomnia l'insonnia f

instant coffee il caffè solubile [kaf-fay sooloobeelay]

instead invece [eenvaychay]
give me that one instead mi dia quello, invece [kwel-lo]
instead of ... invece di...

insulin l'insulina f [eensooleena]

insurance l'assicurazione f [as-seekooratz-yonay]

intelligent intelligente [eentel-leejentay]

interested: I'm interested in ... mi interesso di... [mee eentaires-so]

interesting interessante [eentaires-santay]
that's very interesting è molto interessante [ay]

international internazionale [eentairnatz-yonalay]

interpret interpretare [eentairpretaray]

interpreter l'interprete m/f [eentairpretay]

intersection l'incrocio m [eenkrocho]

interval (at theatre) l'intervallo m [eentairval-lo]

into in

I'm not into ... non m'interesso di...

introduce presentare [present**a**ray]

  may I introduce ...? posso presentarle...? [present**a**rlay]

invitation l'invito **m**

invite invitare [eenveet**a**ray]

Ireland l'Irlanda **f** [eerl**a**nda]

Irish irlandese [eerland**ay**zay]

  I'm Irish sono irlandese

iron (for ironing) il ferro da stiro [**fair**-ro]

  can you iron these for me? me li può stirare? [may lee pwo steer**a**ray]

is* è [ay]

island l'isola **f** [**ee**zola]

it esso

  it is ... è... [ay]

  is it ...? è...?

  where is it? dov'è? [dov**ay**]

  it's him è lui [**loo**-ee]

  it was ... era... [**ai**ra]

Italian (adj) italiano [eetal-y**a**no]

  (language, man) l'italiano **m**

  (woman) l'italiana **f**

  the Italians gli Italiani

Italy l'Italia **f** [eetal-ya]

itch: it itches mi prude [pr**oo**day]

J

jack (for car) il cric

jacket la giacca [**jak**-ka]

jar il vasetto

jam la marmellata

jammed: it's jammed si è inceppato [ay eenchep-p**a**to]

January gennaio [jen-n**a**-yo]

jaw la mascella [mash**el**-la]

jazz il jazz [jetz]

jealous geloso [jel**o**zo]

jeans i jeans

jellyfish la medusa [med**oo**za]

jersey la maglia [m**a**l-ya]

jetty il molo

Jewish ebreo [ebr**ay**-o]

jeweller's la gioielleria [joy-**el**-lair**ee**-a]

jewellery i gioielli [joy-**el**-lee]

job l'impiego **m** [eemp-y**ay**go]

jogging il jogging

  to go jogging andare a fare jogging [and**a**ra a f**a**ray]

joke lo scherzo [sk**ai**rtzo]

  (story) la barzelletta [bartzel-l**et**-ta]

journey il viaggio [vee-**a**j-jo]

  have a good journey! buon viaggio! [bwon]

jug la brocca

  a jug of water una brocca d'acqua [d**a**kwa]

juice il succo [s**oo**k-ko]

July luglio [l**oo**l-yo]

jump (verb) saltare [salt**a**ray]

jumper il maglione [mal-y**o**nay]

jump leads il cavo per collegare due batterie [pair kol-leg**a**ray d**oo**-ay bat-tair**ee**-ay]

junction il bivio [b**ee**v-yo]

June giugno [j**oo**n-yo]

just (only) solo

  just two soltanto due

just for me solo per me [pair may]

just here proprio qui [kwee]

not just now non ora

we've just arrived siamo appena arrivati [s-yamo ap-payna]

K

keep tenere [tenairay]

keep the change tenga il resto

can I keep it? posso tenerlo? [ten-airlo]

please keep it puoi/può tenerlo [pwoy/pwo]

ketchup il ketchup

kettle il bollitore [bol-leetoray]

key la chiave [k-yavay]

the key for room 201, please (la chiave del) duecentuno, per favore

key ring il portachiavi [portak-yavee]

kidneys (in body) i reni [raynee] (food) il rognone [ron-yonay]

kill (verb) uccidere [oocheedairay]

kilo* il chilo [keelo]

kilometre* il chilometro [keelometro]

how many kilometres is it to ...? a quanti chilometri da qui è...? [kwantee – kwee ay]

kind (generous) gentile [jenteelay]

that's very kind of you è molto gentile da parte tua/sua [ay – partay too-a/soo-a]

dialogue

which kind do you want? che tipo vuole? [kay – vwolay]

I want this/that kind questo/quel tipo [kwesto/kwel]

king il re [ray]

kiosk il chiosco [kee-osko] (selling newspapers) l'edicola **f**

kiss il bacio [bacho] (verb) baciare [bacharay]

° kissing
It is customary in Italy to greet friends and relatives by kissing them on both cheeks (the right one first). The exception to this is when men greet each other, when they generally shake hands instead. When meeting somebody for the first time, hand-shaking is sufficient.

kitchen la cucina [koocheena]

kitchenette il cucinino [koocheeneeno]

Kleenex® i fazzolettini di carta [fatzolet-teenee]

knee il ginocchio [jeenok-yo]

knickers le mutande [mootanday]

knife il coltello

knitwear la maglieria [mal-yee-

airee-a]
knock (verb: on door) bussare
[boos-saray]
knock down: he's been
 knocked down è stato
 investito [ay]
knock over (object) far cadere
 [kadairay]
 (pedestrian) investire
 [eenvesteeray]
know (somebody, a place)
 conoscere [kono-shairay]
 (something) sapere [sapairay]
 I don't know non lo so
 I didn't know that non lo
 sapevo [sapayvo]
 do you know where I can
 find ...? sai/sa dove posso
 trovare...? [sa-ee/sa dovay posso trovaray]

L

label l'etichetta f [eteeket-ta]
ladies' (toilets) la toilette
 (delle donne) [twalet del-lay
 don-nay]
ladies' wear l'abbigliamento
 da donna m [ab-beel-yamento]
lady la signora [seen-yora]
lager la birra chiara [beer-ra
 k-yara]
 see beer
lake il lago
lamb l'agnello m [an-yel-lo]
lamp la lampada
lane (motorway) la corsia
 (small road) la stradina

language la lingua [leengwa]
language course un corso di
 lingua
large grande [granday]
last ultimo [oolteemo]
 what time is the last train to
 Trieste? a che ora parte
 l'ultimo treno per Trieste?
 [kay – partay]
 last week la settimana scorsa
 last Friday venerdì scorso
 last night la notte scorsa
late tardi
 sorry I'm late mi scuso del
 ritardo [mee skoozo]
 the train was late il treno era
 in ritardo
 we must go – we'll be late
 dobbiamo andare –
 altrimenti faremo tardi [dob-
 yamo andaray – faraymo]
 it's getting late si sta facendo
 tardi [fachendo]
later più tardi [p-yoo]
 I'll come back later torno più
 tardi
 see you later ci vediamo
 dopo [chee ved-yamo]
 later on poi, più tardi [poy]
latest ultimo [oolteemo]
 by Wednesday at the latest
 ... entro mercoledì al più
 tardi [p-yoo]
laugh (verb) ridere [reedairay]
launderette la lavanderia
 automatica [lavandairee-a owto-
 mateeka]
laundromat la lavanderia
 automatica

laundry (clothes) il bucato
(place) la lavanderia

lavatory il gabinetto

law la legge [lej-jay]

lawn il prato all'inglese
[eenglayzay]

lawyer l'avvocato m

laxative il lassativo

lazy pigro

lead (electrical) il filo (verb)
condurre [kondoor-ray],
guidare [gweedaray]

where does this lead to?
dove porta questo? [dovay –
kwesto]

leaf la foglia [fol-ya]

leaflet il dépliant [dayplee-an]

leak la perdita [pairdeeta]
(verb) perdere [pairdairay]

the roof leaks gocciola
acqua dal tetto [gochola akwa]

learn imparare [eempararay]

least: not in the least per
mente [n-yentay]

at least come minimo
[komay]

leather il cuoio [kwo-yo], la
pelle [pel-lay]

leave (verb: depart) partire
[parteeray]
(leave behind) lasciare [lasharay]

I am leaving tomorrow parto
domani

he left yesterday è partito
ieri [ay – yairee]

may I leave this here? posso
lasciarlo qui? [lasharlo kwee]

I left my coat in the bar ho
lasciato il cappotto al bar [o]

when does the bus for Venice
leave? a che ora parte
l'autobus per Venezia [kay –
partay lowtoboos pair]

leek il porro

left la sinistra [seeneestra]

on the left, to the left a
sinistra

turn left giri a sinistra [jeeree]

there's none left non ce n'è
più nessuno/nessuna [chay
nay p-yoo nes-soono]

left-handed mancino
[mancheeno]

left luggage (office) il
deposito bagagli [bagal-yee]

leg la gamba

lemon il limone [leemonay]

lemonade la gassosa [gas-soza]

lemon tea un tè al limone
[tay al leemonay]

lend prestare [prestaray]

will you lend me your ... ?
può prestarmi il suo/la
sua...? [pwo – soo-o/soo-a]

lens (of camera) l'obiettivo m
[ob-yet-teevo]

lesbian la lesbica

less meno [mayno]

less than meno di

less expensive più a buon
mercato [p-yoo]

lesson la lezione [letz-yonay]

let (allow) permettere [pairmet-
tairay]

will you let me know? mi
faccia sapere [mee facha
sapairay]

I'll let you know ti/le farò

sapere [lay]

let's go for something to eat
andiamo a mangiare
qualcosa [and-y**a**mo a manj**a**ray
kwalk**o**za]

let off far scendere [sh**e**ndairay]

will you let me off at ...? può
farmi scendere a....? [pwo]

letter la lettera [**l**et-taira]

**do you have any letters for
me?** ci sono lettere per me?
[chee s**o**no l**e**t-tairay pair may]

letterbox la buca delle lettere
[b**oo**ka d**e**l-lay]

Letterboxes in Italy are
usually red although there
are some yellow ones.
Per la città means that the box is
for mail within the town.

lettuce la lattuga [lat-t**oo**ga]

lever la leva [**lay**va]

library la biblioteca [beeblee-
ot**ay**ka]

licence il permesso [pairm**e**s-
so]

lid il coperchio [kop**air**k-yo]

lie (verb: tell untruth) mentire
[ment**ee**ray]

lie down stendersi [st**e**ndairsee]

life la vita

lifebelt il salvagente
[salvaj**e**ntay]

lifeguard (man/woman) il
bagnino [ban-y**ee**no], la
bagnina

life jacket il giubbotto di
salvataggio [joob-b**o**t-to dee
salva-t**a**j-jo]

lift (in building) l'ascensore m
[ashens**o**ray]

could you give me a lift? mi
puoi/può dare un
passaggio? [mee pwoy/pwo
d**a**ray oon pas-s**a**j-jo]

would you like a lift?
vuoi/vuole un passaggio?
[vwoy/vw**o**lay]

lift pass lo skipass

a daily/weekly lift pass uno
skipass
giornaliero/settimanale

light la luce [**loo**chay]
(not heavy) leggero [lej-j**ai**ro]

do you have a light? (for
cigarette) puoi/può farmi
accendere? [pwoy/pwo f**a**rmee
ach**e**ndairay]

light green verde chiaro
[k-yaro]

light bulb la lampadina

I need a new light bulb ho
bisogno di una lampadina
nuova [o beez**o**n-yo dee]

lighter (cigarette) l'accendino
m [achen-d**ee**no]

lightning il fulmine
[**foo**lmeenay]

like (verb) piacere [p-yach**ai**ray]

I like it mi piace [mee pee-
achay]

I like going for walks mi
piace fare passeggiate

I like you mi piaci [pee-**a**chee]

I don't like it non mi piace

do you like ...? ti/le piace...?
[tee/lay]

I'd like a beer vorrei una birra [vor-ray]

I'd like to go swimming vorrei andare a fare una nuotata [andaray]

would you like a drink? vuoi/vuole qualcosa da bere? [vwoy/vwolay kwalkoza da bairay]

would you like to go for a walk? ti/le va di fare una passeggiata?

what's it like? com'è? [komay]

like this così [kozee]

I want one like this ne voglio uno/una come questo/questa [nay vol-yo – komay kwesto/kwesta]

lime il lime [la-eem]

line la linea [leen-ay-a]

could you give me an outside line? mi dà la linea, per favore?

lips le labbra

lip salve la pomata per le labbra [pair lay]

lipstick il rossetto

liqueur il liquore [leekworay]

listen ascoltare [askoltaray]

litre* il litro

a litre of white wine un litro di vino bianco

little piccolo

just a little, thanks solo un po', grazie

a little milk un po' di latte

a little bit more ancora un po'

live (verb) vivere [veevairay]

we live together conviviamo [konveev-yamo]

dialogue

where do you live? dove abita? [dovay]

I live in London abito a Londra

lively (person, town) pieno di vita [p-yayno dee veeta]

liver il fegato [faygato]

loaf la pagnotta [pan-yot-ta]

lobby (in hotel) l'atrio m

lobster l'aragosta f

local locale [lokalay]

can you recommend a local wine/restaurant? mi può consigliare un vino/un ristorante del posto? [mee pwo konseel-yaray]

lock la serratura [sair-ratoora] (verb) chiudere a chiave [k-yoodairey a k-yavay]

it's locked è chiuso a chiave [ay k-yoozo]

lock in chiudere dentro

lock out chiudere fuori [fwooree]

I've locked myself out mi sono chiuso/chiusa fuori [k-yoozo]

locker (for luggage etc) l'armadietto m [armad-yet-to]

lollipop il lecca-lecca

Lombardy la Lombardia

London Londra

long lungo [**loo**ngo]
  how long will it take to fix it?
  quanto ci vuole per
  accomodarlo? [kw**a**nto chee
  vv**o**lay pair]
  how long does it take?
  quanto t**e**mpo ci vuole?
  a long time tanto tempo
  one day/two days longer
  anc**o**ra un gi**o**rno/d**u**e
  gi**o**rni
long-distance call l'interurbana **f** [een-tairoorb**a**na]
look: I'm just looking, thanks
  sto s**o**lo d**a**ndo un'occhiata,
  gr**a**zie [ok-y**a**ta]
  you don't look well hai/ha
  una brutta cera [**a**-ee/a **oo**na
  br**oo**t-ta ch**ai**ra]
  look out! attenzione! [at-
  tentz-y**o**nay]
  can I have a look? posso dare
  un'occhiata? [d**a**ray]
look after badare a [bad**a**ray]
look at guardare [gward**a**ray]
look for cercare [chairk**a**ray]
  I'm looking for ... sto
  cercando... [chairk**a**ndo]
look forward to non vedere
  l'ora di [ved**ai**ray]
  I'm looking forward to it non
  vedo l'ora [**vay**do]
loose (handle etc) che si sta
  staccando [kay]
lorry il camion [**kam**-yon]
lose perdere [**pai**rdairay]
  I'm lost, I want to get to ... mi
  sono perso/persa, voglio
  andare a... [**pai**rso – **vol**-yo

andaray]
  I've lost my bag ho perso la
  b**o**rsa [o]
lost property (office) l'ufficio
  oggetti smarriti **m** [oof-**fee**cho
  oj-j**e**t-tee zmar-**ree**tee]
lot: a lot, lots molto
  not a lot non molto
  a lot of Parmesan molto
  parmigiano
  a lot of sauce molta salsa
  a lot of people molta gente
  [j**e**ntay]
  a lot of boys molti ragazzi
  a lot of drinks molte
  bevande
  a lot bigger molto più
  grande [p-yoo]
  I like it a lot mi piace molto
  [mee pee-**a**chay]
lotion la lozione [lotz-y**o**nay]
loud forte [**fo**rtay]
lounge (in house, hotel) il salone
  [sal**o**nay]
  (in airport) la sala d'attesa [at-
  tayza]
love l'amore **m** [am**o**ray]
  (verb) amare [am**a**ray]
  I love Italy mi piace molto
  l'Italia [mee p-y**a**chay]
lovely bello
  (meal) delizioso [deleetz-y**o**zo]
low basso
luck la fortuna [fort**oo**na]
  good luck! buona fortuna!
  [bw**o**na]
luggage i bagagli [bag**a**l-yee]
luggage trolley il carrello
lump (on body) il gonfiore

[gonf-y**o**ray]
lunch il pranzo [pr**a**ntzo]
lungs i polm**o**ni
luxurious lussu**o**so [loos-soo-**o**zo]
luxury il lusso [**loo**s-so]

M

machine la m**a**cchina [mak-**kee**na]
mad (insane) pazzo [p**a**tzo]
(angry) furioso [foor**ee**-**o**zo]
magazine la rivista
maid (in hotel) la cameriera [kamair-y**ai**ra]
maiden name il cognome da nubile [kon-y**o**may da n**oo**beelay]
mail la p**o**sta
see post
(verb) impost**a**re [eempost**a**ray]
is there any mail for me? c'è p**o**sta per me? [chay – may]
mailbox la buca delle lettere [b**oo**ka d**e**l-lay l**e**t-tairay]
see letterbox
main principale [preencheep**a**lay]
main course la portata principale
main post office l'ufficio postale centrale **m** [oof-f**ee**cho post**a**lay chentr**a**lay]
main road (in town) la strada principale [preencheep**a**lay]
(in country) la strada maestra [m**y**stra]
mains switch l'interruttore

generale **m** [eentair-root-t**o**ray jenair**a**lay]
make fare [f**a**ray]
(noun: brand name) la marca
I make it 5,000 lire secondo i miei calcoli sono 5.000 (cinquemila) lire [mee-y**ay** – l**ee**ray]
what is it made of? di che cosa è fatto/fatta? [kay k**o**za]
make-up il trucco [tr**oo**k-ko]
man l'u**o**mo **m** [w**o**mo]
manager il direttore [deeret-t**o**ray]
can I see the manager? posso parlare con il direttore? [parl**a**ray]
manageress la direttrice [deeret-tr**ee**chay]
manual (car with manual gears) la macchina con il cambio manuale [mak-k**ee**na kon eel k**a**mb-yo manoo-**a**lay]
many molti/molte [m**o**ltay]
not many non molti/molte
map (city plan) la pianta [p-y**a**nta]
(road map, geographical) la cartina
March marzo [m**a**rtzo]
margarine la margarina [margar**ee**na]
market il mercato [mairk**a**to]
marmalade la marmellata d'arance [dar**a**nchay]
married: I'm married (said by a man/woman) sono sposato/sposata
are you married? (said to a

man/woman) è sposato/sposata? [ay]

mascara il mascara

match (football etc) la partita

matches i fiammiferi [f-yam-**mee**fairee]

material (fabric) la stoffa

matter: it doesn't matter non importa

what's the matter? che c'è? [kay chay]

mattress il materasso

May maggio [**maj**-jo]

may: may I have another bottle? potrei avere un'altra bottiglia? [pot**ray** av**ai**ray]

may I come in? posso entrare? [entr**a**ray]

may I see it? posso vederlo/vederla? [ved**ai**rlo/ved**ai**rla]

may I sit here? posso sedere qui? [sed**ai**ray kwee]

maybe forse [**for**say]

mayonnaise la maionese [ma-yon**ay**zay]

me*: that's for me è per me [ay pair may]

send it to me mandalo/lo mandi a me

me too anch'io [ank**ee**-o]

meal il pasto

dialogue

did you enjoy your meal? le è piaciuto? [lay ay p-yach**oo**to]

it was excellent, thank you era ottimo, grazie [**ai**ra]

mean (verb) significare [seen-yeefeek**a**ray]

what do you mean? che cosa intendi/intende? [kay k**o**za eent**e**ndee/eent**e**nday]

dialogue

what does this word mean? cosa significa questa parola? [k**o**za seen-**yee**feeka kw**e**sta]

it means ... in English in inglese significa... [eengl**ay**zay]

measles il morbillo [morb**ee**l-lo]

meat la carne [**ka**rnay]

mechanic il meccanico [mek-k**a**neeko]

medicine la medicina [medeech**ee**na]

Mediterranean il Mediterraneo [medeetair-r**a**nay-o]

medium (adj: size) medio [**may**d-yo]

medium-dry semisecco

medium-rare non troppo cotto

medium-sized di taglia media [tal-ya **may**d-ya]

meet (someone) incontrare [eenkontr**a**ray]

(each other) incontrarsi

nice to meet you piacere di conoscerla [pee-achairay dee konoshair-la]

where shall I meet you? dove ci incontriamo? [dovay chee]

meeting la riunione [r-yoon-yonay]

meeting place il luogo d'incontro [lwogo]

melon il melone [melonay]

men gli uomini [wo-meenee]

mend riparare [reepararay]

could you mend this for me? me lo può riparare? [may – pwo]

menswear l'abbigliamento da uomo m [ab-beel-yamento da womo]

mention (verb) nominare [nomeenaray]

don't mention it prego [praygo]

menu il menù [menoo]

may I see the menu, please? mi dà il menù, per favore?

see page 231 for Menu Reader

message il messaggio [mes-saj-jo]

are there any messages for me? ci sono messaggi per me? [chee – pair may]

I want to leave a message for ... vorrei lasciare un messaggio per... [vor-ray lasharay]

metal il metallo

metre* il metro

microwave (oven) il forno a microonde [meekro-onday]

midday mezzogiorno [met-zojorno]

at midday a mezzogiorno

middle: in the middle nel mezzo [metzo]

in the middle of the night in piena notte [p-yayna]

the middle one quello/quella in mezzo [kwel-lo]

midnight mezzanotte [metzanot-tay]

at midnight a mezzanotte

might: I might (not) go può darsi che io (non) ci vada [pwo – kay ee-o non chee]

I might want to stay another day forse dovrò fermarmi ancora un giorno [forsay]

migraine l'emicrania f [emeekran-ya]

Milan Milano [meelano]

mild (taste) leggero [lej-jairo] (weather) mite [meetay]

mile* il miglio [meel-yo]

milk il latte [lat-tay]

milkshake il frappé [frap-pay]

millimetre* il millimetro

minced meat la carne macinata [karnay macheenata]

mind: never mind non fa niente [n-yentay]

I've changed my mind ho cambiato idea [o kamb-yato eeday-a]

dialogue

do you mind if I open the window? le dispiace se apro la finestra? [lay deespee-**a**chay say deespee-**a**chay say]

no, I don't mind no, faccia pure [**f**acha **poo**ray]

mine*: it's mine è mio/mia [ay]

mineral water l'acqua minerale **f** [**a**kwa meen-air**a**lay]

minibar il frigobar

mints le mentine [ment**ee**nay]

minute il minuto [meen**oo**to]

in a minute in un attimo

just a minute un attimo

mirror lo specchio [sp**e**k-yo]

Miss (la) signorina [seen-yor**ee**na]

miss: I missed the bus ho perso l'autobus [o p**ai**rso]

missing smarrito

one of my ... is missing non trovo uno/una dei miei/delle mie... [day mee-**y**ay/del-lay m**ee**-ay]

there's a suitcase missing manca una valigia

mist la nebbiolina [neb-yol**ee**na]

mistake lo sbaglio [zb**a**l-yo]

I think there's a mistake credo ci sia un errore [kr**ay**do chee s**ee**-a oon air-r**o**ray]

sorry, I've made a mistake chiedo scusa, mi sono sbagliato/sbagliata [k-y**ay**do

skooza mee – sbal-y**a**to]

misunderstanding l'equivoco **m** [ekw**ee**-voko]

mix-up: sorry, there's been a mix-up mi dispiace, è successa un po' di confusione [mee deesp-y**a**chay ay sooch**e**s-sa – konfooz-y**o**nay]

mobile phone il telefonino [telayfon**ee**no]

modern moderno [mod**ai**rno]

modern art gallery la galleria d'arte moderna [gal-lair**ee**-a d**a**rtay]

moisturizer l'idratante **m** [ee-drat**a**ntay]

moment: I won't be a moment (won't be long) faccio in un attimo [**f**acho]

monastery il monastero [monast**ai**ro]

Monday lunedì [loon**e**d**ee**]

money i soldi

month il mese [m**ay**zay]

monument il monumento [monoo-m**e**nto]

moon la luna [**loo**na]

moped il motorino

more* più [p-yoo]

can I have some more water, please? vorrei ancora acqua, per favore [vor-r**ay**]

more expensive/interesting più caro/interessante [p-yoo]

more than 50 più di cinquanta

more than that di più

a lot more molto di più

dialogue

would you like some more? ne vuole ancora? [nay vwolay]

no, no more for me, thanks no, basta per me, grazie [pair may]

how about you? e lei? [ay lay]

I don't want any more, thanks non ne voglio più, grazie [nay vol-yo p-yoo]

morning la mattina
this morning questa mattina [kwesta]
in the morning di mattina
mosquito la zanzara [tzantzara]
mosquito repellent l'insettifugo **m** [eenset-teefoogo]
most: I like this one most of all questo/questa mi piace più di tutti/tutte [kwesto – mee p-yachay p-yoo dee toot-tee/toot-tay]
most of the time la maggior parte del tempo [maj-jor partay]
most tourists la maggior parte dei turisti [day]
mostly per lo più [pair lo p-yoo]
mother la madre [madray]
motorbike la motocicletta [moto-cheeklet-ta]
motorboat il motoscafo
motorway l'autostrada **f** [owtostrada]

 Just before joining a motorway, there are machines where you have to collect a card (**lo scontrino**) which you must keep and show at the toll booth at the end of your journey, so that you can be charged accordingly.

mountain la montagna [montan-ya]
in the mountains in montagna
mountaineering l'alpinismo **m**
mouse il topo
moustache i baffi
mouth la bocca
mouth ulcer la stomatite [stomateetay]
move (verb) muovere [mwovairay]
he's moved to another room si è trasferito in un'altra stanza [see ay trasfaireeto]
could you move your car? potrebbe spostare la macchina? [potreb-bay spostaray]
could you move up a little? si può spostare un po' più in là? [see pwo – p-yoo]
where has it been moved to? dove è stato trasferito? [dovay ay]
movie il film [feelm]
movie theater il cinema [cheenema]
see cinema
Mr (il) signor [seen-yor]

Mrs (la) signora [seen-**y**ora]
Ms (la) signora
much molto
 much better/worse molto
 meglio/peggio [**may**l-yo/**pej**-
 jo]
 much hotter molto più
 caldo [p-yoo]
 not much non molto
 not very much non molto
 I don't want very much non
 voglio molto [**vol**-yo]
mud il fango
mug (for drinking) il
 bicchierone [beek-yair**o**nay]
 I've been mugged sono stato
 aggredito [ag-gred**ee**to]
mum la mamma
mumps gli orecchioni [orek-
 yonee]
museum il museo [mooz**ay**-o]

Museums generally open
from 9 a.m. until 1 or 2
p.m., sometimes for an
additional couple of hours in the
afternoon on selected days; almost
all are closed on Mondays. They also
often close early on Sundays,
usually around noon, and for smaller
museums opening hours are
severely cut back during winter.
Museums and galleries charge for
admission.

mushrooms i funghi [**foo**ngee]
music la musica [**moo**zeeka]
musician il/la musicista
 [moozeech**ee**sta]

Muslim (adj) musulmano
mussels le cozze [**kot**zay]
must*: I must devo [**day**vo]
 I mustn't drink alcohol non
 devo bere alcol [**bair**ay]
mustard la senape [**say**napay]
my* il mio, la mia, i miei
 [mee-**yay**], le mie [lay m**ee**-ay]
myself: I'll do it myself lo farò
 da me [may]
 by myself da solo

N

nail (finger) l'unghia f [**oo**ng-
 ya]
 (metal) il chiodo [k-y**o**do]
nail varnish lo smalto per le
 unghie [pair lay **oo**ng-yay]
name il nome [**no**may]

It's quite common to hear
Italians address or greet
each other formally by
their profession: **buonasera
dottore!**; **arrivederla, avvocato
Rossi!** First names are only used in
informal relationships, for example,
between friends and relatives. In
formal situations **signor** or **signora**
(Mr or Mrs/Ms) + surname are used.
It is possible, however, to use
signor/signora + first name in semi-
formal relationships (i.e. to
shopkeepers, bar staff etc).

 my name's John mi chiamo
 John [k-**ya**mo]

what's your name? come si chiama? [**ko**may see k-**ya**ma]

what is the name of this street? come si chiama questa strada? [**kwe**sta]

napkin il tovagliolo [toval-**yo**lo]

Naples Napoli

nappy il pannolino

narrow (street) stretto

nasty (person) antipatico (weather, accident) brutto [br**oo**t-to]

national nazionale [natz-yon**a**lay]

nationality la nazionalità [natz-yonal**ee**ta]

natural naturale [natoor**a**lay]

nausea la nausea [n**ow**zay-a]

navy (blue) blu marino

Neapolitan (adj) napoletano

near vicino a [veech**ee**no]

is it near the city centre? è vicino al centro della città? [ay]

do you go near the Colosseum? passa vicino al Colosseo?

where is the nearest ...? dov'è il... più vicino? [dov**ay** eel ... p-yoo]

nearby vicino [veech**ee**no]

nearly quasi [kw**a**zee]

necessary necessario [neches-**sar**-yo]

neck il collo

necklace la collana

necktie la cravatta

need: I need ... ho bisogno di... [o beez**on**-yo dee]

do I need to pay? devo pagare? [**day**vo pag**a**ray]

needle l'ago m

negative (film) la negativa

neither: neither (one) of them nessuno dei due [nays-s**oo**no day d**oo**-ay]

neither ... nor ... né... né... [nay]

nephew il nipote [neep**o**tay]

net (in sport) la rete [**ray**tay]

Netherlands i Paesi Bassi [pa-**ay**zee]

network map la piantina dei trasporti pubblici [**poob**-bleechee]

never mai [ma-ee]

dialogue

have you ever been to Rome? è mai stato a Roma? [eh]

no, never; I've never been there no, mai; non ci sono mai stato [chee]

new nuovo [nw**o**vo]

news (radio, TV etc) le notizie [not**ee**tzee-ay]

newsagent's il giornalaio [jornal**a**-yo]

newspaper il giornale [jorn**a**lay]

newspaper kiosk l'edicola f

New Year l'anno nuovo **m** [nw**o**vo]

Italians celebrate New Year by going out to expensive dinner-dances (**cenone**). It is traditional to have fireworks at midnight and throw old crockery out of the window, especially in the south.

Happy New Year! felice anno nuovo! [fel**ee**-chay]
New Year's Eve la notte di Capodanno, la notte di San Silvestro [**n**ot-tay dee]
New Zealand la Nuova Zelanda [nw**o**va tzayl**a**nda]
New Zealander: I'm a New Zealander sono neozelandese [nay-otzeland**ay**zay]
next prossimo
  the next turning/street on the left la prossima svolta/strada a sinistra
  at the next stop alla prossima fermata
  next week la settimana prossima
  next to vicino a [veech**ee**no]
nice (food) buono [bw**o**no]
  (looks, view etc) bello
  (person) simpatico
niece la nipote [neep**o**tay]
night la notte [**n**ot-tay]
  at night di notte
  good night buonanotte [bw**o**nan**o**t-tay]

dialogue

do you have a single room for one night? avete una stanza singola per una notte? [av**ay**tay **oo**na st**a**ntza]
yes, madam sì, signora
how much is it per night? quanto si paga per notte? [pair]
it's 60,000 lire for one night 60.000 (sessantamila) lire per notte
thank you, I'll take it grazie, la prendo [gr**a**tzee-ay]

nightclub il night
nightdress la camicia da notte [kam**ee**cha da n**o**t-tay]
night porter il portiere di notte [port-y**ai**ray dee]
no no
  I've no change non ho spiccioli [o sp**ee**ch-yolee]
  there's no ... left non c'è più... [cheh p-yoo]
  no way! assolutamente no!
  oh no! (upset) oh no!
nobody nessuno [nes-s**oo**no]
  there's nobody there non c'è nessuno [chay]
noise il rumore [room**o**ray]
noisy: it's too noisy c'è troppo rumore
non-alcoholic analcolico
none nessuno [nes-s**oo**no]
nonsmoking compartment la carrozza per non fumatori

[kar-ro**tza** pair non foomat**o**ree]

noon mezzogiorno
[medzoj**o**rno]

no-one nessuno [nes-s**oo**no]

nor: nor do I nemmeno io
[nem-m**ay**no **ee**-o]

normal normale [norm**a**lay]

north il nord
 in the north al nord
 north of Rome a nord di
 Roma

northern settentrionale [set-
tentr-yon**a**lay]

Northern Ireland l'Irlanda del
Nord **f** [eerl**a**nda]

Norway la Norvegia [norv**ay**ja]

nose il naso

nosebleed il sangue dal naso
[s**a**ngway]

not* non
 no, I'm not hungry no, non
 ho fame [o f**a**may]
 I don't want any, thank you
 non ne voglio, grazie [nay
 v**o**l-yo]
 it's not necessary non è
 necessario [ay neches-s**a**r-yo]
 I didn't know that non lo
 sapevo [sap**ay**vo]
 not that one – this one non
 quello – questo [kwel-lo –
 kw**e**sto]

note (banknote) la banconota

notebook il notes

notepaper (for letters) la carta
da lettere [**let**-tairay]

nothing niente [n-y**e**ntay]
 nothing for me, thanks per
 me niente, grazie [pair may]

nothing else nient'altro

novel il romanzo [rom**a**ntzo]

November novembre
[nov**e**mbray]

now adesso

number il numero [n**oo**mairo]
 I've got the wrong number
 ho sbagliato numero [o zbal-
 y**a**to]
 what is your phone number?
 qual è il suo numero di
 telefono? [kwal ay eel s**oo**-o]

number plate la targa

nurse (man/woman)
l'infermiere **m** [enfairm-
y**ai**ray]/ l'infermiera **f**

nursery slope la pista per
principianti [pair preencheep-
y**a**ntee]

nut (for bolt) il dado

nuts le noci [n**o**chee]

O

o'clock*: at 7 o'clock alle sette
[**al**-lay]

occupied (toilet) occupato [ok-
koop**a**to]

October ottobre [ot-t**o**bray]

odd (strange) strano

of* di [dee]

off (lights) spento
 it's just off corso Europa è
 una traversa di corso
 Europa [ay – trav**ai**rsa]
 we're off tomorrow partiamo
 domani [part-y**a**mo]

offensive offensivo

office (place of work) l'ufficio m
[oof-**fee**cho]
officer (said to policeman) agente
[a**jen**tay]
often spesso
 not often non spesso
 how often are the buses?
ogni quanto passano gli
autobus? [**on**-yee kw**a**nto]
oil l'olio m [**ol**-yo]
ointment l'unguento m
[oong**wen**to]
OK d'accordo
 are you OK? tutto bene?
[**too**t-to b**ay**nay]
 is that OK with you? ti/le va
bene? [lay]
 is it OK to ...? si può...?
[pwo]
 that's OK thanks va bene
così grazie [ko**zee**]
 I'm OK (nothing for me) io sono
a posto [**ee**-o]
 (I feel OK) sto bene
 is this train OK for ...? questo
treno va bene per...?
[**kwe**sto]
 I said I'm sorry, OK ho
chiesto scusa, va bene? [o
k-y**e**sto sk**oo**za]
old vecchio [**vek**-yo]

dialogue

 how old are you? quanti
anni ha? [kw**a**ntee **a**n-nee a]
 I'm twenty-five ho
venticinque anni [o]
 and you? e lei? [ay lay]

old-fashioned fuori moda
[fw**o**ree]
old town (old part of town) la
città vecchia [cheet-**ta vek**-ya]
 in the old town nella città
vecchia
olive oil l'olio di oliva m [**ol**-
yo]
olives le olive [o**lee**vay]
 black/green olives le olive
nere/verdi [**nai**ray/**vair**day]
omelette la frittata
on* su [soo]
 on the street/beach sulla
strada/sulla spiaggia
 is it on this road? è su questa
strada? [ay soo kw**e**sta]
 on the plane sull'aereo
 on Saturday sabato
 on television alla televisione
 I haven't got it on me non ce
l'ho con me [non chay lo kon
may]
 this one's on me (drink) offro
io da bere [**ee**-o da b**ai**ray]
 the light wasn't on la luce
non era accesa [**loo**chay non
aira ach**ay**za]
 what's on tonight? cosa c'è
da vedere stasera? [**ko**za chay
da ved**ai**ray stas**ai**ra]
once (one time) una volta
 at once (immediately)
immediatamente [eem-med-
yatam**en**tay]
one* uno [**oo**no], una [**oo**na]
 the white one quello bianco,
[**kwel**-lo], quella bianca
one-way ticket: a one-way

105

ticket to ... un biglietto di sola andata per... [beel-yet-to – pair]

onions le cipolle [cheepol-lay]

only solo

only one solo uno

it's only 6 o'clock sono solo le sei

I've only just got here sono appena arrivato [ap-payna]

on/off switch l'interruttore **m** [eentair-root-toray]

open (adj) aperto [apairto]
(verb: door, of shop) aprire [apreeray]

when do you open? quando aprite? [kwando apreetay]

I can't get it open non riesco ad aprirlo/aprirla [r-yesko ad apreerlo/apreerla]

in the open air all'aria aperta

opening times l'orario di apertura **m** [orar-yo dee apairtoora]

open ticket il biglietto aperto [beel-yet-to apairto]

opera l'opera **f** [opaira]

operation (medical) l'operazione **f** [opairatz-yonay]

operator (telephone) il/la centralinista [chentraleeneesta]

opposite: the opposite direction la direzione opposta [deeretz-yonay]

the bar opposite il bar di fronte [frontay]

opposite my hotel di fronte al mio albergo

optician l'ottico **m**

or o

orange (fruit) l'arancia **f** [arancha]
(colour) arancione [aranchonay]

orange juice il succo d'arancia [sook-ko]
(freshly squeezed) la spremuta d'arancia [spremoota]
(fizzy) l'aranciata **f** [aranchata]

orchestra l'orchestra **f**

order: can we order now? (in restaurant) possiamo ordinare ora? [pos-yamo ordeenaray]

I've already ordered, thanks ho già ordinato, grazie [o ja]

I didn't order this non ho ordinato questo [kwesto]

out of order fuori servizio [fworee sairveetz-yo]

ordinary ordinario

other altro

the other one l'altro, l'altra

the other day l'altro giorno

I'm waiting for the others aspetto gli altri [aspet-to l-yee]

do you have any others? ne avete degli altri? [nay avaytay dayl-yee]

otherwise altrimenti

our* il nostro, la nostra, i nostri, le nostre

ours* il nostro, la nostra, i nostri, le nostre

out: he's out è fuori [ay fworee]

three kilometres out of town
tre chilometri fuori città
[keelometree fworee cheet-ta]

outdoors all'aperto [apairto]

outside fuori di [fworee dee]
  can we sit outside?
  possiamo sedere fuori? [pos-yamo sedairay]

oven il forno

over: over here qui [kwee]
  over there lì
  over 500 più di cinquecento [p-yoo]
  it's over è finito/finita [ay]

overcharge: you've overcharged me c'è un errore nel conto [chay oon airroray]

overlook: I'd like a room overlooking the courtyard
vorrei una stanza che dia sul cortile [vor-ray – kay dee-a sool korteelay]

overcoat il soprabito

overnight (travel) di notte [dee not-tay]

overtake sorpassare [sorpas-saray]

owe: how much do I owe you?
quanto le devo? [kwanto lay dayvo]

own: my own ... il mio...
  are you on your own? è da solo/sola? [ay]
  I'm on my own sono da solo/sola

owner (man/woman) il proprietario [propree-etar-yo], la proprietaria

P

pack (verb) fare le valigie [faray lay valeejay]
  a pack of ... un pacco di...

package (small parcel) il pacco

package holiday la vacanza organizzata [vakantza organeetzata]

packed lunch il pranzo al sacco [prantzo]

packet: a packet of cigarettes
un pacchetto di sigarette [pak-ket-to dee seegaret-tay]

padlock il lucchetto [look-ket-to]

Padua Padova [padova]

page (of book) la pagina [pajeena]
  could you page Mr ...? può far chiamare il signor...? [pwo – k-yamaray]

pain il dolore [doloray]
  I have a pain here mi fa male qui [mee fa malay kwee]

painful doloroso

painkillers gli analgesici [analjayzeechee]

paint la vernice [vairneechay]

painting il dipinto

pair: a pair of ... un paio di... [pa-yo]

Pakistani pachistano [pakeestano]

palace il palazzo [palatzo]

pale pallido
  pale blue blu chiaro [k-yaro]

pan la pentola

panties le mutande [moot**a**nday]

pants (underwear: men's/women's) le mutande
(US) i pantaloni

pantyhose il collant [kol-**lan**]

paper la carta
(newspaper) il giornale [jorn**a**lay]
a piece of paper un pezzo di carta [p**e**tzo]

paper handkerchiefs i fazzoletti di carta [fatzol**e**t-tee]

parcel il pacco

pardon (me)? (didn't understand/hear) prego? [pr**ay**go]

parents i genitori [jeneet**o**ree]

parents-in-law i suoceri [sw**o**chairee]

park il parco
(verb: the car) parcheggiare [parkej-j**a**ray]
can I park here? posso parcheggiare qui? [kwee]

Parking is often difficult as there are few car parks. Check the signs and restrictions carefully, and be prepared to pay legal attendants in a **parcheggio a pagamento** (paying car park), or illegal ones for the sake of peace.

parking lot il parcheggio [parkej-jo]

part la parte [p**a**rtay]

partner (boyfriend, girlfriend etc) il/la partner

party (group) il gruppo [gr**oo**p-po]
(celebration) la festa

pass (in mountains) il passo

passenger (man/woman) il passeggero [pas-sej-j**ai**ro], la passeggera

passport il passaporto

If possible, keep your passport with you at all times (as it is compulsory to carry identification). When checking into a hotel, you'll have to surrender your passport briefly, so that the proprietor can register your stay on the necessary police forms.

past: in the past in passato
just past the information office appena dopo l'ufficio informazioni [ap-p**ay**na]

path il sentiero [sent-y**ai**ro]

pattern il motivo

pavement il marciapiede [marchap-y**ay**day]
on the pavement sul marciapiede

pavement café il caffè all'aperto [kaf-f**ay** al-lap**ai**rto]

pay (verb) pagare [pag**a**ray]
can I pay, please? il conto, per favore
it's already paid for è già pagato [ay ja]

dialogue

who's paying? chi paga?
[kee]
I'll pay pago io [**ee**-o]
**no, you paid last time, I'll
pay** no, tu hai pagato
l'altra volta, pago io [**a**-ee]

pay phone il telefono
pubblico
peaceful tranquillo
[trankw**ee**llo]
peach la pesca
peanuts le arachidi
[ara**k**eedee]
pear la perla [**pair**la]
peas i piselli
peculiar strano
pedestrian crossing il
passaggio pedonale [pas-**saj**-
jo pedon**a**lay]
pedestrian precinct la zona
pedonale [**tzo**na]
peg (for washing) la molletta
(for tent) il picchetto [peek-
ket-to]
pen la penna
pencil la matita
penfriend il/la
corrispondente [kor-
reespond**en**tay]
penicillin la penicillina
[peneecheel-**lee**na]
penknife il temperino
[tempair**ee**no]
pensioner (man/woman) il
pensionato [pens-yon**a**to], la
pensionata

people la gente [**jen**tay]
the other people in the hotel
le altre persone all'albergo
[lay **a**ltray pairs**o**nay]
too many people troppa
gente [**trop**-pa]
pepper (spice) il pepe [**pay**pay]
(vegetable) il peperone
[peper**o**nay]
peppermint (sweet) la
caramella alla menta
per: per night a notte [**not**-tay]
how much per day? quanto
(costa) al giorno? [kw**a**nto]
per cent per cento [pair
ch**en**to]
perfect perfetto [pairf**et**-to]
perfume il profumo
[prof**oo**mo]
perhaps forse [**for**say]
perhaps not forse no
period (of time) il periodo
[pair**ee**-odo]
(menstruation) le mestruazioni
[mestroo-atz-y**o**nee]
perm la permanente
[pairman**en**tay]
permit il permesso [pairm**es**-
so]
person la persona [pairs**o**na]
personal stereo il
walkman®
petrol la benzina [bentz**ee**na]

Italy is one of the most
expensive countries in
Europe in which to buy
petrol. For unleaded petrol, look for
the sign: **senza piombo**.

petrol can la latta di benzina [bent**zee**na]

petrol station la stazione di servizio [statz-**yo**nay dee sair**vee**tz-yo]

pharmacy la farmacia [farma**chee**-a]
see **chemist's**

phone il telefono [te**lay**fono]
(verb) telefonare [telefon**a**ray]

 Public telephones, run by Telecom Italia, come in various forms, usually with clear instructions printed on them (in English too).
The most common type takes both coins and phone-cards though in cities you'll come across ones that take cards only. Phonecards (**carte telefoniche**) for L5.000 and L10.000 can be bought from **tabacchi** or newsstands or shops which display the **Telecom Italia carte telefoniche** sticker. If you don't have a card, you'll need L100, L200 or L500 coins, or a token known as a **gettone** (worth L200), available from tabacchi, bars and some newsstands – they're also in use as currency but are becoming rarer by the year.

phone book l'elenco telefonico m
phone box la cabina telefonica
phonecard la scheda telefonica [s**kay**da], la carta

telefonica

phone number il numero di telefono [**noo**mairo dee te**lay**fono]

photo la fotografia [fotograf**ee**-a]

excuse me, could you take a photo of us? scusi, può farci una fotografia? [s**koo**zee, pwo far**chee**]

phrasebook il frasario [fra**zar**-yo]

piano il piano**for**te

pickpocket (man/woman) il borsaiolo [borsa-**yo**lo], la borsa**io**la

pick up: will you be there to pick me up? vieni/viene a prendermi lì?
[vy**ay**nee/vy**ay**nay a pr**en**dairmee]

picnic il picnic

picture (painting) il quadro [**kwa**dro]
(photo) la fotografia [fotograf**ee**-a]

pie (meat) il pasticcio [past**ee**cho]
(fruit) la t**or**ta

piece il pezzo [**pe**tzo]
a piece of ... un pezzo di...

pill la p**i**llola
I'm on the pill prendo la p**i**llola

pillow il cuscino [koo**shee**no]

pillow case la federa [**fay**daira]

pin lo spillo [s**pee**l-lo]

pineapple l'ananas m

pineapple juice il succo d'ananas [**soo**k-ko]

pink rosa
pipe (for smoking) la pipa
(for water) il tubo [**too**bo]
pipe cleaners gli scovolini
pity: it's a pity è un peccato
[ay]
pizza la pizza
place il posto
is this place taken? è
occupato questo posto? [ay
ok-koo**pa**to **kwe**sto]
at your place a casa tua/sua
[**too**-a/**soo**-a]
at his place a casa sua
plain (not patterned) in tinta
unita [oon**ee**ta]
plane l'aereo **m** [a-**ai**ray-o]
by plane in aereo
plant la pianta [p-**ya**nta]
plaster cast il gesso [**jes**-so]
plasters i cerotti [chai**rot**-tee]
plastic la plastica
(credit card) la carta di credito
[**kray**deeto]
plastic bag il sacchetto di
plastica [sak-**ket**-to]
plate il piatto [p-**yat**-to]
platform il marciapiede
[marchapy**ay**day]
which platform is it for Milan,
please? su quale binario
parte il treno per Milano,
per favore? [soo kwa**lay** been**ar**-
yo par**tay** eel **tray**no pair]
play (verb: game, sport) giocare
[**jok**aray]
(instrument) suonare [**swon**aray]
(noun: in theatre) la commedia
[kom-**mayd**-ya]

playground il parco giochi
[**jo**kee]
pleasant piacevole
[p-yach**ay**volay]
please per favore [pair fa**vor**ay]
yes please sì, grazie [see
gratzee-ay]
could you please ...?
potrebbe per favore...?
[po**trayb**-bay]
please don't ... per favore
non...
pleased to meet you piacere
di conoscerla [p-yach**air**ay dee
konosh**air**la]
pleasure il piacere
my pleasure (not at all) non
c'è di che [chay dee kay]
plenty: plenty of ...
molto/molta/molti/molte...
there's plenty of time c'è
(ancora) molto tempo [chay]
that's plenty, thanks basta
così, grazie [ko**zee grat**zee-ay]
pliers le pinze [**peen**tzay]
plug (electrical) la spina
(for car) la candela [kan**day**la]
(in sink) il tappo
plumber l'idraulico **m**
[eedr**ow**leeko]
p.m.* del pomeriggio
[pomai**reej**-jo](in the evening) di
sera [**sai**ra]
poached egg l'uovo in
camicia **m** [l**wo**vo een
kam**ee**cha]
pocket la tasca
point: two point five due
virgola cinque

there's no point è inutile [ay eenooteelay]

points (in car) le puntine [poonteenay]

poisonous velenoso [velenozo]

police la polizia [poleetzee-a] (military police) i carabinieri [karabeen-yairee]

call the police! chiamate la polizia! [k-yamatay]

In Italy the police come in many forms. Drivers may well come up against the **Polizia Urbana**, or town police, who are mainly concerned with directing the traffic and punishing parking offences; the **Polizia Stradale** patrol motorways. You may have some dealings with the **Carabinieri**, with their military-style uniforms and white shoulder belts – they deal with general crime, public order and drug control. They are the most professional of the police forces and the ones to head for if you're in deep trouble. The **Polizia Statale** are the ones to whom thefts should be reported. Dial 113 for the **Polizia** and 112 for the **Carabinieri**.

policeman il poliziotto [poleetz-yot-to]

police station il commissariato

policewoman la donna poliziotto [poleetz-yot-to]

polish il lucido [loocheedo]

polite educato [edookato]

polluted inquinato [eenkweenato]

pony il pony

pool (for swimming) la piscina [peesheena]

poor (not rich) povero [povairo] (quality) scadente [skadentay]

Pope il Papa

pop music la musica pop [moozeeka]

pop singer il/la cantante pop [kantantay]

population la popolazione [popolatz-yonay]

pork il maiale [ma-yalay]

port il porto

porter (in hotel) il portiere [port-yairay]

portrait il ritratto

posh chic [sheek]

possible possibile [posseebeelay]

is it possible to ...? è possibile...? [ay]

as soon as possible al più presto possibile [p-yoo]

post (mail) la posta (verb) impostare [eempostaray]

could you post this for me? potrebbe imbucare questa per me? [potreb-bay eembookaray kwesta pair may]

postal service
The postal service is rather slow and ordinary mail may take weeks to arrive. Things of value should be sent by registered mail (**raccomandata**) or,

if urgent, by special delivery/express mail (**espresso**). Post offices generally open Monday to Saturday from 8.30 a.m. to 2 p.m., but in a few places they also open in the afternoons from 2.30 p.m. to 6.30 p.m or all day from 8.30 a.m. to 7 p.m. If stamps are all you need, buy them at a tobacconist's.

postbox la buca delle lettere [**boo**ka **del**-lay **let**-tairay]
postcard la cartolina
postcode il codice postale [**ko**deechay po**stal**ay]
poster il manifesto
post office l'ufficio postale **m** [oof-**fee**cho po**stal**ay]
poste restante il fermo posta [**fair**mo]
potato la patata
potato chips le patatine [patat**ee**nay]
pots and pans le pentole [**pent**olay]
pottery la ceramica [chair**a**meeka]
pound (money) la sterlina [stair**lee**na]
(weight)* la libbra
power cut l'interruzione della corrente **f** [eentair-rootz-**yo**nay **del**-la kor-**ren**tay]
power point la presa di corrente [**prayz**a dee]
practise: I want to practise my Italian voglio esercitarmi a parlare italiano [**vol**-yo esaircheet**ar**mee a parl**aray**]

prawns i gamberetti [gambair**et**-tee]
prefer: I prefer ... preferisco... [prefair**ee**sko]
pregnant incinta [eench**een**ta]
prescription (for medicine) la ricetta [reech**et**-ta]

 If you're going to use your E111 to get free treatment and prescriptions for medicines at the local rate, there's a complicated procedure to go through first. You have to go to the local **Unità Sanitaria Locale** to exchange the E111 for a 'certificate of entitlement' and a list of doctors, pharmacies and dentists. If you're looking for repeat medication, take empty bottles or capsules with you.

present il regalo
president (of country) il/la presidente [prezeed**en**tay]
pretty grazioso [gratz-**yo**zo]
it's pretty expensive è piuttosto caro [ay p-yoot**os**to]
price il prezzo [**pret**zo]
priest il sacerdote [sachaird**o**tay]
prime minister il primo ministro
printed matter le stampe [**stam**pay]
priority (in driving) la precedenza [preched**en**tza]
prison la prigione [preej**o**nay]
private privato
private bathroom il bagno in

113

camera [ban-yo een kamaira]
probably probabilmente
[probabeelmentay]
problem il problema
[problayma]
no problem! nessun
problema
program(me) il programma
promise: I promise prometto
pronounce: how is this
pronounced? come si
pronuncia? [komay see
pronooncha]
properly (repaired, locked etc)
bene [baynay]
protection factor il fattore di
protezione [fat-toray dee
protetz-yonay]
Protestant protestante
[-tantay]
public convenience i
gabinetti pubblici [poob-
bleechee]
public holiday la festa
nazionale [natzyonalay]
pudding il dessert [des-sair]
pull tirare [teeraray]
pullover il pullover
puncture la foratura [foratoora]
purple viola [v-yola]
purse (for money) il
portamonete [portamonaytay]
(US) la borsetta
push spingere [speenjairay]
pushchair il passeggino [pas-
sej-jeeno]
put mettere [met-tairay]
where can I put ...? dove
posso mettere...? [dovay]

could you put us up for the
night? ci può ospitare per
una notte? [chee pwo ospeetaray
pair]
pyjamas il pigiama [peejama]

Q

quality la qualità [kwaleeta]
quarantine la quarantena
[kwarantayna]
quarter il quarto [kwarto]
quayside: on the quayside
sulla banchina [sool-la
bankeena]
question la domanda
queue la fila
quick veloce [velochay]
that was quick che velocità
[kay velocheeta]
what's the quickest way
there? qual è il modo più
rapido per arrivarci? [kwal ay
eel modo p-yoo rapeedo pair
arreevarchee]
fancy a quick drink? ti/le va
di bere qualcosa
rapidamente? [lay – bairay
kwalkoza rapeedamentay]
quickly velocemente
[velochementay]
quiet (place, hotel) tranquillo
[trankweel-lo]
quiet! silenzio! [seelentz-yo]
quite (fairly) abbastanza [ab-
bastantza]
(very) molto
that's quite right è proprio

giusto [ay – **joo**sto]
quite a lot moltissimo

R

rabbit il coniglio [con**ee**l-yo]
race (for runners, cars) la corsa
racket (tennis, squash) la
  racchetta [rak-k**e**t-ta]
radiator il radiatore [rad-
  yat**o**ray]
radio la radio
  on the radio alla radio
rail: by rail in treno [**tray**no]
railway la ferrovia [fair-
  rov**ee**-a]
rain la pioggia [p-y**o**j-ja]
  in the rain sotto la pioggia
  it's raining piove [p-y**o**vay]
raincoat l'impermeabile **m**
  [eempairmay-**a**beelay]
randy arrapato
rape lo stupro [st**oo**pro]
rare (steak) al sangue
  [s**a**ngway]
rash (on skin) l'eruzione
  cutanea **f** [erootz-y**o**nay
  koot**a**nay-a]
raspberry il lampone
  [lamp**o**nay]
rat il ratto
rate (for changing money) il
  cambio [k**a**mb-yo]
rather: it's rather good è
  piuttosto buono [ay p-yoot-
  t**o**sto bw**o**no]
  I'd rather ... preferirei...
  [prefaireer**ay**]

razor il rasoio [ras**o**-yo]
razor blades le lamette [lamet-
  tay]
read (verb) leggere [l**e**j-
  jairay]
ready pronto
  are you ready? sei/è
  pronto/pronta? [say/ay]
  I'm not ready yet non sono
  ancora pronto/pronta

dialogue

when will it be ready?
quando sarà pronto?
[kw**a**ndo]
it should be ready in a
couple of days dovrebbe
essere pronto tra un
paio di giorni [dovr**e**b-bay
es-sairay – **pa**-yo dee
j**o**rnee]

real reale [ray-**a**lay]
really veramente
  [vairam**e**ntay]
  I'm really sorry sono
  veramente spiacente [spee-
  ach**e**ntay]
  that's really great è proprio
  magnifico
  really? davvero? [dav-v**ai**ro]
rearview mirror lo specchietto
  retrovisore [spek-y**e**t-to
  retroveez**o**ray]
reasonable (prices etc)
  moderato
receipt la ricevuta
  [reechev**oo**ta]

Make sure that you obtain and retain your **ricevuta fiscale** for whatever you pay for, even the smallest transaction. If you are found without one at a random check, both you and the retailer/supplier will be fined heavily. You'll get a receipt for everything you buy, even if it's just a coffee, and shop and bar staff will insist that you take it.

recently recentemente
[rechentem**e**ntay]
reception (in hotel) la
reception
(for guests) il ricevimento
[reecheveem**e**nto]
 at reception alla reception
reception desk la reception
receptionist il/la receptionist
recognize riconoscere
[reekon**o**shairay]
**recommend: could you
recommend ...?** mi potrebbe
consigliare...? [mee potr**e**b-bay
konseel-y**a**ray]
record (music) il disco
red rosso
red wine il vino rosso
refund il rimborso
 can I have a refund? mi può
rimborsare? [pwo
reembors**a**ray]
region la regione [rej**o**nay]
registered: by registered mail
(per) raccomandata
registration number il
numero di

immatricolazione [**noo**mairo
dee eemmatreekolatz-y**o**nay]
relative il/la parente [par**e**ntay]
religion la religione
[releej**o**nay]
remember: I don't remember
non ricordo
 I remember mi ricordo
 do you remember? ti
ricordi/si ricorda?
rent (for apartment etc)
l'affitto **m**
(verb) noleggiare [nolej-j**a**ray]
 to rent a nolo

dialogue

 I'd like to rent a car vorrei
noleggiare una macchina
[vor-r**ay** nolej-j**a**ray **oo**na mak-
keena]
 for how long? per quanto
tempo? [pair kw**a**nto]
 two days due giorni
[j**o**rnee]
 this is our range questa è
la nostra gamma [kw**e**sta
ay]
 I'll take the ... prendo la...
 **is that with unlimited
mileage?** il
chilometraggio è
illimitato? [keelometr**a**j-jo]
 it is sì
 **can I see your licence
please?** posso vedere la
sua patente, per favore?
[ved**ai**ray la s**oo**-a pat**e**ntay]
 and your passport e il

passaporto [ay]
is insurance included?
l'assicurazione è
compresa? [las-seekooratz-
yonay ay komprayza]
**yes, but you pay the first
150,000 lire** sì, ma paga lei
le prime 150.000
(centocinquantamila) lire
[lay lay preemay – leeray]
**can you leave a deposit
of ...?** può lasciare una
caparra di...? [pwo lasharay]

rented car la macchina a
noleggio [mak-keena a
nolej-jo]
repair (verb) riparare
[reepararay]
can you repair it? lo/la può
riparare? [pwo]
repeat ripetere [repetairay]
could you repeat that? può
ripetere? [pwo]
reservation la prenotazione
[prenotatz-yonay]
I'd like to make a reservation
vorrei prenotare [vor-ray
prenotaray]

dialogue

I have a reservation ho
prenotato [o]
yes sir, what name please?
sì, a che nome? [kay
nomay]

reserve prenotare [prenotaray]

dialogue

**can I reserve a table for
tonight?** vorrei prenotare
un tavolo per stasera [vor-ray
– pair stasaira]
**yes madam, for how many
people?** sì, signora, per
quante persone? [seen-yora,
pair kwantay pairsonay]
for two per due
and for what time? per che
ora? [pair kay]
for eight o'clock per le otto
[lay]
**and could I have your name
please?** il suo nome, per
favore? [soo-o nomay]
see **alphabet** for spelling

rest: I need a rest ho bisogno
di riposarmi [o beezon-yo]
the rest of the group il resto
del gruppo
restaurant il ristorante
[reestorantay]

 Restaurants are most
commonly called either
trattoria or **ristorante**.
Traditionally, a trattoria is a less
expensive and more basic purveyor
of home-style cooking (**cucina
casalinga**), while a ristorante is
more upmarket. These days,
however, there is a fine line between
the two, as it is rather chic for an
expensive restaurant to call itself a
trattoria. It's in the rural areas that

you're most likely to come across an old-style trattoria, the sort of place where there's no written menu and no bottled wine. A true ristorante will always have a written menu and a reasonable choice of wines, though even in smart places it's standard to choose the ordinary house wine.

restaurant car il vagone ristorante [vagonay reestorantay]

rest room la toilette [twalet]
see toilet

retired: I'm retired sono in pensione [pens-yonay]

return (ticket) il biglietto di andata e ritorno [beel-yet-to]
see ticket

reverse charge call la telefonata a carico del destinatario

reverse gear la retromarcia [retromarcha]

revolting disgustoso [deezgoostozo]

rib la costola

rice il riso [reezo]

rich (person) ricco [reek-ko]
(food) sostanzioso [sostantz-yozo]

ridiculous ridicolo

right (correct) giusto [joosto]
(not left) destro

you were right avevi/aveva ragione [avayvee/avayva rajonay]

that's right è giusto [ay]

this can't be right non è

possibile [ay pos-seebeelay]

right! d'accordo

is this the right road for ...? è la strada giusta per...? [ay – pair]

on the right a destra

turn right giri a destra [jeeree]

right-hand drive la guida a destra [gweeda]

ring (on finger) l'anello m

I'll ring you ti/le telefono [lay telayfono]

ring back ritelefonare [reetelefonaray]

ripe (fruit) maturo [matooro]

rip-off: it's a rip-off è un furto [ay oon foorto]

rip-off prices i prezzi esorbitanti [pretzee]

risky rischioso [reesk-yozo]

river il fiume [f-yoomay]

road la strada

is this the road for ...? è questa la strada per...? [ay kwesta – pair]

down the road in fondo alla strada

road accident l'incidente stradale m [eencheedentay stradalay]

road map la cartina stradale

roadsign il segnale stradale [sen-yalay]

rob: I've been robbed sono stato derubato/derubata! [dairoobato]

rock la roccia [rocha]
(music) il rock

on the rocks (with ice) con
ghiaccio [g-yacho]
roll (bread) il panino
Roman (adj) romano
the Romans i Romani
Rome Roma
roof il tetto
roof rack il portapacchi
[portapak-kee]
room la camera, la stanza
[stantza]
in my room nella mia stanza
[mee-a]

dialogue

do you have any rooms?
ha una camera? [a]
for how many people? per
quante persone? [pair
kwantay pairsonay]
for one/for two per
una/due
yes, we have rooms free
sì, abbiamo una camera
libera [ab-yamo]
for how many nights will it
be? per quante notti la
vuole? [kwantay – vwolay]
just for one night solo per
una notte [not-tay]
how much is it? quanto
costa? [kwanto]
... with bathroom and ...
without bathroom ... con
bagno e... senza bagno
[ban-yo – sentza]
can I see a room with
bathroom? posso vedere

una camera con
bagno? [vedairay]
OK, I'll take it va bene, la
prendo [baynay]

room service il servizio in
camera [sairveetz-yo een]
rope la corda
rosé il rosé
roughly (approximately)
grossomodo
round: it's my round tocca a
me [may]
roundabout (for traffic) la
rotatoria
round trip ticket il biglietto di
andata e ritorno [beel-yet-to]
see ticket
route il tragitto [trajeet-to]
what's the best route? qual è
il tragitto migliore? [kwalay –
meel-yoray]
rubber (material) la gomma
(eraser) la gomma (per
cancellare) [pair kanchel-laray]
rubber band l'elastico m
rubbish (waste) i rifiuti [reef-
yootee]
(poor quality goods) la porcheria
[porkairee-a]
rubbish! (nonsense)
sciocchezze! [shok-ketzay]
rucksack lo zaino [tza-eeno]
rude sgarbato [zgarbato]
ruins le rovine [roveenay]
rum il rum [room]
rum and coke la
Coca-Cola® col rum
run (verb: person) correre [kor-

rairay]

how often do the buses run?
ogni quanto tempo passa
l'autobus? [**on**-yee kw**a**nto –
lowtoboos]

I've run out of money sono
rimasto senza soldi [**sentza**]

rush hour l'ora di punta f

S

sad triste [**treestay**]
saddle (for bike, horse) la sella
safe (not in danger) sicuro
[seek**oo**ro]
(not dangerous) non
pericoloso [pair**ee**kolozo]
safety pin la spilla di
sicurezza [seek**oo**retza]
sail la vela [**vayla**]
sailboard la tavola a vela
sailboarding il windsurf
salad l'insalata f
salad dressing il condimento
per l'insalata [pair]

sale: for sale vendesi
[vend**ee**see]
salmon il salmone [sal-m**o**nay]
salt il sale [**salay**]
same: the same lo stesso
the same as this come
questo [**ko**may kw**e**sto]
the same again, please un
altro/un'altra, per favore
it's all the same to me per
me è lo stesso [pair may ay]
sand la sabbia
sandals i sandali

sandwich il panino imbottito
sanitary napkins gli
assorbenti igienici [as-
sorb**e**ntee eej**a**yneechee]
sanitary towels gli assorbenti
igienici
sardines le sardine [sard**ee**nay]
Sardinia la Sardegna [sar-d**ayn**-
ya]
Saturday il sabato
sauce la salsa
saucepan la pentola
saucer il piattino [p-yat-**tee**no]
sauna la sauna [**sown**a]
sausage la salsiccia [sals**ee**cha]
say: how do you say ... in
Italian? come si dice... in
italiano? [**ko**may see d**ee**chay ...
een eetal-y**a**no]
what did he/she say? cos'ha
detto? [koz a]
I said ... ho detto... [o]
he/she said ... ha detto... [a]
could you say that again?
puoi/può ripetere, per
favore? [pwoy/pwo reep**e**tairay]
scarf (for neck) la sciarpa
[**sharpa**]
(for head) il foulard [foo**lar**]
scenery il paesaggio [pa-ee-
z**aj**-jo]
schedule (US) l'orario m
scheduled flight il volo di
linea [**lee**nay-a]
school la scuola [sk**wo**la]
scissors: a pair of scissors un
paio di forbici [**pa**-yo dee
forb**ee**chee]
scooter lo scooter

Scotch lo scotch
Scotch tape® lo scotch
Scotland la Scozia [skotz-ya]
Scottish scozzese [skotzayzay]
 I'm Scottish sono scozzese
scrambled eggs le uova
 strapazzate [wova strapatzatay]
scratch il graffio [graf-fyo]
screw la vite [veetay]
screwdriver il cacciavite
 [kachaveetay]
scrubbing brush (for hands) lo
 spazzolino per le unghie
 [spatzoleeno per lay oong-yay]
sea il mare [maray]
 by the sea sul mare [sool]
seafood i frutti di mare
 [froot-tee dee]
seafront il lungomare
 [loongomaray]
 on the seafront sul
 lungomare [sool]
seagull il gabbiano [gab-yano]
search (verb) cercare
 [chairkaray]
seashell la conchiglia
 [konkeel-ya]
seasick: I feel seasick ho mal
 di mare [o – maray]
 I get seasick soffro di mal di
 mare
seaside: by the seaside sul
 mare [sool]
seat il posto
 is this anyone's seat? è
 libero questo posto? [ay
 leebairo kwesto]
seat belt la cintura di
 sicurezza [cheentoora dee

 seekooretza]
sea urchin il riccio di mare
 [reecho dee maray]
seaweed le alghe marine
 [algay mareenay]
secluded isolato
second (adj) secondo
 (of time) il secondo
 just a second! un attimo!
second class (travel) in
 seconda classe [klassay]
second floor (UK) il secondo
 piano(US) il primo piano
second-hand di seconda
 mano
see vedere [vedairay]
 can I see? posso vedere?
 have you seen ...? hai/ha
 visto... [a-ee/a]
 I see (I understand) capisco
 I saw him this morning l'ho
 visto stamattina [lo]
self-catering apartment
 l'appartamento (per le
 vacanze) m [pair lay vakantzay]
self-service il self-service
sell vendere [vendairay]
 do you sell ...? avete...?
 [avaytay]
Sellotape® lo scotch
send mandare [mandaray]
 I want to send this to England
 voglio mandare questo in
 Inghilterra [vol-yo – kwesto een
 eengeeltair-ra]
senior citizen (man/woman) il
 pensionato, la pensionata
separate separato
separated: I'm separated sono

separato/separata

separately (pay) a parte [par**tay**]

(travel) separatamente [separata**may**ntay]

September settembre [set-**tem**bray]

septic infetto

serious serio [**sair**-yo]

service charge (in restaurant) il servizio [sair**veetz**-yo]

service station la stazione di servizio [statz-**yo**nay dee sair**veetz**-yo]

serviette il tovagliolo [toval-**yo**lo]

set menu il menù fisso [me**noo**]

several diversi [deev**air**see]

sew cucire [kooch**ee**ray]

could you sew this back on? potrebbe riattaccarlo? [potreb-bay r-yat-tak-**kar**lo]

sex il sesso

(sexual intercourse) il rapporto sessuale [ses-swa**lay**]

sexy sexy

shade: in the shade all'ombra

shake: to shake hands stringersi la mano [str**een**jairsee]

shallow (water) poco profondo

shame: what a shame! che peccato! [kay]

shampoo lo shampoo

shampoo and set shampoo e messa in piega [ay – p-y**ay**ga]

share (verb: room, table etc) dividere [deev**ee**dairay]

sharp (knife) tagliente [tal-**yen**tay]

(taste) aspro

(pain) acuto [ak**oo**to]

shattered (very tired) distrutto [deestr**oo**t-to]

shaver il rasoio [raz**o**-yo]

shaving foam la schiuma da barba [sk-**yoo**ma]

shaving point la presa per il rasoio [pr**ay**za pair eel raz**o**-yo]

she* lei [lay]

is she here? è qui? [ay kwee]

sheet (for bed) il lenzuolo [lentz-w**o**lo]

shelf lo scaffale [skaf-**fa**lay]

shellfish i frutti di mare [fr**oo**t-tee dee ma**ray**]

sherry lo sherry

ship la nave [n**a**vay]

by ship con la nave

shirt la camicia [kam**ee**cha]

shit! merda! [m**air**da]

shock lo shock

I got an electric shock from the ... ho preso la scossa dal... [o pr**ay**zo]

shock-absorber l'ammortizzatore *m* [am-morteetzat**o**ray]

shocking scandaloso

shoe la scarpa

a pair of shoes un paio di scarpe [p**a**-yo dee sk**ar**pay]

shoelaces i lacci

shoe polish il lucido per le scarpe [l**oo**cheedo pair lay sk**ar**pay]

shoe repairer il calzolaio

[kalzola-yo]

shop il negozio [negotz-yo]

Shop opening times vary from place to place and from season to season. Shops generally open some time between 8 and 9 a.m. (food shops tend to open earlier than other shops) and close for lunch at some time between 12.30 and 1 p.m., re-opening at 3.30 or 4 p.m. They then remain open until 7 or 8 p.m. Some big department stores and supermarkets are open at lunchtime. Shops in holiday resorts don't always close for lunch and often remain open until very late at night. Frequently in winter, and sometimes in summer, shops have a weekly closing day or afternoon.

shopping: I'm going shopping vado a far compere [kompairay]

shopping centre il centro commerciale [chentro kommairchalay]

shop window la vetrina

shore la riva

short (person) basso

(time) poco

(journey) corto

shortcut la scorciatoia [skorchato-ya]

shorts i calzoncini [kaltzoncheenee]

should: what should I do? cosa dovrei fare? [koza dovray faray]

he shouldn't be long non ci dovrebbe mettere tanto [chee dovreb-bay met-tairay]

you should have told me avresti dovuto dirmelo [dovooto deermelo]

shoulder la spalla

shout (verb) gridare [greedaray]

show (in theatre) lo spettacolo

could you show me? mi può far vedere? [mee pwo far vedairay]

shower (in bathroom) la doccia [docha]

with shower con doccia

shower gel il gel per la doccia [pair]

shut (verb) chiudere [k-yoodairay]

when do you shut? quando chiudete? [kwando k-yoodaytay]

when do they shut? quando chiudono? [k-yoodono]

they're shut sono chiusi [k-yoosee]

I've shut myself out mi sono chiuso fuori [k-yoozo fworee]

shut up! stai zitto! [sty tzeet-to]

shutter (on camera) l'otturatore **m** [ot-tooratoray]

(on window) l'imposta **f**

shy timido

Sicily la Sicilia [seecheel-ya]

sick (US) malato

I'm going to be sick (vomit) sto per vomitare [pair

123

vomeet**aray**]

see ill

side il lato

the other side of town l'altra parte della città [partay del-la cheet-**ta**]

side lights le luci di posizione [**loo**chee dee poseetz-**yo**nay]

side salad l'insalata f

side street la stradina [strad**ee**na]

sidewalk il marciapiede [marchap-**yay**day]

see pavement

sight: the sights of ... le attrazioni turistiche di... [at-tratz-**yo**nee too**ree**steekay]

sightseeing: we're going sightseeing andiamo a fare un giro turistico [and-**yamo** a faray oon **jee**ro]

sightseeing tour il giro turistico

sign (roadsign etc) il segnale [sen-**yalay**]

signal: he didn't give a signal non ha segnalato [a sen-yal**ato**]

signature la firma

signpost il cartello stradale [strad**ala**y]

silence il silenzio [seelentz-yo]

silk la seta [**sayta**]

silly sciocco [**shok**-ko]

silver l'argento m [ar**jento**]

silver foil la stagnola [stan-**yola**]

similar simile [**seemeelay**]

simple (easy) semplice [**sempleechay**]

since: since yesterday da ieri [**yairee**]

since I got here da quando sono arrivato/arrivata [kw**ando**]

sing cantare [kant**aray**]

singer il/la cantante [kant**antay**]

single: a single to ... un biglietto di sola andata per... [beel-yet-to – pair]

I'm single (man/woman) sono celibe/nubile [**chay**lee-bay/**noo**beelay]

single bed il letto a una piazza [p-**yatza**]

single room la camera singola

sink (in kitchen) l'acquaio m [akw**a**-yo]

sister la sorella

sister-in-law la cognata [kon-**yata**]

sit: can I sit here? posso sedere qui? [sed**airay** kwee]

is anyone sitting here? è libero questo posto? [ay **lee**bairo kwesto]

sit down sedersi [sed**airsee**]

size la taglia [**tal**-ya]

ski lo sci [shee]

(verb) sciare [shee-**aray**]

a pair of skis un paio di sci [**pa**-yo dee]

ski boots gli scarponi da sci

skiing lo sci

we're going skiing andiamo a sciare [and-**yamo** a shee-**aray**]

ski instructor (man/woman) il
maestro di sci [**my**stro dee
shee]/la maestra di sci
ski-lift lo ski-lift
skin la pelle [**pel**-lay]
skin-diving l'immersione
senza attrezzature f [eem-
mairs-**yo**nay s**e**ntza at-trez-
zat**oo**ray]
skinny mingherlino
[meengairl**ee**no]
ski-pants i calzoni da sci
[kaltz**o**nee da shee]
ski-pass lo ski-pass
ski pole la racchetta da sci
[rak-k**e**t-ta da shee]
skirt la gonna
ski run la pista da sci [shee]
ski slope il campo da sci
ski wax la sciolina [shee-
ol**ee**na]
sky il cielo [ch**ay**lo]
sleep (verb) dormire
[dorm**ee**ray]
did you sleep well? hai/ha
dormito bene? [**a**-ee/a –
b**ay**nay]
I need a good sleep ho
bisogno di fare una buona
dormita [o beez**o**n-yo dee f**a**ray
oona bw**o**na]
sleeper (on train) il vagone
letto [vag**o**nay]
sleeping bag il sacco a pelo
[**pay**lo]
sleeping car il vagone letto
[vag**o**nay]
sleeping pill il sonnifero [son-
n**ee**fairo]

sleepy: I'm feeling sleepy ho
sonno [o]
sleeve la manica
slide (photographic) la
diapositiva
slip (under dress) la sottoveste
[sot-to-v**e**stay]
slippery scivoloso [sheevol**o**zo]
Slovenia la Slovenia [slo-**vayn**-
ya]
slow lento
slow down! (driving) rallenta!
(speaking) parla/parli più
lentamente! [p-yoo
lentam**e**ntay]
slowly lentamente
could you say it slowly?
puoi/può dirlo più
lentamente? [pwoy/pwo d**eer**lo
p-yoo]
very slowly molto
lentamente
small piccolo
smell: it smells (smells bad)
puzza [**poo**tza]
smile (verb) sorridere [sor-
r**ee**dairay]
smoke il fumo [**foo**mo]
do you mind if I smoke? le/ti
dispiace se fumo? [lay/tee
deespee**a**chay say]
I don't smoke non fumo
do you smoke? fuma/fumi?
snack: I'd just like a snack
vorrei fare uno spuntino
[vor-r**ay** f**a**ray **oo**no spoon-**tee**no]
sneeze lo sternuto [stairn**oo**to]
snorkel il respiratore
[respeerat**o**ray]

snow la neve [**nay**vay]
 it's snowing nevica [**nay**veeka]
 so: it's so expensive è così
 caro [ay]
 it's so good è proprio
 buono [bw**o**no]
 not so fast più piano [p-yoo]
 so am I anch'io [ank**ee**-o]
 so do I anch'io
 so-so così così
soaking solution (for contact
 lenses) la soluzione
 conservante e disinfettante
 per le lenti a contatto
 [soloot-z-y**o**nay konsairv**a**ntay ay
 deeseenfet-t**a**ntay pair lay]
soap il sapone [sap**o**nay]
soap powder il detersivo (in
 polvere) [detairs**ee**vo een
 p**o**lvairay]
sober sobrio
sock il calzino [kaltz**ee**no]
socket (electrical) la presa
 [**pray**sa]
soda (water) il seltz
sofa il divano
soft (material etc) morbido
soft-boiled egg l'uovo alla
 coque [**wo**vo **a**l-la kok]
soft drink la bibita
 (analcolica)
soft lenses le lenti morbide
 [m**o**rbeeday]
sole la suola [**swo**la]
 could you put new soles on
 these? può risuolare queste
 scarpe? [pwo reeswol**a**ray
 kw**e**stay sk**a**rpay]
some: can I have some

water/rolls? potrei avere
 dell'acqua/dei panini?
 [potr**ay** av**a**iray – day]
 can I have some? posso
 averne un po'? [av**a**irnay]
somebody, someone
 qualcuno [kwal-k**oo**no]
something qualcosa [kwalk**o**za]
 something to drink qualcosa
 da bere [b**a**iray]
sometimes qualche volta
 [kw**a**lkay]
somewhere da qualche parte
 [p**a**rtay]
son il figlio [**feel**-yo]
song la canzone [kantz**o**nay]
son-in-law il genero [**jay**nairo]
soon presto
 I'll be back soon torno fra
 poco
 as soon as possible al più
 presto possibile [p-yoo – pos-
 s**ee**beelay]
sore: it's sore mi fa male
 [**ma**lay]
sore throat il mal di gola
sorry: (I'm) sorry scusa/mi
 scusi [sk**oo**za/mee sk**oo**zee]
 sorry? (didn't understand)
 prego? [**pray**go]
sort: what sort of ...? che tipo
 di...? [kay]
soup la minestra, la zuppa
 [tz**oo**p-pa]
sour (taste) aspro
south il sud [sood]
 in the south al sud
South Africa il Sudafrica
 [sood**a**freeka]

South African (adj)
sudafricano [soodafree-kano]
I'm South African
(man/woman) sono
sudafricano/sudafricana
southeast il sud-est [soodest]
southwest il sud-ovest
[soodovest]
souvenir il souvenir
spanner la chiave inglese
[k-yavay eenglayzay]
spare part il pezzo di
ricambio [petzo dee reekamb-yo]
spare tyre la gomma di scorta
spark plug la candela
[kandayla]
speak: do you speak English?
parla inglese? [eenglayzay]
I don't speak ... non parlo...

dialogue

can I speak to Roberto?
posso parlare con
Roberto? [parlaray]
who's calling? chi parla?
[kee]
it's Patricia sono Patricia
I'm sorry, he's not in, can I
take a message? mi
dispiace, non c'è; vuole
lasciare un messaggio?
[mee deesp-yachay, non chay;
vwolay lasharay oon mes-saj-jo]
no thanks, I'll call back
later no, grazie, richiamo
più tardi [reek-yamo p-yoo]
please tell him I called gli

dica che ho chiamato,
per favore [l-yee – kay o
k-yamato]

spectacles gli occhiali [ok-yalee]
speed la velocità [velocheeta]
speed limit il limite di
velocità [leemee-tay dee]
speedometer il tachimetro
[takeemetro]
spell: how do you spell it?
come si scrive? [komay see
skreevay]
see alphabet
spend spendere [spendairay]
spider il ragno [ran-yo]
spin-dryer la centrifuga
[chentreefooga]
splinter la scheggia [skej-ja]
spoke (in wheel) il raggio [raj-jo]
spoon il cucchiaio [kook-ya-yo]
sport lo sport
sprain: I've sprained my ... mi
sono slogato... [zlogato]
spring (season) la primavera
[preema-vaira]
(of car, seat) la molla
square (in town) la piazza
[p-yatza]
stairs le scale [skalay]
stale (bread) raffermo [raf-fairmo]
(taste) sa di vecchio [vek-yo]
stall: the engine keeps stalling
il motore si spegne in
continuazione [motoray see

St

127

spen-yay een konteenoo-atz-yonay]
stamp il francobollo

Stamps can be bought at tobacconists' shops and sometimes from stalls and shops selling postcards. Avoid post offices, unless you require a special postal service, as it's likely you will have to queue.

dialogue

a stamp for England, please un francobollo per l'Inghilterra, per favore [pair]
what are you sending? per che cosa? [kay koza]
this postcard per questa cartolina [kwesta]

standby (flight) il volo stand-by
star la stella
start l'inizio **m** [eeneetz-yo] (verb) cominciare [komeencharay]
when does it start? quando comincia? [kwando komeencha]
the car won't start la macchina non parte [mak-keena]
starter (of car) lo starter
(food) l'antipasto **m**
starving: I'm starving sto morendo di fame [famay]
state (in country) lo stato
the States (USA) gli Stati

Uniti [l-yee – ooneetee]
station la stazione [statz-yonay]
statue la statua [statoo-a]
stay: where are you staying? dove'è alloggiato/alloggiata? [dovay ay al-loj-jato]
I'm staying at ... sono (alloggiato/alloggiata) a...
I'd like to stay another two nights vorrei fermarmi ancora due notti [vor-ray fair-marmee]
steak la bistecca
steal rubare [roobaray]
my bag has been stolen mi hanno rubato la borsa [mee an-no roobato]
steep (hill) ripido
steering lo sterzo [stairtzo]
step: on the steps sui gradini
stereo lo stereo [stairay-o]
sterling la sterlina [stairleena]
steward (on plane) lo steward
stewardess la hostess
sticking plaster il cerotto [chairot-to]
still ancora
I'm still waiting sto ancora aspettando
is he still there? è ancora lì? [ay]
keep still! sta' fermo/ferma! [fairmo]
sting: I've been stung sono stato punto [poonto]
stockings le calze [kaltzay]
stomach lo stomaco
stomach ache il mal di stomaco

128

stone (rock) la pietra
[p-y**e**tra]

stop (verb) fermare [fairm**a**ray]
please, stop here (to taxi driver etc) fermi qui, per fav**o**re
[**fair**mee kwee]
do you stop near ...? ferma vicino a...? [veech**ee**no]
stop doing that! smettila!
[zm**e**t-teela]

stopover la s**o**sta

storm la temp**e**sta

straight: straight ahead avanti diritto
a straight whisky un whisky liscio [**lee**sho]

straightaway immediatamente [eem-med-yatam**e**ntay]

strange (odd) strano

stranger (man/woman) lo straniero [stran-y**ai**ro]/la stran**i**era
I'm a stranger here non s**o**no di qui [kwee]

strap (on watch) il cinturino [cheentoor**ee**no]
(on dress) la spallina
(on suitcase) la cinghia
[ch**ee**ng-ya]

strawberry la fragola

stream il ruscello [roosh**e**l-lo]

street la strada
on the street sulla strada
[s**oo**l-la]

streetmap la piantina della città [p-yant**ee**na d**e**l-la cheet-t**a**]

string lo spago

strong forte [**for**tay]

stuck bloccato
the key's stuck la chiave si è bloccata [k-y**a**vay see ay]

student (man/woman) lo studente/la studentessa
[stood**e**ntay/stood**e**nt**e**s-sa]

stupid stupido [st**oo**peedo]

suburb la periferia

subway (US) la metropolitana

suddenly improvvisamente
[eemprov-veezam**e**ntay]

suede la pelle scamosciata
[p**e**l-lay skamo-sh**a**ta]

sugar lo zucchero [tz**oo**k-kairo]

suit il completo [kompl**ay**to]
it doesn't suit me (jacket etc) non mi sta bene [**bay**nay]
it suits you ti sta bene

suitcase la valigia [val**ee**ja]

summer l'estate f [est**a**tay]
in the summer d'estate

sun il sole [s**o**lay]
in the sun al sole
out of the sun all'ombra

sunbathe prendere il sole
[pr**e**ndairay eel s**o**lay]

sunblock (cream) la crema a protezione totale [kr**ay**ma a protetz-y**o**nay tot**a**lay]

sunburn la scottatura [skot-tat**oo**ra]

sunburnt scottato

Sunday la domenica
[dom**ay**neeka]

sunglasses gli occhiali da sole [ok-y**a**lee da s**o**lay]

sun lounger (chair) il lettino

sunny assolato
it's sunny c'è il sole [chay eel

solay]
sun roof (in car) il tetto
apribile [apree-beelay]
sunset il tramonto
sunshade il parasole
[parasolay]
sunshine la luce del sole
[loochay del solay]
sunstroke il colpo di sole
suntan l'abbronzatura f [ab-
brontzatoora]
suntan lotion la lozione
solare [lotz-yonay solaray]
suntanned abbronzato [ab-
brontzato]
suntan oil l'olio solare m [ol-
yo solaray]
super fantastico
supermarket il supermercato
[soopair-mairkato]
supper la cena [chayna]
supplement (extra charge) il
supplemento [soop-plemento]
sure sicuro [seekooro]
are you sure? sei/è
sicuro/sicura? [say/ay]
sure! certo! [chairto]
surname il cognome [kon-
yomay]
swearword la parolaccia
[parolacha]
sweater il maglione [mal-
yonay]
sweatshirt la felpa
Sweden la Svezia [zvetzee-a]
Swedish (adj) svedese
[zvedayzay]
sweet (taste) dolce [dolchay]
(noun: dessert) il dolce

sweets le caramelle [karamel-
lay]
swelling il gonfiore [gonf-
yoray]
swim (verb) nuotare [nwotaray]
I'm going for a swim vado a
fare una nuotata [faray oona
nwotata]
let's go for a swim andiamo
a fare una nuotata [and-
yamo]
swimming costume il
costume da bagno
[kostoomay da ban-yo]
swimming pool la piscina
[pee-sheena]
swimming trunks il costume
da bagno [kostoomay da ban-
yo]
Swiss svizzero [zveetzairo]
switch l'interruttore m
[eentair-root-toray]
switch off (engine, TV, lights)
spegnere [spen-yairay]
switch on (engine, TV, lights)
accendere [achendairay]
Switzerland la Svizzera
[sveetzaira]
swollen gonfio [gonf-yo]

T

table il tavolo
a table for two un tavolo per
due [pair]
table cloth la tovaglia [toval-
ya]
table tennis il ping-pong

table wine il vino da tavola

tailback (of traffic) la coda

tailor il sarto

take (pick up, catch) prendere
[pr**e**ndairay]

(accept) accettare [achet**a**ray]

can you take me to the
airport? può portarmi
all'aerop**o**rto?

do you take credit cards?
accettate carte di credito?
[achet-t**a**tay k**a**rtay dee kr**ay**deeto]

fine, I'll take it va bene, lo/la
prendo [b**ay**nay]

can I take this? (leaflet etc)
posso prenderlo/prenderla?

how long does it take?
quanto ci vuole? [kw**a**nto chee
vw**o**lay]

it takes three hours ci
vogliono tre ore [chee v**o**l-
yono]

is this seat taken? è
occupato questo posto? [ay
ok-koop**a**to kw**e**sto]

pizza to take away una pizza
da portare via [port**a**ray v**ee**-a]

can you take a little off here?
(to hairdresser) può tagliare un
po' qui? [pwo tal-y**a**ray oon po
kwee]

talcum powder il talco

talk (verb) parlare [parl**a**ray]

tall alto

tampons i tamponi

tan l'abbronzatura f [ab-
brontzat**oo**ra]

to get a tan abbronzarsi [ab-
brontz**a**rsee]

tank (of car) il serbatoio
[sairbat**o**-yo]

tap il rubinetto [roobeen**e**t-to]

tape (cassette) la cassetta
(sticky) il nastro adesivo
[adez**ee**vo]

tape measure il metro a
nastro

tape recorder il registratore
[rejeestrat**o**ray]

taste il gusto [g**oo**sto]

can I taste it? posso
assaggiarlo/assaggiarla? [as-
saj-j**a**rlo]

taxi il taxi

will you get me a taxi? mi
può chiamare un taxi? [pwo
k-yam**a**ray]

where can I find a taxi? dove
posso prendere un taxi?
[d**o**vay – pr**e**ndairay]

dialogue

to the airport/to Hotel
Centrale please
all'aerop**o**rto/all'alb**e**rgo
Centr**a**le, per fav**o**re

how much will it be?
quanto verrà a costare?
[kw**a**nto – kost**a**ray]

50,000 (cinquantamila)
lire

that's fine, right here,
thanks va bene qui,
grazie [b**ay**nay kwee]

taxi-driver il tassista

taxi rank il posteggio dei taxi

[postej-jo day]
tea (drink) il tè [tay]
 tea for one/two, please
 un/due tè, per favore
teabags le bustine di tè
 [boost**ee**nay dee tay]
teach: could you teach me?
 mi puoi/può insegnare?
 [mee pwoy/pwo eensen-y**a**ray]
teacher l'insegnante **m/f**
 [eensen-y**a**ntay]
team la squadra [skw**a**dra]
teaspoon il cucchiaino da tè
 [kook-kee-a-**ee**no da tay]
tea towel lo strofinaccio
 [strofeen**a**cho]
teenager l'adolescente **m/f**
 [adolesh**e**ntay]
telegram il telegramma
telephone
 see **phone** and **speak**
television la televisione
 [televeez-y**o**nay]
tell: could you tell him ...?
 potresti/potrebbe dirgli...?
 [potr**e**b-bay d**ee**rl-yee]
temperature (weather) la
 temperatura [tempairat**oo**ra]
 (fever) la febbre [**f**eb-bray]
temple (building) il tempio
tennis il tennis
tennis ball la palla da tennis
tennis court il campo da
 tennis
tennis racket la racchetta da
 tennis [rak-k**e**t-ta]
tent la tenda
term (at university, school) il
 trimestre [treem**e**stray]

terminus (rail) il capolinea
 [kapol**ee**nay-a]
terrible terribile [tair-r**ee**beelay]
terrific fantastico
than* di [dee]
 smaller than più piccolo di
 [p-yoo]
thanks, thank you grazie
 [gr**a**tzee-ay]
 thank you very much grazie
 mille [m**ee**l-lay]
 thanks for the lift grazie del
 passaggio
 no thanks no grazie

dialogue

 thanks grazie [gr**a**tzee-ay]
 that's OK, don't mention it
 prego [pr**ay**go]

that: that man quell'uomo
 [kwel w**o**mo]
 that woman quella donna
 [kw**e**l-la]
 that one quello/quella lì
 [kw**e**l-lo]
 I hope that ... spero che...
 [sp**a**iro kay]
 that's nice (food) è
 buono/bu**o**na [bw**o**no]
 is that ...? (quello/quella)
 è...?
 that's it (that's right)
 esattamente [ezat-tam**e**ntay]
the* il, lo, la [eel]; i, gli, le
 [l-yee, lay]
theatre il teatro [tay-**a**tro]
their(s)* il loro, la loro, i loro,

le loro

them*: for them per loro

with them con loro

I gave it to them l'ho dato a loro [lo]

who? – them chi? – loro [kee]

then (at that time) allora

(after that) poi [poy]

there là

over there laggiù [laj-joo]

up there lassù [las-soo]

is there ...? c'è...? [chay]

are there ...? ci sono...? [chee]

there is ... c'è...

there are ... ci sono...

there you are (giving something) ecco qua [kwa]

thermometer il termometro [tairmometro]

thermos flask il thermos [tairmos]

these: these men questi uomini [kwestee]

these women queste donne [kwestay]

can I have these? vorrei questi/queste [vor-ray]

they* loro

thick spesso

(stupid) ottuso [ot-toozo]

thief il ladro

thigh la coscia [kosha]

thin sottile [sot-teelay]

(person) magro

thing la cosa [koza]

my things le mie cose [lay mee-ay kozay]

think pensare [pensaray]

I think so penso di sì

I don't think so non credo [kraydo]

I'll think about it ci penserò [chee pensairo]

third party insurance l'R.C.A. [lair-ray chee a]

thirsty: I'm thirsty ho sete [o saytay]

this questo/questa [kwesto]

this man quest'uomo

this woman questa donna

this one questo/questa (qui) [kwee]

this is my wife questa è mia moglie [mol-yay]

is this ...? (questo/questa) è...?

those quelli/quelle [kwel-lee/kwel-lay]

those men quegli uomini [kwayl-yee]

those women quelle donne

those children quei bambini [kway]

which ones? – those quali? – quelli/quelle [kwalee]

thread il filo

throat la gola

throat pastilles le pastiglie per la gola [pasteel-yay pair]

through attraverso [at-travairso]

does it go through ...? (train, bus) passa per...? [pair]

throw (verb) gettare [jet-taray]

throw away (verb) buttare via [boot-taray]

thumb il pollice [pol-leechay]

thunderstorm il temporale
[temporal-ay]
Thursday il giovedì [jovedee]
ticket il biglietto [beel-yet-to]

dialogue

a return to Rome un
biglietto di andata e
ritorno per Roma [pair]
coming back when? il
ritorno per quando?
[kwando]
today/next Tuesday
oggi/martedì prossimo
[oj-jee]
that will be 48,000
quarantottomila lire

ticket office la biglietteria
[beel-yet-tairee-a]
tide la marea [maray-a]
tie (necktie) la cravatta
tight (clothes etc) attillato
it's too tight è troppo stretto
[ay]
tights il collant [kol-lan]
till la cassa
time* il tempo
what's the time? che ore
sono? [kay oray]
this time questa volta
[kwesta]
last time l'ultima volta
[loolteema]
next time la prossima volta
four times quattro volte
[kwat-tro voltay]
timetable l'orario m

tin (can) il barattolo
tinfoil la carta stagnola [stan-
yola]
tin opener l'apriscatole m
[apree-skatolay]
tiny piccolo
tip (to waiter etc) la mancia
[mancha]

 Although service is
included (usually 10-15%
of the bill), it is customary
to leave a tip in restaurants, when
satisfied with the service. A small tip
is often left in bars as well, and
given to hotel porters. Taxi drivers
are not usually tipped.

tired stanco
I'm tired sono stanco/stanca
tissues i fazzolettini di carta
[fatzolet-teenee]
to: to Naples/London a
Napoli/Londra
to Italy/England in
Italia/Inghilterra [een
eetal-ya/ eenghil-tair-ra]
to the post office all'ufficio
postale [oof-feecho postalay]
toast (bread) il pane tostato
[panay]
today oggi [oj-jee]
toe il dito del piede
[p-yayday]
together insieme [eens-
yaymay]
we're together (in shop etc)
siamo insieme [s-yamo]
can we pay together?

possiamo pagare insieme?
[pos-**ya**mo pagar**ay**]

toilet la toilette [twa**let**]

where is the toilet? dov'è la
toilette? [do**vay**]

I have to go to the toilet devo
andare alla toilette [**day**vo
and**ar**ay]

Public toilets are rare in
Italy, especially in the less
touristy places. You will
have to take advantage of toilets in
restaurants and bars or toilets at
railway stations and in museums
etc. Toilet paper is not always
supplied and, in public toilets, you
will need coins for the attendants.

toilet paper la carta igienica
[eej**ay**neeka]

token (for phone, shower) il
gettone [jet-**to**nay]

tomato il pomodoro

tomato juice il succo di
pomodoro [**soo**k-ko]

tomato ketchup il ketchup

tomorrow domani

tomorrow morning domani
mattina

the day after tomorrow
dopodomani

toner (cosmetic) il tonico

tongue la lingua [**leen**gwa]

tonic (water) l'acqua tonica **f**
[**ak**wa]

tonight (before 10 p.m.) stasera
(after 10 p.m.) stanotte [stan**ot**-
tay]

tonsillitis la tonsillite [tonseel-
leetay]

too (excessively) troppo
(also) anche [**an**kay]

too hot troppo caldo

too much troppo

me too anch'io [an**kee**-o]

tooth il dente [**den**tay]

toothache il mal di denti

toothbrush lo spazzolino da
denti [spatzol**ee**no]

toothpaste il dentifricio
[denteef**ree**cho]

top: on top of ... su... [soo]

at the top in cima [**chee**ma]

top floor l'ultimo piano
[**ool**teemo]

topless in topless

torch la torcia elettrica
[**tor**cha]

total il totale [tota**lay**]

tour (noun) il giro [**jee**ro]

is there a tour of ...? ci sono
visite guidate di...? [chee –
veezeetay gweed**at**ay]

tour guide la guida [**gwee**da]

tourist il/la turista [too**ree**sta]

tourist information office
l'ufficio informazioni **m**
[oof-**fee**cho eenformatz-**yo**nay]

tour operator l'operatore
turistico **m** [opairat**o**ray
too**ree**steeko]

towards verso [**vair**so]

towel l'asciugamano **m**
[ashooga**ma**no]

tower la torre [**tor**-ray]

town la città [**cheet**ta]

in town in città

135

just out of town appena
fuori città [ap-**pay**na f**wo**ree]
town centre il centro (della
città) [chentro del-la cheeta]
town hall il municipio
[mooneech**ee**p-yo]
toy il giocattolo [jok**at**-tolo]
track (US) il marciapiede
[marchapy**ay**day]
see **platform**
tracksuit la tuta da ginnastica
[**too**ta da jeenn**a**steeka]
traditional tradizionale
[tradeetz-yon**a**-lay]
traffic il traffico
traffic jam l'ingorgo **m**
traffic lights il semaforo
trailer (for carrying tent etc) il
rimorchio [reem**or**k-yo]
(US) la roulotte [rool**o**t]
trailer park il campeggio per
roulotte [kamp**e**j-jo pair]
train il treno [**tray**no]
by train in treno

The following services are
available:
EC (**Eurocity**) fast international train; a supplement must be
paid in advance
IC (**Intercity**) fast national train; a
supplement must be paid in
advance
Espresso long-distance fast train
Diretto long-distance train stopping
at main stations
Regionale local train stopping at all
stations
Some trains require a **prenotazione**

obbligatoria (compulsory
reservation). This will be indicated
on the timetable.

dialogue

is this train for ...? questo
treno va a...? [k**we**sto]
sure sì
**no, you want that platform
there** no, deve andare a
quel binario [**day**vay
and**a**ray a kwel been**ar**-yo]

trainers (shoes) le scarpe da
ginnastica [sk**ar**pay da
jeenn**a**steeka]
train station la stazione
ferroviaria [statz-**yo**nay fair-rov-
yar-ya]
tram il tram
translate tradurre [trad**oor**-ray]
could you translate that?
puoi/può tradurlo?
[pwoy/pwo]
translation la traduzione
[tradootz-**yo**nay]
translator (man/woman) il
traduttore [tradoot-**to**ray], la
traduttrice [tradoot-**tree**chay]
trashcan la pattumiera [pat-
toom-**yai**ra]
travel viaggiare [v-yaj-j**a**ray]
we're travelling around
stiamo visitando la regione
[st-**ya**mo – rej**o**nay]
travel agent's l'agenzia di
viaggi **f** [ajentz-ya dee vee-**aj**-
jee]

traveller's cheque il traveller's cheque

tray il vassoio [vas-so-yo]

tree l'albero **m** [albairo]

tremendous fantastico

trendy alla moda

trim: just a trim please (to hairdresser) solo una spuntatina per favore [spoontateena]

trip (excursion) la gita [jeeta]
 I'd like to go on a trip to ... vorrei fare una gita a... [vor-ray faray]

trolley il carrello

trouble i problemi [problaymee]
 I'm having trouble with ... ho difficoltà con... [o]
 sorry to trouble you scusi il disturbo [skoozee eel deestoorbo]

trousers i pantaloni

true vero [vairo]
 that's not true non è vero [ay]

trunk il bagagliaio [bagal-ya-yo]

trunks (swimming) il costume da bagno [kostoomay da ban-yo]

try (verb) provare [provaray]
 can I have a try? posso provare?

try on provare
 can I try it on? posso provarlo/provarla?

T-shirt la maglietta [mal-yet-ta]

Tuesday il martedì [martedee]

tuna il tonno

tunnel il tunnel [toon-nel]

Turin Torino [toreeno]

turn: turn left/right giri a sinistra/destra [jeeree]

turn off: where do I turn off? dove devo girare? [dovay dayvo jeeraray]
 can you turn the heating off? può spegnere il riscaldamento? [pwo spen-yairay]

turn on: can you turn the heating on? può accendere il riscaldamento? [achendairay]

turning (in road) la svolta

Tuscany la Toscana [toskana]

TV la TV [tee voo]

tweezers le pinzette [peentzet-tay]

twice due volte [doo-ay voltay]
 twice as much il doppio [dop-yo]

twin beds i letti gemelli [jemel-lee]

twin room la camera a due letti [doo-ay]

twist: I've twisted my ankle mi sono slogato la caviglia [mee sono zlogato la kaveel-ya]

type il tipo
 a different type of ... un tipo diverso di... [deevairso]

typical tipico

tyre lo pneumatico [p-nay-oomateeko]

Tyrrhenian Sea il Mar Tirreno [teer-rayno]

U

ugly brutto [**broo**tto]

ulcer l'ulcera f [**oo**lchaira]

umbrella l'ombrello m

uncle lo zio [**tzee**-o]

unconscious privo di sensi

under (in position) sotto

(less than) meno di [**mayno**]

underdone (meat) al sangue [**sa**ngway]

underground (railway) la metropolitana

underpants le mutande [**moo**tanday]

understand capire [kap**ee**ray]

I understand capisco

I don't understand non capisco

do you understand? capisci/capisce? [kap**ee**shee/kap**ee**shay]

unemployed disoccupato [deezok-koop**a**to]

United States gli Stati Uniti [st**a**tee oon**ee**tee]

university l'università f [ooneevair**see**ta]

unleaded petrol la benzina senza piombo [bent**zee**na s**e**nza p-y**o**mbo]

unlimited mileage il chilometraggio illimitato [keelometr**a**j-jo]

unlock aprire [apr**ee**ray]

unpack disfare le valigie [deesf**a**ray lay val**ee**jay]

until finché [feenk**ay**]

unusual insolito

up su [soo]

up there lassù [las-s**oo**]

he's not up yet (not out of bed) non si è ancora alzato [non see ay – altz**a**to]

what's up? che c'è? [kay chay]

upmarket chic [sheek]

upset stomach il disturbo di stomaco

upside down sottosopra

upstairs al piano superiore [soopair-y**o**ray]

urgent urgente [oorj**e**ntay]

us* noi [noy], ci [chee]

with us con noi

for us per noi [pair]

USA gli USA [oo-sa]

use (verb) usare [ooz**a**ray]

may I use ...? posso usare...?

useful utile [**oo**teelay]

usual solito

the usual (drink etc) il solito

V

vacancy: do you have any vacancies? (hotel) avete camere libere? [av**ay**tay kam**a**iray l**ee**bairay] see room

vacation la vacanza [vak**a**ntza] see holiday

(from university) le vacanze [vak**a**ntzay]

vaccination il vaccino [vach**ee**no]

vacuum cleaner

l'aspirapolvere **m**
[aspeerap**o**lvairay]

valid (ticket etc) valido

  how long is it valid for? per quanto tempo è valido? [pair kw**a**nto – ay]

valley la valle [v**a**l-lay]

valuable (adj) di valore [val**o**ray]

  can I leave my valuables here? posso lasciare qui i miei oggetti di valore? [lash**a**ray kwee ee mee-y**ay** oj-jet-tee dee]

value il valore [val**o**ray]

van il furgone [foorg**o**nay]

vanilla la vaniglia [van**ee**l-ya]

  a vanilla ice cream un gelato alla vaniglia [jel**a**to]

vary: it varies dipende [deep**e**nday]

vase il vaso [v**a**zo]

Vatican City la Città del Vaticano [cheet**a** del vateek**a**no]

veal il vitello

vegetables la verdura [vaird**oo**ra]

vegetarian (man/woman) il vegetariano [vejetar-y**a**no], la vegetariana

vending machine il distributore automatico [deestreeboot**o**ray owtom**a**teeko]

Venetian (adj) veneziano [venetz-y**a**no]

Venice Venezia [ven**ay**tz-ya]

very molto

  very little for me per me molto poco [pair may]

I like it very much mi piace moltissimo [mee pee-**a**chay]

vest (under shirt) la canottiera [kanot-ty**ai**ra]

via la via [**vee**-a]

video (film) la videocassetta (recorder) il videoregistratore [veeday-o-rejeestrat**o**ray]

view la vista

villa la villa

village il paese [pa-**ay**zay]

vinegar l'aceto **m** [ach**e**to]

vineyard la vigna [v**ee**n-ya]

visa il visto

visit (verb) visitare [veezeet**a**ray]

  I'd like to visit ... mi piacerebbe visitare... [mee pee-achair**e**b-bay]

  see **hospitality**

vital: it's vital that ... è di vitale importanza che... [ay dee veet**a**lay eemport**a**ntza kay]

vodka la vodka

voice la voce [v**o**chay]

volcano il vulcano

voltage il voltaggio [volt**a**j-jo]

The supply is 220V, though anything requiring 240V will work.

vomit vomitare [vomeet**a**ray]

W

waist la vita

waistcoat il gilet [jeel**ay**]

wait (verb) aspettare [aspet-taray]

wait for me aspettami/mi aspetti

don't wait for me non aspettarmi/mi aspetti

can I wait until my wife/partner gets here? posso aspettare fino a quando arriva mia moglie/la mia partner? [kwando]

can you do it while I wait? può farlo adesso? [pwo]

could you wait here for me? mi può aspettare qui? [kwee]

waiter il cameriere [kamair-yairay]

waiter! cameriere!

waitress la cameriera [kamair-yaira]

waitress! cameriera!

wake: can you wake me up at 5.30? mi può dare la sveglia alle cinque e mezza? [pwo daray la svayl-ya]

wake-up call la sveglia [svayl-ya]

Wales il Galles [gal-les]

walk: is it a long walk? ci si mette molto a piedi? [chee see met-tay – p-yayday]

it's only a short walk è a due passi da qui [ay a doo-ay – kwee]

I'll walk vado a piedi

I'm going for a walk vado a fare una passeggiata [faray oona pas-sej-jata]

Walkman® il walkman

wall il muro [mooro]

wallet il portafoglio [porta-fol-yo]

wander: I like just wandering around mi piace andarmene in giro [mee pee-achay andarmenay een jeero]

want: I want a ... voglio un/uno/una... [vol-yo]

I don't want any ... non voglio nessun/nessuno/nessuna... [nes-soon]

I want to go home voglio andare a casa [andaray]

I don't want to non voglio

he wants to ... vuole... [vwolay]

what do you want? cosa vuole?

ward (in hospital) la corsia [korsee-a]

warm caldo

I'm so warm sento molto caldo

was*: he/she/it was ... era... [aira]

wash (verb) lavare [lavaray]

can you wash these? può lavare questi/queste? [pwo – kwestee/kwestay]

washer (for bolt etc) la rondella

washhand basin il lavabo

washing (clothes) il bucato

washing machine la lavatrice [lavatreechay]

washing powder il detersivo per bucato [detairseevo pair]

washing-up liquid il detersivo

liquido per i piatti
[**lee**kweedo pair ee p-y**a**t-tee]

wasp la vespa

watch (wristwatch) l'orologio
m [orol**o**jo]

**will you watch my things for
me?** può dare un'occhiata
alla mia roba? [pwo d**a**ray oon
ok-y**a**ta **a**lla m**ee**-a]

watch out! attenzione! [at-
tentz-y**o**nay]

watch strap il cinturino
(dell'orologio) [cheentoor**ee**no
del orol**o**jo]

water l'acqua **f** [**a**kwa]

may I have some water?
vorrei un po' d'acqua [vor-
r**ay**]

water bus (in Venice) il
vaporetto

waterproof (adj)
impermeabile [eempairmay-
abeelay]

waterskiing lo sci acquatico
[shee akw**a**-teeko]

wave (in sea) l'onda **f**

**way: could you tell me the way
to ...?** mi può indicare
come si arriva a...? [mee pwo
eendeek**a**ray k**o**may]

it's this way da questa parte
[kw**e**sta p**a**rtay]

it's that way da quella parte
[kw**e**l-la]

is it a long way to ...?... è
molto lontano/lontana?
[ay]

no way! assolutamente no!
[as-solootam**e**ntay]

dialogue

**could you tell me the way
to ...?** come si fa per
andare a...? [k**o**may – pair
and**a**ray]

**go straight on until you
reach the traffic lights**
vada dritto fino al
semaforo

turn left giri a sinistra
[**jee**ree]

take the first on the right
prenda la prima a destra

see **where**

we* noi [noy]

weak (person, drink) debole
[**day**bolay]

weather il tempo

dialogue

**what's the weather
forecast?** come sono le
previsioni del tempo?
[k**o**may – lay preveez-y**o**nee]

it's going to be fine farà
bel tempo

it's going to rain pioverà
[p-yovair**a**]

it'll brighten up later si
rasserenerà più tardi
[p-y**oo**]

wedding il matrimonio

wedding ring la vera [**vai**ra]

Wednesday il mercoledì
[mairkoled**ee**]

week la settimana
a week (from) today oggi a otto [oj-jee]
a week (from) tomorrow domani a otto
weekend il fine settimana [feenay]
at the weekend durante il fine settimana
weight il peso [payzo]
weird strano
weirdo il tipo strano
welcome: welcome to ... benvenuto a... [benvenooto]
you're welcome (don't mention it) prego [praygo]
well: I don't feel well non mi sento bene [baynay]
she's not well non sta bene
you speak English very well parla inglese molto bene [eenglay-zay]
well done! bravo!
this one as well anche questo/questa [ankay kwesto]
well well! (surprise) guarda, guarda! [gwarda]

dialogue

how are you? come va? [komay]
very well, thanks benissimo, grazie
– and you? – è lei? [ay lay]

well-done (meat) ben cotto
Welsh gallese [gal-layzay]
I'm Welsh sono gallese

were*: we were eravamo
west l'ovest m
in the west ad ovest
West Indian (adj) delle Indie occidentali [del-lay eendee-ay ocheedentalay]
wet umido [oomeedo], bagnato [ban-yato]
what? cosa?
what's that? cos'è? [kozay]
what should I do? cosa dovrei fare? [dovray faray]
what a view! che vista! [kay]
what bus is it? che autobus è? [kay – ay]
wheel la ruota [rwota]
wheelchair la sedia a rotelle [sayd-ya a rotel-lay]
when? quando? [kwando]
when we get back quando torniamo
when's the train/ferry? a che ora parte il treno/il traghetto? [kay – partay]
where? dove? [dovay]
I don't know where it is non so dov'è [dovay]

dialogue

where is the cathedral? dov'è il duomo? [dovay]
it's over there è laggiù [ay laj-joo]
could you show me where it is on the map? puoi/può farmi vedere dov'è sulla cartina? [pwoy/pwo – vedairay dovay]

it's just here è proprio qui
[kwee]
see **way**

dialogue

which one? quale? [kwalay]
that one quello/quella
[kwel-lo/kwel-la]
this one? questo/questa?
[kwesto]
no, that one no,
quello/quella

while: while I'm here mentre
sono qui [mentray – kwee]
whisky il whisky
white bianco [b-yanko]
white wine il vino bianco
who? chi? [kee]
who is it? chi è? [ay]
the man who ... l'uomo
che... [lwomo kay]
whole: the whole week tutta
la settimana [toot-ta]
the whole lot tutto
whose: whose is this? di chi
è questo/questa? [dee kee ay
kwesto]
why? perché? [pairkay]
why not? perché no?
wide largo
wife la moglie [mol-yay]
will*: will you do it for me? lo
farà per me? [pair may]
wind il vento

window (of house) la finestra
(of shop) la vetrina
near the window vicino alla
finestra [veecheeno]
in the window (of shop) in
vetrina
window seat il posto vicino
al finestrino [veecheeno]
windscreen il parabrezza
[parabretza]
windscreen wipers i
tergicristalli [tairjeekreestal-lee]
windsurfing il windsurf
windy: it's windy c'è vento
[chay]
wine il vino
can we have some more
wine? ancora vino, per
favore
wine list la lista dei vini [day]
winter l'inverno m [eenvairno]
in the winter d'inverno
winter holiday le vacanze
invernali [va-kantzay
eenvairnalee]
wire il filo di ferro [fair-ro]
(electric) il filo (elettrico)
wish: best wishes tanti
auguri [owgooree]
with con
I'm staying with ... sono
ospite di... [ospeetay]
without senza [sentza]
witness il/la testimone
[testeemonay]
will you be a witness for me?
può farmi da testimone?
[pwo]
woman la donna

143

women
Italy has a reputation for sexual harassment against women that is well-known and well-founded. Generally it's worse the further south you travel, where if you're travelling on your own, or with another woman, you can expect to be tooted and hissed at in towns every time you step outside the hotel door. This persistent pestering is not usually made with any kind of violent intent, but it's annoying and frustrating nevertheless. Indifference is often the most effective policy, as is looking as confident as possible, a purposeful stride and firmly directed gaze.

wonderful meraviglioso [mairaveel-y**o**zo]

won't*: it won't start non parte [**pa**rtay]

wood (material) il legno [l**en**-yo]
(forest) il bosco

wool la lana

word la parola

work il lavoro
it's not working non funziona [foontz-y**o**na]
I work in ... lavoro a/in...

world il mondo

worry: I'm worried sono preoccupato/preoccupata [pray-ok-koop**a**to]

worse: it's worse è peggio [ay p**e**j-jo]

worst il peggio [p**e**j-jo]

worth: is it worth a visit? vale la pena di visitarlo/visitarla? [v**a**lay la p**a**yna]

would: would you give this to ...? può dare questo/questa a...? [pwo d**a**ray kw**e**sto]

wrap: could you wrap it up? può incartarlo? [pwo]

wrapping paper la carta da pacchi [**pa**k-kee]

wrist il polso

write scrivere [skr**ee**vairay]
could you write it down? può scrivermelo? [pwo skr**ee**vairmelo]
how do you write it? come si scrive? [**ko**may see skr**ee**vay]

writing paper la carta da lettere [**let**-tairay]

wrong: it's the wrong key è la chiave sbagliata [ay la k-y**a**vay zbal-y**a**ta]
this is the wrong train questo è il treno sbagliato [kw**e**sto]
the bill's wrong c'è un errore nel conto [chay oon air-r**o**ray]
sorry, wrong number mi scusi, ho sbagliato numero [mee sk**oo**zee o – n**oo**mairo]
sorry, wrong room mi scusi, ho sbagliato camera
there's something wrong with ... c'è qualcosa che non va nel/nello/nella... [chay kwalk**o**za kay]
what's wrong? cosa c'è che non va? [**ko**za chay kay]

X

X-ray i raggi X [raj-jee eeks]

Y

yacht lo yacht
yard* lo yard
 (backyard etc) il cortile
 [kort**ee**lay]
year l'anno **m**
yellow giallo [j**a**l-lo]
yes sì
yesterday ieri [y**ai**ree]
 yesterday morning ieri
 mattina
 the day before yesterday
 l'altro ieri
yet ancora

dialogue

 is it here yet? è (già)
 arrivato? [ay ja]
 no, not yet no, non ancora
 you'll have to wait a little
 longer yet devi/deve
 aspettare ancora un po'
 [**day**vay aspet-t**a**ray]

yoghurt lo yogurt [y**o**goort]
you* (singular, polite) lei [lay]
 (singular, familiar) tu
 (plural) voi [voy]
 this is for you questo/questa
 è per te/lei [kw**e**sto – ay pair
 tay/lay]

with you con te/lei

In Italian, when you
address people you don't
know, or with whom you
have a formal relationship, you
should use the **Lei** form of 'you',
which takes the third person
singular of the verb. **Tu** (you), the
second person singular, is used to
address family, friends, children and
informal acquaintances.

young giovane [j**o**vanay]
your(s)* (singular, polite) (il) suo
 [s**oo**-o], (la) sua, (i) suoi
 [swoy], (le) sue [s**oo**-ay]
 (singular, familiar) (il) tuo [t**oo**-
 o], (la) tua, (i) tuoi [twoy], le
 tue [t**oo**-ay]
 (plural) (il) vostro, (la) vostra,
 (i) vostri, (le) vostre [v**o**stray]
youth hostel l'ostello della
 gioventù **m** [jovent**oo**]

Z

zero lo zero [tz**ai**ro]
zip la cerniera lampo [chairn-
 y**ai**ra]
 could you put a new zip on?
 potrebbe cambiare la
 cerniera lampo? [potr**e**b-bay
 kamb-y**a**ray]
zip code il codice postale
 [k**o**deechay postalay]
zoo lo zoo [tz**o**-o]

Italian

→

English

A

a* at; in; to; per
 a persona per person
abbaglianti full beam
abbassare [ab-bas-saray] to
 lower, to pull down
abbastanza [ab-bastantza]
 enough; quite, rather
abbiamo* we have
abbigliamento da bambino m
 [ab-beel-yamento] children's
 wear
abbigliamento da donna
 ladies' wear
abbigliamento da uomo
 menswear
abbigliamento per signora
 ladies' clothing
abbonamento m [ab-bonamento]
 season ticket
abbonamento mensile
 [menseelay] monthly ticket
abbronzante m [ab-brontzantay]
 suntan lotion
abbronzarsi [ab-brontzarsee] to
 get a tan
abbronzato [ab-brontzato]
 tanned
abbronzatura f [ab-brontzatoora]
 suntan
abile [abeelay] skilful
abitante m/f [abeetantay]
 inhabitant
abitare [abeetaray] to live
abiti mpl [abeetee] clothes
abito m [abito] dress; suit
abitudine f [abeetoodeenay]
 habit

a.C. (avanti Cristo) B.C.
accanto beside
acceleratore m [achelairatoray]
 accelerator
accendere [achendairay] to
 switch on; to light
 mi fa accendere? have you
 got a light?
accendere i fari switch on
 headlights
accendino m [achendeeno]
 lighter
accensione m [achens-yonay]
 ignition
accento m [achento] accent
accessori moda mpl fashion
 accessories
accesso riservato ai
 viaggiatori muniti di biglietto
 access only for passengers
 in possession of tickets
accettare [achet-taray] to
 accept
accettazione f [achet-tatz-yonay]
 check-in
acciaio m [acha-yo] steel
accidenti! [acheedentee] damn!
accomodati come in; take a
 seat
accomodi: si accomodi [ak-
 komodee] come in; take a
 seat
accompagnare [ak-kompan-
 yaray] to accompany
accompagnatore m [ak-
 kompan-yatoray],
 accompagnatrice f [ak-
 kompan-yatreechay] tour leader

acconciatore m ladies' hairdresser

accordo m agreement
d'accordo all right, OK
essere d'accordo (con) [es-sairay] to agree (with)

accreditare [ak-kraydeetaray] to credit

acetone m [achetonay] nail polish remover

A.C.I. (Automobile Club d'Italia) m [achee] Italian Automobile Association

acqua f [akwa] water

acqua di Colonia [dee kolon-ya] eau de Cologne

acquaio m [akwa-yo] sink

acqua potabile [potabeelay] drinking water

addormentarsi to fall asleep

addormentato [ad-dormentato] asleep

adesso now

adolescente m/f [adoleshentay] teenager

adulto m adult

aereo (m) [a-airay-o] plane; air (adj)
andare in aereo to fly

aerobica f [a-airobeeka] aerobics

aeromobile m [a-airomobeelay] aeroplane

aeroplano m [a-airoplano] aeroplane

aeroporto m [a-airoporto] airport

aerostazione f [a-airostatz-yonay] air terminal

affamato starving

affari mpl business

affermare [af-fermaray] to maintain

afferrare [af-fer-raray] to catch

affettare [af-fet-taray] to slice

affittare [af-feet-taray] to rent

affittasi to let, to rent

affitto m rent
dare in affitto to let
prendere in affitto to hire, to rent

affollato crowded

affondare [af-fondaray] to sink

affrancare [af-frankaray] to stamp; to frank

affrancatura f postage

affrancatura per l'estero postage abroad

affrettarsi to hurry

agenda f [ajenda] diary

agenzia f [ajentzee-a] agency

agenzia di viaggi(o) [dee vee-aj-jee-o] travel agency

agenzia immobiliare [eem-mobeel-yaray] estate agent

agenzia turistica travel agency

aggiungere [aj-joonjairay] to add

aggiustare [aj-joostaray] to mend

aggressivo aggressive

agitare prima dell'uso shake before use

agitato [ajeetato] agitated

agli* [al-yee] at the; to the; with

ago m [ago] needle

agosto m August

agricoltore m [agreekolt**o**ray] farmer

ai* [a-ee] at the; to the; with

ai binari to the platforms/tracks

ai treni to the trains

aiutare [a-yoot**a**ray] to help

aiuto m [a-y**oo**to] help

al* at the; to the

ala f wing

alba f sunrise

albergo m hotel

albergo a 5/4/3/2 stelle 5/4/3/2-star hotel

albergo di categoria lusso [kataygor**ee**-a] luxury hotel

albero m [**a**lbairo] tree

albero a gomiti m crankshaft

alghe marine fpl [**a**lgay mar**ee**nay] seaweed

alimentari mpl groceries

alla* at the; to the; with

allacciare le cinture fasten your seat belts

allarme m [al-l**a**rmay] alarm

allattare [al-lat-t**a**ray] to breastfeed

alle* [**a**l-lay] at the; to the; with

allegria f [al-legr**ee**-a] cheerfulness

allegro cheerful

allenarsi to train

allievo m, **allieva** f [al-l-y**e**vo] pupil

allo* at the; to the

alloggiare [al-loj-j**a**ray] to stay

alloggio m [al-l**o**j-jo] accommodation

allora then

e allora? so what?

allungare [al-loong**a**ray] to stretch; to extend

almeno [al-m**a**yno] at least

Alpi fpl [**a**lpee] Alps

al... piano on/to ... floor

alpinismo m [alpeen**ee**zmo] mountaineering

alpinista m/f mountaineer

al portatore to the bearer

alt stop, halt

alternatore m [al-tairnat**o**ray] alternator

altitudine f [alteet**oo**deenay] altitude

alto high, tall

altopiano m plateau

altra, altri, altre [**a**ltray] other

altrimenti [altreem**e**ntee] otherwise

altro other

un altro another

alunno m, **alunna** f pupil

alzare [altz**a**ray] to lift, to raise

alzarsi [altz**a**rsee] to get up, to stand up

amare [am**a**ray] to love

amaro bitter

ambasciata f [ambash**a**ta] embassy

ambiente m [amb-y**e**ntay] environment

ambulanza f [ambool**a**ntza] ambulance

ambulatorio m [amboolat**o**r-yo] out-patients' department; surgery

americano (m), americana (f) American

amico m, amica f friend

ammalato ill, (US) sick

ammettere [am-met-tairay] to admit

ammobiliato [am-mobeel-yato] furnished

ammortizzatore m [am-morteedzatoray] shock absorber

amore m [amoray] love
fare l'amore [faray] to make love

ampere: da 15 ampere [ampairay] 15-amp

anabbaglianti mpl dipped headlights

analgesico m [analjayzeeko] painkiller

A.N.A.S. f (Azienda Nazionale Autonoma delle Strade) national road maintenance authority

anche [ankay] also; even
anche a te/lei [a tay/lay] the same to you

ancora f [ankora] anchor

ancora [ankora] still
ancora più... [p-yoo] even more ...
ancora un/uno/una... another/one more ...
ancora (una volta) (once) again
non ancora not yet

andare* [andaray] to go

andarsene [andarsenay] to go away

andarsene in fretta to rush away

andar via to go away

andate* [andatay] you go

andato* gone

andiamo* we go

anello m ring

angolo m corner; angle

animale m [aneemalay] animal

annegare [an-negaray] to drown

anniversario di matrimonio m wedding anniversary

anno m year

annoiarsi [an-noyarsee] to be bored

anno nuovo m [nwovo] New Year

annullare [an-nool-laray] to cancel

annullato cancelled

antenato m ancestor

antenna f aerial

antibiotico m antibiotic

anticamera f waiting room

Antica Roma f Ancient Rome

antichità fpl [anteekeeta] antiques

anticipo: in anticipo [een anteecheepo] in advance; early

antico ancient

antidolorifico m painkiller

antigelo m [anteejelo] antifreeze

antiquariato m [anteekwar-yato] antique; antiques shop

antisettico m antiseptic

antistaminico m

antihistamine

aperto* open

apparecchio m [ap-par**ek**-yo] phone

apparecchio m **acustico** [ak**oo**steeko] hearing aid

apparire [ap-par**ee**ray] to appear

appartamento m flat, apartment

appartamento ammobiliato furnished flat/apartment

appassionato (di) very keen (on)

appena [ap-p**ay**na] just; hardly, scarcely

appeso [ap-p**ay**so] hanging

appetito m [ap-pet**ee**to] appetite

appoggiato [ap-poj-j**a**to] leaning

approvare [ap-prov**a**ray] to approve

appuntamento m [ap-poon-tam**en**to] appointment

apre alle... opens at ...

apribottiglie m [apreebot-**teel**-yay] bottle opener

aprile m [apr**ee**lay] April

aprire* [apr**ee**ray] to open

apriscatole m [apreesk**a**tolay] tin opener

AR (andata e ritorno) return (ticket), round trip ticket

AR (avviso di ricevimento) receipt for registered letters which you return to sender

arancione [aranch**o**nay] orange

arbitro m referee

arco m arch

area di servizio f [serv**ee**tz-yo] service area

argento m [ar**j**ento] silver

argomento m topic, subject

aria f [**ar**-ya] air

avere l'aria... to look ...

aria condizionata f [konditz-yon**a**ta] air-conditioning

armadietto m [armad-**yet**-to] locker; cupboard

armadio m [armad-yo] cupboard; wardrobe

arrabbiarsi [ar-rab-**yar**see] to get angry

arrabbiato angry

arrestare [ar-rest**a**ray] to arrest

arrivare [ar-reev**a**ray] to arrive

arrivederci [ar-reeved**air**chee] goodbye

arrivo m arrival

arrivo previsto per le ore... expected time of arrival ...

arrogante [ar-rog**a**ntay] arrogant

arroganza f [ar-rog**a**ntza] arrogance

arrostire [ar-rost**ee**ray] to roast

arte f [**a**rtay] art

articoli da regalo mpl gifts

articoli per la casa household goods

articoli per la cucina kitchen articles

articoli sportivi sports gear

artificiale [arteefeech**a**lay] artificial

artigianato m [arteejan**a**to] crafts

artista m/f artist

ascensore f [ashensoray] lift, elevator

asciugacapelli m [ashoogakapel-lee] hair dryer

asciugamano m [ashoogamano] towel

asciugamano da bagno bath towel

asciugamano piccolo hand towel

asciugare [ashoogaray] to dry

asciugarsi [ashoogarsee] to dry oneself

asciugarsi le mani to dry one's hands

asciugatrice f [ashoogatreechay] tumble dryer

asciugatura con fon f [ashoogatoora] blow-dry

asciutto [ashoot-to] dry

ascoltare [askoltaray] to listen

asilo m [azeelo] nursery school

asilo nido crèche

asino m donkey

asma f [azma] asthma

aspettare [aspet-taray] to wait (for)

aspirapolvere m [aspeerapolvairay] vacuum cleaner

passare l'aspirapolvere to vacuum

aspirina f [aspeereena] aspirin

aspro sour

assaggiare [as-saj-jaray] to taste

asse da stiro m [as-say da steero] ironing board

assegno m [as-sen-yo] cheque, (US) check

pagare con un assegno to pay by cheque

assente [as-sentay] absent

assicurata f [as-seekoorata] registered letter

assicurazione f [as-seekooratz-yonay] insurance

assicurazione di viaggio [vee-aj-jo] travel insurance

assistenza auto repairs

associazione f [as-sochatz-yonay] society, association

assolato sunny

assolutamente [as-solootamentay] absolutely

assorbente igienico m [as-sorbentay eejeneeko] sanitary towel, sanitary napkin

atlante (geografico) f [atlantay jay-ografeeko] atlas

atlante stradale [stradalay] road atlas

atleta m/f [atlayta] athlete

atletica f [atlayteeka] athletics

attaccapanni m coat rack

attaccato stuck

attenda wait

attenti al cane beware of the dog

attento careful, attentive

attenzione f [at-tentz-yonay] care, attention

attenzione! look out!; caution!

attenzione: per l'uso leggere attentamente le istruzioni

interne warning: before use read instructions inside carefully

atterraggio m [at-tair-r**a**j-jo] landing

atterraggio di fortuna emergency landing

atterrare [at-tair-r**a**ray] to land

attillato tight

attimo: un attimo just a minute

attraente [at-tra-**e**ntay] attractive

attraversare [at-travairs**a**ray] to go through; to cross

attraverso [at-trav**a**irso] through

attrezzatura f [at-tretzat**oo**ra] equipment

auguri: tanti auguri [tant**ee** owg**oo**ree] best wishes

aula f [**ow**la] classroom

aumentare [owment**a**ray] to increase

australiano (m) [owstral-y**a**no], **australiana** (f) Australian

austriaco (m) [owstr**ee**-ako], **austriaca** (f) Austrian

autentico [owt**e**nteeko] genuine

autista m/f [owt**ee**sta] driver

auto f [**ow**to] car

autoambulanza f [owtoambul**a**ntza] ambulance

autobus m [**ow**toboos] bus

autofficina f garage (for repairs)

autogrill m [owtogr**ee**l] motorway/highway restaurant

autolavaggio m [owtolav**a**j-jo]

car wash

automobilista m/f [owtomobeel**ee**sta] car driver

autonoleggio m car rental

autorimessa f [owtoreem**e**s-sa] garage

autostop: fare l'autostop to hitchhike

autostrada f motorway, freeway, highway

autunno m [owt**oo**n-no] autumn, Fall

avanti come in; cross now **avanti diritto** straight ahead **più avanti** further on

avere m [av**a**iray] credit

avere* to have

avete* [av**ay**tay] you have

avuto* had

Avv. (avvocato) lawyer

avventura f [av-vent**oo**ra] adventure

avviarsi [av-vee-**a**rsee] to set off

avvicinarsi [av-veecheen**a**rsee] to approach

avviso m [av-v**ee**zo] notice

avvocato m lawyer

azioni fpl [atz-y**o**nee] shares, stocks

azzurro [adz**oo**r-ro] sky-blue

B

bacio m [b**a**cho] kiss

baffi mpl moustache

bagagli mpl [bag**a**l-yee] luggage, baggage

bagagliaio m [bagal-**ya**-yo] boot, trunk; left luggage, baggage check

bagaglio a mano m [bag**al**-yo] hand luggage/baggage

bagaglio in eccesso [ech**es**-so] excess baggage

bagnato [ban-y**a**to] wet

bagnato fradicio [fra**dee**cho] soaked

bagnino m [ban-y**ee**no], **bagnina** f lifeguard

bagno m [ban-yo] bath; bathroom

andare in bagno to go to the bathroom/toilet/rest room

fare il bagno to have a bath; to have a swim

bagnoschiuma m [ban-yosk-y**oo**ma] bubble bath

baia f [b**a**-ya] bay

balconata f balcony, dress-circle

balcone m [bal**ko**nay] balcony

ballare [bal-l**a**ray] to dance

balletto m ballet

ballo m dancing; dance

balsamo m conditioner

bambino m, **bambina** f child

bambola f doll

banca f bank

banchina f [bank**ee**na] platform, (US) track; quayside

banchina non transitabile soft verge

banco m desk

banco informazioni [eenformatz-y**o**nee] information desk

bancomat® m cash dispenser, automatic teller

banconota f banknote, (US) bill

bandiera f [band-y**ai**ra] flag

barare [bar**a**ray] to cheat

barattolo m tin

barba f beard

farsi la barba to shave

barbiere m [barb-y**ai**ray] barber's

barca (a motore) f [mot**o**ray] (motor) boat

barca a remi [**ray**mee] rowing boat

barca a vela [**vay**la] sailing boat

basket m basketball

basso low

basta (così)! [ko**zee**] that's enough!

bastare [bast**a**ray] to be enough

battello m passenger ferry; steamer

battere [bat-t**ai**ray] to beat

batteria f [bat-tair**ee**-a] battery; drums

beauty-case m toilet bag(s)

bebè m/f [be**bay**] baby

belga (m/f) Belgian

Belgio m [**bel**jo] Belgium

bello beautiful

bene [b**ay**nay] good; fine; well

bene, grazie [gr**a**tzee-ay] fine, thanks

ti sta bene! it serves you right!

va bene! that's fine!, it's

OK!; that's right
benissimo! excellent!
benvenuto! [benv**ay**nooto]
welcome!
benzina f [bendz**ee**na] petrol,
(US) gas
benzina normale [norm**a**lay]
two- or three-star petrol,
regular gas
benzina senza piombo [s**e**ntza
p-y**o**mbo] unleaded
petrol/gas
benzina super four-star
petrol, premium
benzina verde [v**a**irday]
unleaded petrol/gas
bere* [b**a**iray] to drink
berretto m [bair-r**e**t-to] cap
beve* [b**ay**vay] he/she/it
drinks; you drink
bevete* [bev**ay**tay] you drink
bevi* [b**ay**vee] you drink
beviamo* we drink
bevo* [b**ay**vo] I drink
bevono* they drink
bevuto* drank
biancheria da bambino f
[b-yankair**ee**-a] children's
underwear
biancheria da donna ladies'
lingerie
biancheria da letto bed linen
biancheria da uomo men's
underwear
biancheria intima underwear
biancheria per la casa
household linen
bianco [b-y**a**nko] white
bianco e nero [ay n**a**iro] black

and white
bibita f [b**ee**beeta] soft drink
biblioteca f [beebl-yot**e**ka]
library
bicchiere m [beek-y**a**iray] glass
bicicletta f [beecheekl**e**t-ta]
bicycle
andare in bicicletta to cycle
bidello m [beed**e**l-lo], **bidella f**
caretaker
bigiotteria f [bijot-tair**ee**-a]
costume jewellery
bigliettaio m [beel-yet-t**a**-yo]
conductor
biglietteria f [beel-yet-tair-**ee**-a]
ticket office; box-office
biglietteria automatica
[owtom**a**teeka] ticket vending
machine
biglietto m [beel-y**e**t-to] ticket;
banknote, (US) bill
biglietto chilometrico
[keelom**e**treeko] ticket
allowing travel up to a
maximum specified
distance
biglietto d'accesso ai treni
[dach**e**s-so **a**-ee tr**a**ynee]
platform ticket
biglietto da visita business
card
biglietto di andata e ritorno
[reet**o**rno] return (ticket),
round trip ticket
biglietto di auguri [owg**oo**ree]
(greetings/birthday) card
biglietto di sola andata single
(ticket), one-way ticket
biglietto per viaggi in comitiva

[vee-**aj**-jee] group/party ticket

biglietto ridotto [reed**ot**-to] reduced rate ticket

biglietto valido per più corse [val**ee**do pair p-yoo korsay] multi-journey ticket

bilancia (pesapersone) f [beel**an**chee-a payzapairs**o**nay] (bathroom) scales

bilanciatura gomme f [beelanchat**oo**ra g**o**m-may] wheel-balancing

binario m [been**ar**-yo] platform, (US) track

biondo [b-y**o**ndo] blond

birreria f [beer-rair**ee**-a] bar specializing in beer

bisogno: ho bisogno di [o beez**o**n-yo] I need

bivio m [b**ee**v-yo] junction

bloccato blocked; stuck

blocchetto di biglietti m [blok-**ket**-to dee beel-**yet**-tee] book of tickets

boa f [b**o**-a] buoy

bocca f mouth

bollire [bol-l**ee**ray] to boil; to be boiling

bomba f bomb; type of ice cream; doughnut

bonifico bancario m [bon**ee**feeko bank**ar**-yo] credit transfer

bordo: a bordo on board

borgo medioevale m [med-yo-ayv**a**lay] medieval village

borsa f bag

borsa dell'acqua calda [del-lakwa] hot-water bottle

borsaiolo m [borsa-y**o**lo], **borsaiola f** pickpocket

borsellino m purse

borsetta f handbag, (US) purse

bosco m wood, forest

bottiglia f [bot-**teel**-ya] bottle

bottone m [bot-**to**nay] button

braccialetto m [brachal**et**-to] bracelet

braccio m [br**a**cho] arm

branda f campbed

bravo good; skilful

bravo! well done!

bravura f skilfulness

breve [br**ay**vay] short, brief

brillante [breel-l**a**ntay] brilliant

britannico British

brocca f jug

bruciare [brooch**a**ray] to burn

brutto [br**oot**-to] ugly

buca delle lettere f [del-lay let-tairay] letter box, mailbox

bucato f laundry

fare il bucato to do the washing

buco m hole

buffet m snack bar(s); sideboard(s)

buffo [b**oo**f-fo] funny

buio (m) [b**oo**-yo] dark

buona fortuna! [bw**o**na fort**oo**na] good luck!

buonanotte [bwonan**ot**-tay] good night

buon appetito! [bwon ap-pet**ee**to] enjoy your meal!

buonasera [bwonas**ai**ra] good

evening

buon compleanno! [komplay-**an**-no] happy birthday!

buongiorno [bwon**jo**rno] good morning

buono [bw**o**no] good

buon viaggio! [vee-**aj**-jo] have a good trip!

bussola f [b**oo**s-sola] compass

busta f [b**oo**sta] envelope

busta imbottita [eembot-t**ee**ta] padded envelope

butano m [b**oo**tano] camping gas

buttare via [boot-t**a**ray v**ee**-a] to throw away

C

C (caldo) hot

C (Celsius) C

cabina f cabin; beach hut

cabina telefonica [telef**o**neeka] phone box

caccia f [k**a**cha] hunting

andare a caccia to go hunting

cacciavite m [kacha**vee**tay] screwdriver

cadere [kad**ai**ray] to fall

far cadere to drop

caduta massi falling rocks

caffè m [kaff**ay**] coffee(s); café(s)

caffetteria f [kaf-fet-tair**ee**-a] coffee bar, coffee house

caffettiera f [kaf-fet-y**ai**ra] coffeepot; coffee maker

C.A.I. m (Club Alpino Italiano) Italian Alpine Club

calciatore m [kalchat**o**ray], **calciatrice** f [kalchatr**ee**chay] football player

calcio m [k**a**lcho] football; kick

giocare a calcio [jok**a**ray] to play football

calcolare [kalkol**a**ray] to calculate

calcolatore m [kalkolat**o**ray] calculator

caldo (m) heat; warm; hot

avere caldo to be warm

fa caldo it's warm/hot

calendario m [kalend**a**r-yo] calendar

calmarsi to calm down

calvo bald

calzature fpl [kaltzat**oo**ray] footwear

calze fpl [k**a**ltzay] socks; stockings

calzini mpl [kaltz**ee**nee] socks

calzolaio m [kaltzol**a**-yo] shoe repairer's

calzoleria f [kaltzolair**ee**-a] shoe repairer's

calzoncini mpl [kaltzonch**ee**nee] shorts

calzoni mpl [kaltz**o**nee] trousers, (US) pants

cambiare [kamb-y**a**ray] to change

cambiarsi [kamb-y**a**rsee] to change

cambiavalute m [kamb-yaval**oo**tay] bureau de change

cambio m [kamb-yo] change; bureau de change; gears

camera f [kamaira] room

camera da letto bedroom

camera d'aria [dar-ya] inner tube

camera doppia [dop-ya] double room

camera doppia con bagno/servizi [ban-yo/sairveetzee] double room with bathroom

camera doppia senza bagno [sentza] double room without bathroom

camera singola [seengola] single room

cameriera f [kamair-yaira] maid; waitress

cameriere m [kamair-yairay] waiter

camiceria f [kameechairee-a] shirt shop

camicetta f [kamichet-ta] blouse

camicia f [kameecha] shirt

camicia da notte [not-tay] nightdress

caminetto m fireplace

camino m chimney

camion m [kam-yon] lorry

camminare [kam-meenaray] to walk

campagna f [kampan-ya] countryside; campaign

campana f bell (church)

campanello m bell; doorbell

campeggio m [kampej-jo] camping; campsite

campeggio per roulotte [roolot] caravan site, trailer park

campionato m [kamp-yonato] championship

campione senza valore sample, no commercial value

campo m course; court; field

campo da golf golf course

campo da hockey hockey field

campo da tennis tennis court

campo di calcio [kalcho] football pitch

campo sportivo [sporteevo] sports ground

canadese (m/f) [kanadayzay] Canadian

canale m [kanalay] canal; channel

cancellato [kanchel-lato] cancelled

cancello m [kanchel-lo] gate

candela f [kandayla] candle; spark plug

candeliere m [kandel-yairay] candlestick

cane m [kanay] dog

canna da pesca f fishing rod

cannuccia f [kan-noocha] straw

canoa f [kano-a] canoe; canoeing

canottaggio m [kanot-taj-jo] rowing; canoeing

canotto m (rubber) dinghy

cantare [kantaray] to sing

cantina f cellar

canto m singing

canzone f [kantzonay] song

C.A.P. (Codice di Avviamento Postale) **m** postcode, zip code

cap. (capitolo) chapter

caparra f deposit

capelli mpl hair

capire [kap**ee**ray] to understand

capisco: non capisco [kap**ee**sko] I don't understand

capitale f [kapeet**a**lay] capital city

capitano m captain

capo m boss

capolavoro m masterpiece

capolinea m [kapol**ee**nay-a] terminus

cappella f chapel

cappello m hat

cappotto m coat

capra f goat

carabinieri mpl [karabeen-y**ai**ree] military police force

carattere m [kar**a**t-tairay] character

carburatore m [karboorat**o**ray] carburettor

carcere m [k**a**rchairay] prison

carino nice, pleasant

carnevale m [karnev**a**lay] carnival

caro dear, expensive

carreggiata f [kar-rej-j**a**ta] roadway

carrello m (luggage/baggage) trolley

carrozza f [kar-r**o**tza] coach, carriage, car

carrozza cuccette [koochet-tay] sleeping car

carrozza letti [l**e**t-tee] sleeping car

carrozza ristorante [reestor**a**ntay] restaurant car

carrozzeria f [kar-rotzair**ee**-a] car body shop

carrozzina f [kar-rotz**ee**na] pram

carta f card; paper

carta assegni [as-s**e**n-yee] cheque/check card

carta da disegno [dees**e**n-yo] drawing paper

carta da lettere [l**e**t-tairay] writing paper

carta da pacchi [p**a**k-kee] brown paper

carta d'argento [dar**j**ento] senior citizens' railcard for reduced fares

carta di credito [kr**ay**deeto] credit card

carta d'identità identity card

carta d'imbarco boarding pass

carta geografica [jay-ogr**a**feeka] map

carta igienica [eej**e**neeka] toilet paper

carta verde [v**ai**rday] under-26 reduced fare railcard

carte fpl [k**a**rtay] cards

cartella f school-bag; briefcase

cartina f map

cartoleria f [kartolair**ee**-a] stationer's

cartolibreria f [kartoleebrair**ee**-a] stationery and book shop

cartolina f postcard

cartone m [kart**o**nay] cardboard

casa f [k**a**za] house

casalinga f [kazal**ee**nga] housewife

casalinghi mpl household goods

cascata f waterfall

caseggiato m [kasej-j**a**to] block (of apartments)

casella postale f [post**a**lay] P.O. Box

casello autostradale m [kaz**e**l-lo owtostrad**a**lay] motorway/highway toll booth

caserma dei carabinieri f [kas**a**irma day karabeen-y**a**iree] military police station

caserma dei vigili del fuoco [v**ee**jeelee del fw**o**ko] fire station

caso: per caso [pair k**a**zo] by chance

in caso di emergenza rompere il vetro in case of emergency break the glass

in caso di sosta in galleria accendere i fari e spegnere il motore if stopping in tunnel, switch on headlights and switch off engine

cassa f [k**a**s-sa] till, cashdesk, cashier

cassa automatica

[owtom**a**teeka] cash dispenser, automatic teller

cassa continua [kont**ee**nwa] cash dispenser, automatic teller

cassetta f box; cassette

cassetta delle lettere [d**e**l-lay l**e**t-tairay] postbox, mailbox

cassetta di sicurezza [seekoor**e**tza] safe-deposit box

cassetto m drawer

cassettone m [kas-set-t**o**nay] chest of drawers

cassiere m [kas-sy**a**iray], **cassiera** f cashier, teller

castello m castle

catena f [kat**ay**na] chain

catenaccio m [katen**a**cho] bolt

catino m basin

cattedrale f [kat-taydr**a**lay] cathedral

cattiveria f [kat-teev**air**-ya] nastiness; naughtiness

cattivo [kat-t**ee**vo] bad

cattolico Catholic

causa f [k**ow**za] cause

cavallo m horse

andare a cavallo to go horse riding

cavatappi m corkscrew

caviglia f [kav**ee**l-ya] ankle

cazzo m prick

CC (Carabinieri) military police force

c/c (conto corrente) m [kor-r**e**ntay] current account

CE f [chay] EC

c'è [chay] there is

non c'è he/she/it is not

here

non c'è... there is no ...

celeste [chelestay] light blue

celibe [chayleebay] single (man)

cena f [chayna] dinner (evening meal); supper

cenare [chenaray] to have dinner

cenno m [chen-no] sign

centinaia fpl [chenteena-ya] hundreds

cento [chento] hundred

centralino m [chentraleeno] local exchange, operator

centrifuga f [chentreefooga] spin-dryer

centro m [chentro] centre

centro città [cheet-ta] city centre

centro commerciale [kommerchalay] shopping centre

centro culturale [kooltooralay] arts centre

centro della città [cheet-ta] city centre

centro (di) informazioni turistiche [eenformatz-yonee tooreesteekay] tourist information office

centro sportivo sports centre

centro storico old town

ceramica f [cherameeka] pottery

cera per auto f [chaira pair owto] car wax

cercare [chairkaray] to look for

cerchio m [chairk-yo] circle

cerniera lampo f [chairn-yaira]

zip

cerotto m [cherot-to] sticking plaster, Bandaid®

certamente [chairtamentay] certainly

cestino m [chesteeno] basket; wastepaper basket

cfr. (confronta) cf.

charter: il volo charter m charter flight

che [kay] that, which; than

che? what?

check-in: fare il check-in to check in

chi? [kee] who?

chiacchierare [k-yak-yairaray] to chat

chiacchierone (m) [k-yak-yaironay], chiacchierona (f) chatterbox; talkative

chiamare [k-yamaray] to call

come si chiama? [komay see k-yama] what's your name?

come ti chiami? what's your name?

chiamata f [k-yamata] call

chiamata a carico del destinatario [kareeko del desteenatar-yo] reverse charge call

chiamata in teleselezione [teleseletz-yonay] direct dialling

chiamata interurbana [eentairoorbana] long-distance call

chiamata urbana [oorbana] local call

chiaro [k-yaro] clear; light

chiave f [k-yavay] key; spanner

chiave inglese [eenglayzay] wrench

chiedere [k-yaydairay] to ask

chiesa f [k-yayza] church

chilo m [keelo] kilo

chilometro m [keelometro] kilometre

chimica f [keemeeka] chemistry

chiodo m [k-yodo] nail (metal)

chirurgia f [keeroorjee-a] surgery

chirurgo m [keeroorgo] surgeon

chitarra f [keetar-ra] guitar

chiude alle... closes at ...

chiudere [k-yoodairay] to close

chiudere a chiave [k-yavay] to lock

chiudere bene dopo l'uso close tightly after use

chiudi il becco! [k-yoodee eel bek-ko] shut up!

chiuso* (dalle... alle...) [k-yoozo] closed (from ... to ...)

chiuso per ferie closed for holidays/vacation

chiuso per turno closing day

chiusura settimanale... closed on ...

ci* [chee] here; there; us; each other; to us; ourselves

ci sono there are

ciao! [chow] hello!; cheerio!, goodbye!

ciascuno [chaskoono], ciascuna

each

cibo m [cheebo] food

ciclismo m [cheekleesmo] cycling

ciclista m/f [cheekleesta] cyclist

cieco [chee-ayko] blind

cielo m [chaylo] sky

ciglia fpl [cheel-ya] eyelashes

cima: in cima (a) [cheema] at the top (of)

cimitero m [cheemeetairo] cemetery

cinghia della ventola f [cheeng-ya] fan belt

cinquanta [cheenkwanta] fifty

cinque [cheenkway] five

cintura f [cheentoora] belt

cintura di sicurezza [dee seekooretza] seat belt

ciò [cho] this; that

circa [cheerka] about

circonvallazione f [cheerkonval-latz-yonay] ring road

C.I.T. (Compagnia Italiana Turismo) m [cheet] Italian tourist organization

città f [cheet-ta] town(s); city, cities

per la città local mail only

cittadina f [cheet-tadeena] citizen; city dweller; town

cittadino m citizen; city dweller

clacson m horn

classe f [klas-say] class; classroom

classe economica economy class

clienti: i clienti sono pregati di

lasciare libere le camere entro le ore 12 del giorno di partenza on day of departure, guests are requested to vacate rooms before midday

clima m climate

clinica f clinic

coda f tail; queue

coda del treno [**tray**no] rear of the train

code traffic queues ahead

codice della strada m [**ko**deechay] highway code

codice di avviamento postale [av-yam**e**nto post**a**lay] postcode, zip code

cofano m bonnet, (US) hood

cognata f [kon-y**a**ta] sister-in-law

cognato m brother-in-law

cognome m [kon-y**o**may] surname

coi [**koy**] with the

coiffeur m hair stylist

coincidenza f [ko-eencheed**e**ntza] connection (travelling)

col with the

colazione f [kolatz-y**o**nay] breakfast

colla f glue

collana f necklace

collant m [kol-**lan**] tights, pantyhose

collasso m collapse

collasso cardiaco heart failure

colle m [**ko**l-lay] hill

collegamenti internazionali international connections

collegio m [kol-**lay**jo] boarding school

colletto m collar

collezionare [kol-letz-yon**aray**] to collect

collezione f [kol-letz-y**o**nay] collection (stamps etc)

collina f hill

collo m neck

colloquio m [kol-l**o**kw-yo] interview; conversation

colonna f column

colore m [kol**o**ray] colour

colorificio m [koloreef**ee**cho] paint and dyes shop

colpa: è colpa mia it's my fault

colpi di sole mpl [**so**lay] highlights

colpire [kolp**ee**ray] to hit; to knock

colpo di sole m [**so**lay] sunstroke

coltello m knife

coltello da cucina [kooch**ee**na] kitchen knife

coltello da pane [**pa**nay] bread knife

comandante m/f [komand**a**ntay] pilot

comando dei vigili del fuoco m [day v**ee**jeelee del f**wo**ko] fire department headquarters

comando dei vigili urbani [oorb**a**nee] municipal headquarters of traffic police

come [komay] like; as
come? how?; what?; sorry?,
pardon me?, what did you
say?
come, scusi? [skoozee]
pardon?, pardon me?
come stai/sta/state? [sta-
ee/sta/statay] how are you?
come va? how are things?
comico (m) [komeeko] comic;
comedy; comedian
cominciare [komeencharay] to
start
comitiva f group
commedia f [kom-mayd-ya]
play; comedy
commesso m, commessa f
shop assistant
commissariato (di polizia) m
[kom-mees-sar-yato dee poleetzee-
a] police station
comodo comfortable
compact (disc) m compact
disc
compagna f [kompan-ya]
schoolfriend; partner
compagnia aerea f [kompan-
yee-a a a-airay-a] airline
compagno m [kompan-yo]
schoolfriend; partner
comperare [kompairaray] to
buy
compere: andare a fare le
compere [kompairay] to go
shopping
competizione f [kompeteetz-
yonay] competition; race
compilare [kompeelaray] to fill
in

compleanno m [komplay-an-no]
birthday
completamente [kompleta-
mentay] completely, entirely
completo m [komplayto] suit;
outfit
completo full; no vacancies
complicato complicated
complimento m compliment
comporre [kompor-ray] to dial
comportamento m behaviour
comportarsi to behave
composizione [kompozeetz-
yonay] medicinal
composition
comprare [kompraray] to buy
compreso [komprayzo]
included
compressa f tablet
comune m [komoonay] town
hall; municipal district
comunicazione f [komooneekatz-
yonay] phone call
comunque [komoonkway]
however
con with
concerto m [konchairto]
concert
concessionario m [konches-
yonar-yo] agent, dealer
conchiglia f [konkeel-ya] shell
condoglianze fpl [kondol-
yantzay] condolences
condotta f behaviour
conducente m/f [kondoochentay]
driver
conferenza f [konfairentza]
lecture; conference
conferma: dare conferma to

confirm
confermare [konfairmaray] to confirm
confetto m sugar-coated pill; sugar-coated almond
confezione f [konfetz-yonay] pack; packaging
confine m [konfeenay] border
confusione f [konfooz-yonay] confusion; mess
congelatore m [konjelatoray] freezer
congratulazioni! [kongratoolatz-yonee] congratulations!
congresso m conference
conoscere [konoshairay] to know
consegnare [konsen-yaray] to deliver
conservare in frigo keep refrigerated
conservare in luogo asciutto keep in a dry place
consigliare [konseel-yaray] to recommend
consolato m consulate
consumarsi: da consumarsi preferibilmente entro... best before ...
contagioso [kontajozo] infectious
contanti mpl cash
 pagare in contanti to pay cash
contare [kontaray] to count
contascatti m [kontaskat-tee] time-unit counter(s)
contatto: mettersi in contatto con to contact

contenere [kontenairay] to contain
contento happy; pleased
contenuto m [kontenooto] contents
continuare [konteenwaray] to continue, to go on
continui [konteenwee] keep going
continuo [konteenwo] continuous
conto m bill, (US) check
conto corrente [kor-rentay] current account
conto in banca bank account
contraccettivo m [kontrachet-teevo] contraceptive
contraccezione f [kontra-chetz-yonay] contraception
contraddire [kontrad-deeray] to contradict
contrario a [kontrar-yo] opposed to
contrassegno IVA [kontras-sen-yo eeva] proof that VAT has been paid
contro against
controllare [kontrol-laray] to check
controllo automatico della velocità m automatic speed check
controllo bagagli [bagal-yee] baggage control
controllo biglietti ticket inspection
controllo passaporti passport control
controllo radar della velocità

radar speed check
controllore m [kontrol-**lo**ray] ticket inspector; bus conductor
conversare [konvairs**a**ray] to converse
conversazione f [konvairsatz-**yo**nay] conversation
convincente [konveen**che**ntay] convincing
convincere [kon**vee**nchairay] to convince, to persuade
convinto convinced
coperchio m [kop**ai**rk-yo] lid
coperta f [kop**ai**rta] blanket
coperto m cover charge
 al coperto indoors
coppa f cup
copriletto m bedspread
coraggioso [koraj-**jo**zo] brave
corda f rope
cordiale [kord-**ya**lay] friendly
cornice f [korn**ee**chay] frame
coro m choir
corpo m body
corrente (f) [kor-**re**ntay] current; draught

correnti pericolose fpl dangerous currents
correre [kor-**rai**ray] to run
corridoio m [kor-reed**o**-yo] corridor; aisle
corridore m [kor-reed**o**ray] runner
corriera f [kor-**ya**ira] coach, long-distance bus
corrispondente m/f [kor-reespond**e**ntay] penfriend
corrispondenza f [kor-reespond**e**ntza] mail; correspondence
corruzione f [kor-rootz-**yo**nay] corruption
corsa f race; running
corsa semplice [s**e**mpleechay] one way (ticket)
corsia di emergenza f [emairj**e**ntza] emergency lane
corso m course; main street
corso di lingua [**lee**ngwa] language course
cortile m [kort**ee**lay] courtyard
corto short
cosa f [k**o**za] thing
 cosa? what?
 cosa hai/ha detto? what did you say?
coscia f [k**o**sha] thigh
così [koz**ee**] like this; so
 così grande [gr**a**nday] so big
 così così so-so
costa f coast
costare [kost**a**ray] to cost
costola f rib
costruire [kostroo-**ee**ray] to build
costume m [kost**oo**may] custom
costume da bagno [kost**oo**may da b**a**n-yo] swimsuit; swimming trunks
cotone m [kot**o**nay] cotton
cotone idrofilo [eedr**o**feelo] cotton wool
cotto: ben cotto well done
 poco cotto underdone
 troppo cotto overdone
C.P. (Casella Postale) f P.O.

Box
cravatta f tie, necktie
credenza f [kredentza] dresser; cupboard
credere [kraydairay] to believe, to think
 non posso crederci! [kredairchee] I can't believe it!
credito m [kraydeeto] credit
crema f [krayma] (for face etc) cream; custard
crema detergente [detairjentay] cleansing cream
crema idratante [eedratantay] moisturizer
crema solare [solaray] suntan lotion
cremeria f [kremairee-a] dairy shop, also selling ice cream and cakes
cretino (m) idiot; fool; stupid
C.R.I. (Croce Rossa Italiana) f Italian Red Cross
cric m jack
criminalità f crime(s)
crisi f [kreezee] crisis, crises
critica f criticism
criticare [kreeteekaray] to criticize
crociera f [krochaira] cruise
crudele [kroodaylay] cruel
cruscotto m [krooskot-to] dashboard
cuccetta f [koochet-ta] couchette
cucchiaino m [kook-ya-eeno] teaspoon; coffeespoon
cucchiaio m [kook-ya-yo]

spoon
 un cucchiaio (di) a spoonful (of)
cucina f [koocheena] kitchen; cooker; cooking, cookery
cucinare [koocheenaray] to cook
cucire [koocheeray] to sew
cuffia da bagno f [ban-yo] bathing cap
cugino m [koojeeno], **cugina f** cousin
cultura f [kooltoora] culture
cunetta o dosso dips or blind summits
cuoca f [kwoka] cook
cuocere [kwochairay] to cook; to bake
cuoco m [kwoko] cook
cuoio m [kwo-yo] leather
cuore m [kworay] heart
cupola m dome, cupola
curioso m [koor-yozo] curious
curva f [koorva] bend
curva pericolosa dangerous bend
cuscino m [koosheeno] pillow; cushion
CV (cavallo vapore) h.p.

D

da* from; by; at; to
dà* he/she it gives; you give
da consumarsi entro... use by ...
dado m nut (for bolt); dice
dagli* [dal-yee] from the; by

the

dai* [da-ee] from the; by the; you give

dallo, dal, dalla, dalle* [dal-lay] from the; by the

dama f draughts

danese (m/f) [danayzay] Danish; Dane

Danimarca f Denmark

danneggiare [dan-nej-jaray] to damage

danno* (m) they give; damage

dappertutto [dap-pairtoot-to] everywhere

dare* (m) [daray] to give; debit

data f date

data di nascita [nasheeta] date of birth

date* [datay] you give

davanti m [davantee] front (part)
  davanti a in front of
  passare davanti (a) to pass, to go past

da vendersi dietro presentazione di ricetta medica to be sold on prescription only

da vendersi entro... sell by ...

davvero [dav-vairo] really?
  ah, davvero? is it?; do they? etc

d.C. (dopo Cristo) A.D.

debito m [daybeeto] debt

debole [daybolay] weak

decidere [decheedairay] to decide

decimo (m) [daycheemo] tenth

decollare [dekol-laray] to take off

decollo m take-off

degente m/f [dejentay] in-patient

del, dei [day], degli* [dayl-yee] some; of the

delfino m dolphin

delicato frail, delicate

delizioso [deleetz-yozo] lovely, delicious; charming

dello, della, delle* [del-lay] some; of the

deltaplano m hang-gliding

deludere [deloodairay] to disappoint

deluso [deloozo] disappointed

denaro m money

dente m [dentay] tooth

dentiera f [dent-yaira] dentures

dentifricio m [denteefreecho] toothpaste

dentista m/f dentist

dentro inside

dépliant m [dayplee-ant] brochure(s); leaflet(s)

deposito m [depozeeto] deposit

deposito bagagli [bagal-yee] left luggage, baggage check

deposito bancario [bankar-yo] deposit account

depresso depressed

deputato m, deputata f MP

descrivere [deskreevairay] to describe

desidera? [dezeedaira] what would you like?; can I help you?

destinatario m [desteenatar-yo]

addressee

destinazione f [desteenatz-
yonay] destination

destra f right

a destra on/to the right

detersivo liquido per i piatti m
[detairseevo leekweedo pair ee p-
yat-ti] washing-up liquid

detersivo per bucato [bookato]
washing powder

detestare [detestaray] to hate

deve* [dayvay] he/she/it
must; you must

devi* [dayvee] you must

deviazione f [dev-yatz-yonay]
diversion

devo* [dayvo] I must

devono* they must

di* of; than

diabetico [dee-abayteeko]
diabetic

dialetto m dialect

diamante m [dee-amantay]
diamond

diamo* we give

diapositiva f [dee-apozeeteeva]
slide

diario m [dee-ar-yo] diary

diarrea f [dee-ar-ray-a]
diarrhoea

dibattito m debate

dica? yes?

dice* [deechay] he/she/it says;
you say

dicembre m [deechembray]
December

dichiarare [deek-yararay] to
declare

dichiarazione f [deek-yaratz-

yonay] statement

dici* [deechee] you say

diciamo* [deech-yamo] we say

diciannove [deechan-no-vay]
nineteen

diciassette [deechas-set-tay]
seventeen

diciotto [deechot-to] eighteen

dico* I say

dicono* they say

dieci [dee-aychee] ten

dieta f [d-yayta] diet

essere a dieta to be on a
diet

dietro m [d-yaytro] back, rear;
at the back

dietro (a) behind

difendere [deefendairay] to
defend

difettoso [deefet-tozo] faulty

difficile [deef-feecheelay]
difficult

diligente [deeleejentay] hardworking

dimenticare [deementeekaray]
to forget

dimenticarsi to forget

diminuire [deemeenweeray] to
lessen

dimostrazione f [deemostratz-
yone] demonstration

dintorni mpl environs

nei dintorni di in the vicinity
of

Dio m [dee-o] God

Dio mio! my God!

dipendere: dipende
[deependay] it depends

dipingere [deepeenjairay] to

paint

dipinto m painting

dire* [**dee**ray] to say; to tell

diretto (m) direct; through train

direttore m [deeret-**to**ray] manager; headmaster

direttrice f [deeret-**tree**chay] manageress; headmistress

direzione f [deeretz-**yo**nay] direction

disaccordo m [deezak-**kor**do] disagreement

disastro m [dee**za**stro] disaster

discesa f [deesh**ay**sa] descent; slope; exit

disco m record

discorso m speech

discoteca f disco

discreto [deeskr**ay**to] discreet

discutere (di) [deesk**oo**tairay] to discuss; to argue

disegnare [deesen-**ya**ray] to draw

disegno m [dees**e**n-yo] drawing

disfare: disfare le valigie [deesf**a**ray lay val**ee**jay] to unpack

disinfettante m [deezeenfet-**tan**tay] disinfectant, antiseptic

disoccupato [deezok-koop**a**to] unemployed

disoccupazione f [deezok-koopatz-**yo**nay] unemployment

disordinato [deezordeen**a**to] untidy

dispiacere: le dispiace se...? [lay deesp-**ya**chay say] do you mind if I ...?

mi dispiace (tanto)! I'm (so) sorry!

dispiaciuto [deesp-yach**oo**to] sorry

disporsi su due file get into two lanes

dispositivo m [deespozeet**ee**vo] device

dispositivo di emergenza emergency button/handle

distante [deest**an**tay] far away

distanza f [deest**an**tza] distance

disteso [deest**ay**zo] lying down

distinta di versamento f [deest**ee**nta dee vairsam**e**nto] paying-in slip

distratto absent-minded; inattentive

distribuire [deestreebw**ee**ray] to distribute

distribuito da... [deestreebw**ee**to] distributed by ...

distributore m [deestreeboot**o**ray] distributor, dispenser; petrol station, gas station

distributore (automatico) di biglietti [owtom**a**teeko dee beel-**yet**-tee] ticket machine

disturbare [deestoorb**a**ray] to disturb

disuguale [deezoogw**a**lay] unequal

ditale m [deet**a**lay] thimble

dite* [**dee**tay] you say

dito m finger

dito del piede [p-yayday] toe

ditta f [deet-ta] firm, company

divano m [deevano] sofa

diversi [deevairsee], diverse [deevairsay] several

diverso different

divertente [deevairtentay] amusing

divertirsi [deevairteersee] to enjoy oneself

dividere [deeveedairay] to divide

divieto di accesso no entry

divieto di accesso ai non addetti ai lavori no access – works only

divieto di accesso – escluso residenti/bus/taxi residents/buses/taxis only

divieto di affissione stick no bills

divieto di balneazione no bathing

divieto di fermata no stopping

divieto di pesca no fishing

divieto di sosta no parking

divieto di transito no thoroughfare

divorziato [deevortz-yato] divorced

dizionario m [deetz-yonar-yo] dictionary

do* I give

dobbiamo* we must

docce fpl [dochay] showers

doccia f [docha] shower

fare la doccia to have a shower

dodici [doh-deechee] twelve

Dogana f Customs

Dogana merci Customs for freight

Dogana passeggeri passenger Customs

dolce (m) [dolchay] sweet; cake

dolci mpl [dolchee] confectionery; cakes

dollaro m dollar

dolore m [doloray] pain

doloroso [dolorozo] painful

domanda f question

domandare [domandaray] to ask

domani [domanee] tomorrow

a domani see you tomorrow

domenica f [domayneeka] Sunday

la domenica on Sundays

la domenica e i giorni festivi Sundays and public holidays

donna f woman

donne ladies (toilet), ladies rest room

dopo after; afterwards

dopobarba m aftershave

doposciampo m [doposhampo] conditioner

doppio [dop-yo] double

dormire [dormeeray] to sleep

andare a dormire to go to bed

dottore (Dott.) m [dot-toray] doctor

dottoressa (Dott.ssa) f doctor

dove? [dovay] where?

173

dove si trova...? where is ...?

dovere* (m) [dov**ai**ray] to have to, must; to owe; duty

dovete* [dov**ay**tay] you must

dovuto* had to

dozzina f [dodz**ee**na] dozen

(una) dozzina (di) a dozen (of)

drammatico dramatic

dritto straight on

droga f drug(s)

drogheria f [drogair**ee**-a] grocer's

dubitare [doobeet**a**ray] to doubt

due [d**oo**-ay] two

due pezzi mpl [p**e**tzee] bikini

dune fpl [d**oo**nay] sand dunes

dunque [d**oo**nkway] therefore, so; well (then)

duomo m [d**wo**mo] cathedral

durante [door**a**ntay] during

durante la marcia reggersi agli appositi sostegni please hold on while vehicle is in motion

duro m [d**oo**ro] hard

E

e [ay] and

è* [ay] he/she/it is; you are

ebreo [ebr**ay**-o] Jewish

ecc. (eccetera) etc

eccetto [ech**e**t-to] except

ecco [**e**k-ko] here is/are; here you are; that's it

ecco qua! [kwa] here you are!

edicola f newsagent's

edificio m [edeef**ee**cho] building

educato [edook**a**to] polite

effettua: si effettua dal... al... this service is available from ... until ...

Egr.Sig. (egregio signore) Mr (in letters)

elastico (m) rubber band; elastic

elenco telefonico m [tel**ay**foneeko] telephone directory

elettrauto m [elet-tr**ow**to] workshop for car electrical repairs

elettricista m [elet-treech**ee**sta] electrician

elettricità f [elet-treecheet**a**] electricity

elettrico [el**e**t-treeko] electric

elettrodomestici mpl [elet-trodom**e**steechee] electrical appliances

elicottero m helicopter

emergenza f [emairj**e**ntza] emergency; emergency lane

emissione del biglietto take your ticket here

emozionante [emotz-yon**a**ntay] exciting

E.N.I.T. (Ente Nazionale Italiano per il Turismo) m [**e**neet] Italian national tourist board

enorme [en**o**rmay] enormous

enoteca f [enot**ay**ka] wine-tasting shop

entrare [entr**a**ray] to go in; to come in

entrata f entrance

entrata con abbonamento o biglietto già convalidato entry for those with season tickets or with validated tickets

entrata libera admission free

entusiasmante [entooz-yazm**a**ntay] fascinating; exciting

E.P.T. (Ente Provinciale per il Turismo) m Italian local tourist board

equipaggio m [ekeep**a**j-jo] crew

equitazione f [ekweetatz-y**o**nay] horse riding

equivoco m [ekw**ee**voko] misunderstanding

erba f [**a**irba] grass

errore m [er-r**o**ray] mistake

esagerare [esajair**a**ray] to exaggerate

esame m [es**a**may] examination

esattamente [esat-tam**e**ntay] exactly

esatto [es**a**t-to] correct

esaurito sold out

esausto [es**ow**sto] exhausted

escluso frontisti residents only

escluso sabato e festivi except Saturdays and Sundays/holidays

escursione f [eskoors-y**o**nay] excursion, outing; hike

esempio m [es**e**mp-yo] example

  per esempio for example

esente da tasse [es**e**ntay da tas-say] duty-free

esercizio m [ezairch**ee**tz-yo] exercise; shop

espresso m strong black coffee; express letter; express train

esprimere [espr**ee**mairay] to express

essere* [**e**s-sairay] to be

esso [**e**s-so] it

est m east

estate f [est**a**tay] summer

estero: all'estero [al-l**e**stairo] abroad

estetista f beautician

estintore m [esteent**o**ray] fire extinguisher

età f [ayt**a**] age

etichetta f [eteek**e**t-ta] label

etto(grammo) m hundred grams

Eurocity m international fast train

europeo [ay-ooroop**ay**-o] European

evitare [eveet**a**ray] to avoid

F

F (freddo) cold

fa* he/she/it does; you do; ago

fabbrica f factory

facchino m [fak-**kee**no] porter

faccia f [**fa**cha] face

facciamo* [fa**cha**mo] we do

faccio* [**fa**cho] I do

facile [**fa**cheelay] easy

fai* [**fa**-ee] you do

fai da te m [da tay] DIY

falso false

fame: avere fame [av**ai**ray **fa**may] to be hungry

famiglia f [fam**eel**-ya] family

famoso famous

fanno* they do

fantastico (m) terrific; fantasy film/movie

fa' pure! [**poo**ray] do as you please!; please, do!

fare* [**fa**ray] to make; to do

farfalla f butterfly

fari mpl headlights

fari posteriori [postair-**yo**ree] rear lights

farmacia f [farmach**ee**-a] chemist's, pharmacy

farmacia di turno duty chemist's, late-night pharmacy

faro m light; lighthouse

fasciatura f [fasha**too**ra] bandage

fastidio m [fast**eed**-yo] nuisance

fate* [**fa**tay] you do

fatica f [fat**ee**ka] hard work; strain

fatto a mano handmade

fattoria f farm

fattura f [fat-**too**ra] invoice

favore m [fa**vo**ray] favour

per favore please

favorevole a [favor**ay**volay] in favour of

fazzolettini di carta mpl [fatzolet-**tee**nee] tissues, Kleenex®

fazzoletto m [fatzol**et**-to] handkerchief

febbraio m [feb-bra-yo] February

febbre f [f**eb**-bray] temperature

febbre da fieno f [f-y**ay**no] hay fever

federa f [**fay**daira] pillowcase

fegato m [**fay**gato] liver

felice [fel**ee**chay] happy

feriale: giorno feriale [**jo**rno fair-y**a**lay] working day

feriali mpl working days

ferita f wound

ferito injured

fermare [fair**ma**ray] to stop

fermarsi to stop

fermata (dell'autobus) f [fair**ma**ta del-**low**toboos] (bus) stop

fermata a richiesta [reek-y**es**ta] request stop

fermata facoltativa [fakoltat**ee**va] request stop

fermata obbligatoria [ob-bleegat**o**r-ya] compulsory stop

fermata prenotata bus or tram stopping

fermo! [**fair**mo] don't move!

fermo per manutenzione closed for repairs

fermo posta m poste restante

ferragosto m August 15th (public holiday)

ferramenta f hardware store(s)

ferro m [**fair**-ro] iron; knitting needle

ferro da stiro [st**ee**ro] iron (for ironing)

ferrovia f [fair-rov**ee**-a] railway

Ferrovie dello Stato fpl [fair-rov**ee**-ay] Italian State Railways

festa f party; holiday, vacation

festivi mpl public holidays

fetta f slice

FFSS (Ferrovie dello Stato) fpl Italian state railways

fiala f [f-y**a**la] phial

fiammifero m [f-yam-m**ee**fairo] match (light)

fianco m [f-y**a**nko] side; hip

fidanzata f [feedantz**a**ta] fiancée

fidanzato (m) fiancé; engaged

fidarsi to trust

fido m credit

fiera f [f-y**a**ira] funfair; trade fair

fiero proud

figlia f [**fee**l-ya] daughter

figlio m son

figlio di puttana! [dee] son of a bitch!

fila f queue

  fare la fila to queue

film m film, movie

filo m thread

filo di ferro wire

filtro m filter

finale f [feen**a**lay] final

finalmente [feenalm**e**ntay] at last

finché [feenk**ay**] until

fine (f) [**fee**nay] end; thin; fine (blade, pen etc); refined

fine del tratto autostradale end of motorway/highway

fine settimana [set-teem**a**na] weekend

finestra f window

finestrino m window (on plane, train)

finire [feen**ee**ray] to finish

fino thin; fine (blade, pen etc); even

  fino a until

finocchio m [feen**o**k-yo] fennel; poof

fioraio m [f-yora-yo] florist

fiore m [f-y**o**ray] flower

fiorentino m [f-yorent**ee**no] Florentine

Firenze f [feer**e**ntzay] Florence

firma f signature

firmare [feerm**a**ray] to sign

fischio m [**fee**sk-yo] whistle

fisica f [**fee**zeeka] physics

fiume m [f-y**oo**may] river

flacone m [flak**o**nay] medicine bottle

foglia f [**fo**l-ya] leaf

folla f crowd

fon m hair dryer

fondo m bottom

  in fondo a at the end/bottom of

fondotinta m [fondot**ee**nta]

foundation cream

fontana f fountain

footing m jogging

foratura f [forat**oo**ra] puncture

forbici mpl [f**o**rbeechee] scissors

forchetta f [forket-ta] fork

foresta f forest

forfora f dandruff

forma f form

in forma fit

formica f [form**ee**ka] ant

fornaio m [forn**a**-yo] baker's

fornello m cooker; hob

fornire [forn**ee**ray] to supply

forniture per ufficio fpl office
supplies

forno m oven

forno a microonde [meekro-
onday] microwave (oven)

forse [f**o**rsay] maybe, perhaps

forte [f**o**rtay] strong; loud

fortuna f [fort**oo**na] luck

fortunatamente
[fortoonatam**e**ntay] fortunately

foruncolo m spot

fotografare [fotografaray] to
photograph

fotografia f [fotograf**ee**-a]
photograph; photography

fare fotografie [fotograf**ee**-ay]
to take photographs

fotografo m photographer

fotoottica f camera shop and
optician

foulard m [fool**a**r] headscarf

fra between; in; through

fra l'altro besides

fragile [fr**a**jeelay] frail

francamente [frankam**e**ntay]

frankly

francese (m/f) [franch**ay**zay]
French; Frenchman;
Frenchwoman

Francia f [fr**a**ncha] France

franco m franc

francobollo m [frankob**o**l-lo]
stamp

frasario m [fraz**a**r-yo]
phrasebook

frase f [fr**a**zay] sentence

fratello m brother

frattura f [frat-t**oo**ra] fracture

frazione f [fratz-y**o**nay]
fraction; administrative
division of a municipality

freccia f [fr**e**cha] indicator;
arrow

freddo (m) cold

fa freddo it's cold

avere freddo to be cold

freno m [fr**ay**no] brake

freno a mano handbrake

fresco fresh; cool (weather)

friggere [fr**ee**j-jairay] to fry

friggitrice f [freej-jeetr**ee**chay]
deep-fat fryer

frigo m fridge

frigobar m minibar

frigorifero m [freegoreef**a**iro]
fridge

frizione f [freetz-y**o**nay] clutch;
friction

fronte f [fr**o**ntay] forehead

di fronte a opposite; in front
of

frontiera f [front-y**a**ira] border

frullatore m [frool-lat**o**ray] mixer

frusta f whisk

fruttivendolo m [froot-teevendolo] greengrocer's

FS (Ferrovie dello Stato) fpl Italian state railways

f.to (firmato) signed

fucile m [foocheelay] gun; rifle

fumare [foomaray] to smoke

fumatori smokers

fumetto m comic; strip cartoon

fumo m [foomo] smoke

fune f [foonay] rope

funivia f [fooneevee-a] cable car

funzionare [foontz-yonaray] to work

fuochi d'artificio mpl [fwokee darteefeecho] fireworks

fuoco m [fwoko] fire

fuori [fworee] outside

fuori servizio out of order

furgone m [foorgonay] van

furioso [foor-yozo] furious

fusibile m [foozeebeelay] fuse

G

gabinetto m [gabeenet-to] toilet, rest room

andare al gabinetto to go to the toilet/rest room

galleria f [gal-lair-ee-a] tunnel; balcony; circle

galleria d'arte [dartay] art gallery

Galles m [gal-les] Wales

gallese (m/f) [gal-layzay] Welsh; Welshman; Welshwoman

gamba f leg

gara f sporting event; race; competition

garanzia f [garantzee-a] guarantee

gasolio m [gazol-yo] diesel oil

gasolio invernale [eenvairnalay] diesel containing anti-freeze

gatto m cat

gelateria f [jelatairee-a] ice cream parlour

gelato (m) [jelato] frozen; ice cream

gelo m [jaylo] frost

gelosia f [jelozee-a] jealousy

geloso [jelozo] jealous

gemelli mpl [jemel-lee] twins

generalmente [jenairalmentay] generally

genere m [jaynairay] type

in genere mostly, generally

genero m [jaynairo] son-in-law

genitori mpl [jeneetoree] parents

gennaio m [jen-na-yo] January

Genova f [jenova] Genoa

gente f [jentay] people

gentile [jenteelay] kind

gentilezza f [jenteeletza] kindness

Germania f [jerman-ya] Germany

gesto m [jesto] gesture

gettare [jet-taray] to throw

gettare via to throw away

gettoni mpl [jet-tonee] telephone tokens

ghiacciaio m [g-yacha-o]

glacier
ghiaccio m [g-yacho] ice
già [ja] already
giacca f [jak-ka] jacket
giacca a vento anorak
giallo (m) [jal-lo] yellow;
thriller
giardini pubblici mpl [poob-
bleechee] public gardens
giardino m [jardeeno] garden
ginecologo m [jeenaykologo]
gynaecologist
Ginevra f [jeenevra] Geneva
ginnastica f [jeen-nasteeka]
gymnastics; PE
ginocchio m [jeenok-yo] knee
giocare [jokaray] to play
giocatore m [jokatoray] player
giocatrice f [jokatreechay]
player
giocattolo m [jokat-tolo] toy
giochi per il computer mpl
[j-yokee] computer games
gioco m [joko] game
gioco di società [dee socheta]
board game
gioielleria f [jo-yel-lairee-a]
jeweller's
gioielli mpl [jo-yel-lee]
jewellery
gioielliere m [jo-yel-yairay]
jeweller
giornalaio m [jornala-yo]
newsagent's
giornale m [jornalay]
newspaper
giornata f [jornata] day
giorni feriali mpl weekdays
giorni festivi public holidays

giorno m [jorno] day
giorno di chiusura [k-yoozoora]
closing day
giovane (m/f) [jovanay] young;
young person
giovedì m [jovaydee] Thursday
giradischi m [jeeradeeskee]
record player
girare [jeeraray] to turn
girarsi to turn
giri a destra [jeeree] turn
right
giri a sinistra [seeneestra] turn
left
giro m [jeero] turn; walk,
stroll; tour
a giro di posta by return
mail
andare a far un giro to go for
a stroll/drive
fare un giro in bicicletta
[beecheeklet-ta] to go for a
cycle ride
giro a piedi [p-yaydee] walk,
stroll
giro in barca boat trip
giro in macchina [mak-keena]
drive
gita f [jeeta] excursion,
outing; hike
gita in pullman coach trip
gita organizzata [organeedzata]
package tour
gita scolastica [skolasteeka]
school trip
giù [joo] down
**giubbotti salvagente sotto la
poltrona** lifejackets are
under the seat

180

giugno **m** [**joo**n-yo] June

giusto [**joo**sto] right, correct; fair

gli* [l-yee] the; to him; to them

goccia **f** [**go**cha] drop

gola **f** throat

golf **m** golf; jumper

gomito **m** elbow

gomma **f** rubber; tyre

gomma a terra flat tyre

gomma di scorta spare tyre

gommista **m/f** tyre repair specialist

gommone **m** [gom-m**o**nay] (rubber) dinghy

gonfio [**go**nf-yo] swollen

gonna **f** skirt

gorgo **m** whirlpool

governativo governmental; state

governo **m** government

gradino **m** step

grado **m** degree, level

grammatica **f** grammar

grammo **m** gramme

Gran Bretagna **f** [bretan-ya] Great Britain

granchio **m** [gr**a**nk-yo] crab

grande [gr**a**nday] big

grande magazzino **m** [magadz**ee**no] department store

grandine **f** [gr**a**ndeenay] hail

grasso fat

gratis free

grato grateful

grattacielo **m** [grat-tach**ay**lo] skyscraper

grattugiare [grat-tooj**a**ray] to grate

gratuito [grat**oo**-eeto] free

grazie [gr**a**tzee-ay] thank you

grazie a Dio! thank God!

grazie, anche a te/lei [**a**nkay a tay/lay] thank you, the same to you

grazie mille [m**ee**l-lay] thank you very much

grazioso [gratz-y**o**zo] pretty

Grecia **f** [gr**e**cha] Greece

greco (**m**) Greek

gridare [greed**a**ray] to shout

grigio [gr**ee**jo] grey

grosso big, large; thick

grotta **f** cave

gruccia **f** [gr**oo**cha] coathanger

gruppo **m** group

gruppo sanguigno [sangw**ee**n-yo] blood group

guancia **f** [gw**a**ncha] cheek

guanti **mpl** [gw**a**ntee] gloves

guanto di spugna **m** [dee sp**oo**n-ya] flannel

guardare [gward**a**ray] to look (at)

guardare in su [een soo] to look up

guardaroba **m** [gwardar**o**ba] wardrobe; cloakroom

guasto (**m**) [gw**a**sto] breakdown; broken, out of order; rotten

guerra **f** [gw**ai**r-ra] war

guida **f** [gw**ee**da] guide; guidebook

guidare [gweed**a**ray] to lead; to drive

guidare a passo d'uomo [dwomo] drive at walking speed

guida telefonica f [gweeda] telephone directory

guscio m [goosho] shell

gusto m taste

H

ha* [a] he/she it has; you have

hai* [a-ee] you have

hanno* [an-no] they have

ho* [o] I have

I

i* [ee] the

idea f [eeday-a] idea

idiota m/f [eed-yota] idiot

idraulico m [eedrowleeko] plumber

ieri [yairee] yesterday

il* [eel] the

imbarazzante [eembaratzantay] embarrassing

imbarazzato [eembaratzato] embarrassed

imbarazzo m [eembaratzo] embarrassment

imbarcarsi [eembarkarsee] to board, to embark

imbarco m [eembarko] boarding

imbarco immediato now boarding

imbrogliare [eembrol-yaray] to cheat

imbucare [eembookaray] to post, to mail

immediatamente [eem-med-yata-mentay] immediately

immersione f [eem-mers-yonay] skin-diving

immigrato m [eem-meegrato], immigrata f immigrant

imparare [eempararay] to learn

impaziente [eempatz-yentay] impatient

impermeabile (m) [eempairmay-abeelay] raincoat; waterproof

importante [eemportantay] important; significant; sizeable

importare: non importa [eemporta] it doesn't matter

imposta f tax

impostare [eempostaray] to post, to mail

imposte fpl [eempostay] shutters

improvvisamente [eemprov-veezamentay] suddenly

in in; into; to

in macchina [mak-keena] by car

incartare [eencartaray] to wrap

incassare [eenkas-saray] to cash

incidente m [eencheedentay] accident

incinta [eencheenta] pregnant

incontro m meeting

incrocio m [eenkrocho] junction; crossroads,

intersection

incrocio pericoloso dangerous junction

indicare [eendeekaray] to indicate; to point at; to show

indietro [eend-yaytro] behind; back

 faccia marcia indietro [facha marcha] reverse

indirizzo m [eendeereetzo] address

indubbiamente [eendoob-yamentay] undoubtedly

infarto m heart attack

infelice [eenfeleechay] unhappy

infermeria f [eenfairmairee-a] infirmary

infermiere m [eenfairm-yairay], **infermiera f** nurse

infezione f [eenfetz-yonay] infection

influenzare [eenfloo-entzaray] to influence

informare [eenformaray] to inform

informarsi (su) to get information (about)

informazioni fpl [eenformatz-yonee] (tourist) information

informazioni elenco abbonati directory enquiries

Ing. (ingegnere) engineer

ingannare [eengan-naray] to deceive

ingegnere m [eenjen-yairay] engineer

ingenuo [eenjaynwo] naïve

Inghilterra f [eengheeltair-ra]

England

inglese (**m/f**) [eenglayzay] English; Englishman; Englishwoman

ingoiare [eengo-yaray] to swallow

ingorgo m traffic jam

ingrandimento m enlargement

ingrassaggio m [eengras-saj-jo] oiling, lubrication

ingresso m entrance (hall)

ingresso gratuito/libero admission free

iniezione f [eenyetz-yonay] injection

inizio m [eeneetz-yo] beginning

innumerevole [een-noomairayvolay] innumerable

inoltrare [eenoltraray] to forward

inquilino m [eenkweeleeno], **inquilina f** tenant

inquinato [eenkweenato] polluted

insegnante m/f [eensen-yantay] teacher

insegnare [eensen-yaray] to teach

inserire le monete insert coins

insettifugo m [eenset-teefoogo] insect repellent

insetto m [eenset-to] insect

insieme [eens-yaymay] together

insistere [eenseestairay] to insist

insonnia f [eenson-ya] insomnia

interessante [eentaires-santay] interesting

interessarsi di/a [eentaires-sarsee dee] to be interested in

internazionale [eentairnatz-yonalay] international

interno internal; inside
all'interno inside

intero whole

interruttore m [eentair-root-toray] switch

interruzione della corrente f [eentair-rootz-yonay del-la kor-rentay] power cut

intervallo m [eentairval-lo] interval; break; half-time

intervista f [eentairveesta] interview

intorno (a) around

intossicazione alimentare f [eentos-seekatz-yonay aleementaray] food poisoning

introdurre un biglietto alla volta insert only one ticket at a time

invalido disabled
per invalidi for disabled people

inverno m winter

investire [eenvesteeray] to invest; to knock over

inviare [eenv-yaray] to send; to post, to mail

invidioso [eenveed-yozo] envious

invitare [eenveetaray] to invite

invito m invitation

io* [ee-o] I

Irlanda f [eerlanda] Ireland

Irlanda del Nord Northern Ireland

irlandese (m/f) [eerlandayzay] Irish; Irishman; Irishwoman

isola f [eezola] island

istituto m institute; secondary school; department

istruttore di nuoto m [eestroot-toray dee nwoto] swimming instructor

istruttrice di nuoto f [eestroot-treechay] swimming instructor

istruzioni per l'uso instructions for use

Italia f [eetal-ya] Italy

italiano (m) [eetal-yano], **italiana** (f) Italian

itinerario m [eeteenairar-yo] route, itinerary

I.V.A. (Imposta sul Valore Aggiunto) f [eeva] VAT

I.V.A. compresa [komprayza] inclusive of VAT

K

K-way® m cagoule

L

L pound, £; lira

l (litro) litre

la* the; her; it; you

là there

di là [dee] over there; that way; in the other room; from there

labbro m [lab-bro] lip

lacca per capelli f [kapel-lee] hair spray

lacci per le scarpe mpl [lachee pair lay skarpay] shoe laces

ladro m thief

laggiù [laj-joo] over there

lago m lake

laguna f lagoon

lamentarsi to complain

lametta f razor blade

lampada f lamp

lampada da comodino bedside lamp

lampadina f light bulb

lampione m [lamp-yonay] street lamp

lana f wool

lanciare [lancharay] to throw

largo wide

lasciare [lasharay] to leave; to let, to allow

lassativo m laxative

lato m side

latte detergente m [lat-tay detairjentay] skin cleanser

latteria f [lat-tairee-a] dairy shop

lattina f can

laurea f [lowray-a] degree

lavabo m washbasin

lavanderia (automatica) f [lavandairee-a owtomateeka] launderette

lavandino m sink

lavare [lavaray] to wash

lavare a mano wash by hand

lavare a secco dry-clean only

lavare i panni to do the washing

lavare i piatti [p-yat-tee] to do the washing up

lavare la biancheria [b-yan-kairee-a] to do the washing

lavare separatamente wash separately

lavarsi [lavarsee] to wash, to have a wash

lavarsi i denti to brush one's teeth

lavasecco m dry-cleaner's

lavastoviglie f [lavastoveel-yay] dishwasher

lavatrice f [lavatreechay] washing machine

lavorare [lavoraray] to work

lavori in corso mpl roadworks

lavori stradali roadworks

lavoro m work

le* [lay] the; to her; to you

legare [legaray] to tie

legge f [lej-jay] law

leggere [lej-jairay] to read

leggero [lej-jairo] light

legno m [len-yo] wood

lei* [lay] she; her; you

lentamente [lentamentay] slowly

lenti a contatto fpl contact lenses

lenti morbide fpl [morbeeday] soft lenses

lenti rigide fpl [reejeeday] hard

lenses
lenti semi-rigide fpl [saymee]
gas permeable lenses
lento slow
lenzuolo m [lentzwolo] sheet
lettera f [let-taira] letter
lettera tassata excess postage
to be paid
letti a castello mpl bunk beds
lettino m cot; sun lounger
lettino pieghevole [p-yayggay-volay] lounger; campbed
letto m bed
  andare a letto to go to bed
  (ri)fare il letto to make the
  bed
letto a due piazze [doo-ay p-yatzay] double bed
letto a una piazza [p-yatza] single bed
leva del cambio f [layva del kamb-yo] gear lever
levare [layvaray] to remove
levata f [layvata] collection
lezione f [letz-yonay] lesson;
class
li [lee] them
lì [lee] there
libbra f pound
libero vacant, free
libertà f freedom
libreria f [leebrairee-a]
bookshop, bookstore;
bookcase
libretto degli assegni m [dayl-yee as-sen-yee] cheque book,
checkbook
libro m book
liceo m [leechay-o] secondary

school
lima f [leema] file
lima per le unghie [oong-yay]
nailfile
limite delle acque sicure m
end of safe bathing area
limite di velocità speed limit
linea f [leenay-a] line
linea aerea [a-airay-a] airline
linea ferroviaria railway line
lingua f [leengwa] tongue;
language
liquido tergicristallo m [leekweedo tairjeekreestal-lo]
screen wash
liquori mpl [leekworee] spirits
lira sterlina f [stairleena] pound
sterling
liscio [leesho] smooth; neat
lista f list; menu
listino dei cambi m exchange
rates
L(it). (lire italiane) Italian lire
lite f [leetay] fight
litigare [leeteegaray] to argue,
to quarrel
litigio m [leeteejo] argument,
quarrel
litro m litre
livido m bruise
lo* the; him; it
località f locality
locanda f guesthouse, hotel
loggione m [loj-jonay] gallery,
the gods
londinese (m/f) [londeenayzay]
London (adj); Londoner
Londra f London
lontano far away

loro* they; them; you
il/la loro their(s); your(s)
lozione idratante f [lotz-yonay
eedratantay] moisturizer
lozione solare [solaray] suntan
lotion
L.st. (lira sterlina) pound
luce f [loochay] light
lucidare [loocheedaray] to
polish
luci di posizione mpl [loochee
dee pozeetz-yonay] sidelights
lucido per le scarpe m
[loocheedo pair lay skarpay] shoe
polish
luglio m [lool-yo] July
lui* [loo-ee] he; him
luna f [loona] moon
luna di miele [m-yelay]
honeymoon
luna park m funfair
lunedì m [loonaydee] Monday
lunghezza f [loongetza] length
lungo long; along
lungomare m [loongomaray]
esplanade, promenade
luogo di nascita m [lwogo dee
nasheeta] place of birth

M

M (Metropolitana)
underground, (US) subway
m (metro) metre
ma but
macchia f [mak-ya] stain
macchina f [mak-keena] car;
machine

macchina da scrivere
[skreevairay] typewriter
macchina del caffè [kaf-fay]
coffee-maker
macchina fotografica camera
macchina obliteratrice
[obleetairatreechay] ticket-
stamping machine
macelleria f [machel-lairee-a]
butcher's
macinacaffè m [macheena-kaf-
fay] coffee grinder
madre f [madray] mother
maestra f [ma-aystra] primary
school teacher; instructor
maestra di sci [shee] ski
instructor
maestro m [ma-aystro]
primary school teacher;
instructor
maestro di sci [shee] ski
instructor
maggio m [maj-jo] May
maggior: la maggior parte (di)
[maj-jor partay] most (of)
maggiore [maj-joray] bigger
maglia f [mal-ya] sweater,
pullover
lavoro a maglia m knitting
maglietta f [mal-yet-ta] T-shirt
maglione m [mal-yonay]
sweater, jumper
mai [ma-ee] never
malato ill
malattia f disease
malattia venerea [vaynairay-a]
VD
maldestro clumsy
mal di denti m [dentee]

toothache
mal di gola sore throat
mal di mare [ma**ra**y] seasickness
mal di testa headache
male m [**ma**lay] pain, ache
male badly
  far male to hurt
maledetto damned, cursed
maledizione! [maledeetz-**yo**nay] damn!
maleducato rude
malgrado despite
malinteso m [maleent**ay**zo] misunderstanding
malizia f [mal**ee**tz-ya] mischief; malice
malizioso [maleetz-**yo**zo] mischievous
mancia f [**ma**ncha] tip (in restaurant etc)
mancino [manch**ee**no] left-handed
mandare [mand**a**ray] to send
mangiacassette m [manjakas-**set**-tay] portable cassette player
mangianastri m [manja-**na**stree] cassette player
mangiare [manj**a**ray] to eat
manica f sleeve
manifesto m poster
maniglia f [man**ee**l-ya] handle; door knob
mano f hand
  di seconda mano second-hand
mansarda f attic room
Mantova f Mantua

manuale di conversazione m [man**wa**lay dee konvairsatz-**yo**nay] phrasebook
maratona f marathon
Marche fpl [**ma**rkay] Marches
marcia a senso unico alternato temporary one way system in operation
marcia normale normal speed lane
marciapiede m [marchap-**yay**day] pavement, sidewalk; platform, (US) track
marco m mark
mare m [**ma**ray] sea
  sul mare at the seaside
marea f [mar**ay**-a] tide
  alta/bassa marea high/low tide
mar Ionio m [ee-**on**-yo] Ionian Sea
marito m husband
mar Mediterraneo m [medeetair-**ra**nay-o] Mediterranean
marmo m marble
marrone [mar-**ro**nay] brown
martedì m Tuesday
martello m hammer
mar Tirreno m [teer-**ray**no] Tyrrhenian Sea
marzo m [**ma**rtzo] March
mascella f [mash**el**-la] jaw
maschera f [**ma**skaira] mask
maschilista m [maskeel**ee**sta] male chauvinist
massa: una massa (di gente) f a crowd (of people)
massimo: al massimo at the most

materassino (gonfiabile) m [gonfee-**a**beelay] air mattress, Lilo®

materasso m mattress

materia f [mat**ai**r-ya] subject

matita f pencil

matrimonio m wedding

mattina f morning
 la/alla mattina in the morning
 ogni mattina [**o**n-yee] every morning

mattino m morning
 il/al mattino in the morning

maturo [mat**oo**ro] ripe

ma va? really?
 ma va! I don't believe it!

mazza f [m**a**tza] club; bat

me* [may] me

meccanico m [mek-k**a**neeko] mechanic

medaglia f [med**a**l-ya] medal

media f [m**a**yd-ya] average

medicina f [medeech**ee**na] medicine

medico (di turno) m [m**a**ydeeko dee t**oo**rno] doctor (on duty)

medio [m**a**yd-yo] average; medium

Medioevo m [med-yo-**ay**vo] Middle Ages

Mediterraneo m [medeetair-r**a**nay-o] Mediterranean

medusa f [med**oo**za] jellyfish

meglio [m**a**yl-yo] better
 meglio così [k**o**zee] so much the better

meno (di) [m**a**yno dee] less (than)

mento m chin

mentre [m**e**ntray] while

menzionare [mentz-yon**a**ray] to mention

meraviglioso [meraveel-y**o**zo] wonderful

mercato m [mairk**a**to] market
 a buon mercato [bwon] cheap, inexpensive

merce f [m**ai**rchay] goods
 la merce venduta non si cambia senza lo scontrino goods are not exchanged without a receipt

merceria f [mairchair**ee**-a] haberdashery

mercoledì m [mairkoled**ee**] Wednesday

merda! [m**ai**rda] shit!

merenda f afternoon snack
 far merenda to have an afternoon snack

mese m [m**a**yzay] month

messa f mass

messaggio m [mes-s**a**j-jo] message

messa in piega f [p-y**a**yga] set
 messa in piega con il fon blow-dry

mestiere m [mest-y**ai**ray] job

mestruazioni fpl [mestrwatz-y**o**nee] period (menstruation)

metà f half
 metà prezzo [pr**e**tzo] half price

metallo m metal

metro m metre

metrò m underground, (US) subway

metropolitana f underground, (US) subway

mettere [met-tairay] to put

mettersi in viaggio [met-tairsee een v-yaj-jo] to set off on a journey

mezza: mezza dozzina (di) [medza dodzeena dee] half a dozen (of)

mezzanotte f [medzanot-tay] midnight

mezza pensione f [medza pens-yonay] half board

mezzo (m) [medzo] half; middle

in mezzo a in the middle of

mezzogiorno m [medzojorno] midday

mezz'ora f [medzora] half an hour

mi* [mee] me; myself; to me

mia* [mee-a] my; mine

mi dica [mee deeka] yes?; what would you like?

mie* [mee-ay] my; mine

miei* [m-yay-ee] my; mine

migliaia fpl [meel-ya-ya] thousands

migliorare [meel-yoraray] to improve

migliori [meel-yoree], **migliore** [meel-yoray] best; better

milanese (m/f) [meelanayzay] Milanese; person from Milan

milione [meel-yonay] million

mille [meelay] thousand

mingherlino [meengairleeno] skinny

minimo least, slightest

come minimo [komay] at least

ministero m ministry; board; office

minuto m minute

mio* [mee-o] my; mine

mirino m viewfinder

mi scusi [skoozee] excuse me; sorry

mi spiace [spee-achay] I'm sorry

misto lana [meesto] wool mixture

misurare [meezooraray] to measure

mitt. (mittente) sender

mittente m [meet-tentay] sender

mobili mpl [mobeelee] furniture

moda f fashion

di moda fashionable

modulo m form

moglie f [mol-yay] wife

molla f spring (mechanical)

molletta (da bucato) f clothes peg

molo m quay; pier; jetty

molta a lot, much; very

molti, molte [moltay] a lot; much; very; many, lots of

molto a lot; much; very

molto bene, grazie [baynay] very well, thank you

momento: un momento, prego [praygo] one moment, please

mondo m world

moneta f [monayta] coin; small change

monolocale m [monolokalay]

studio flat/apartment
montagna f [montan-ya] mountain
monumento ai caduti war memorial
moquette f [moket] (fitted) carpet
morbido soft
morbillo m measles
morire [moreeray] to die
morso m bite
morte f [mor-tay] death
morto dead
mosca f fly
moschea f [moskay-a] mosque
moscone m [moskonay] twin-hulled rowing boat
mostra f exhibition; show
mostrare [mostraray] to show
moto f motorbike
motore m [motoray] engine
motorino m moped
motoscafo m motorboat
movimenti mpl transactions
movimento m movement
mucca m cow
multa f fine
municipio m [mooneecheep-yo] town hall
munitevi di un carrello/cestino please take a trolley/basket
muovere [mwovairay] to move
muoversi [mwovairsee] to move
muoviti! [mwoveetee] hurry up!
muro m wall
muscolo m muscle
museo m [moozay-o] museum

musica f [moozeeka] music
mutande fpl [mootanday] underpants; pants, panties
mutuo m [mootwo] mortgage; bank loan

N

nafta f diesel oil
napoletano Neapolitan
Napoli f Naples
nascita f [nasheeta] birth
nascondere [naskondairay] to hide
nascondersi to hide
naso m [nazo] nose
nastro m tape; ribbon
nastro adesivo adhesive tape
nastro trasportatore [trasportatoray] conveyor belt
Natale m [natalay] Christmas
 Buon Natale! [bwon] Merry Christmas!
natale native
nato born
natura f nature
naturale: al naturale [natooralay] (food) plain; natural
naturalmente [natooralmentay] naturally, of course
naturista m/f naturist, nudist
nausea: avere la nausea [avairay nowzay-a] to feel sick/queasy
nave f [navay] ship
nave di linea [leen-ya] liner
nave passeggeri [pas-sej-jairee]

passenger ship

navigare [naveegaray] to sail

nazionale [natz-yonalay] national; domestic

nazionalità f [natz-yonaleeta] nationality

nazione f [natz-yonay] nation

ne* [nay] of him/her/them/it; about him/her/them/it

non ne ho [o] I don't have any

prendine [prendeenay] take some

né: né... né... [nay] neither ... nor ...

neanche [nay-ankay] not even

nebbia f fog

nebbioso [neb-yozo] foggy

necessario [neches-sar-yo] necessary

negare [negaray] to deny

negli* [nayl-yee] in the

negoziante m/f [negotz-yantay] shopkeeper

negozio m [negotz-yo] shop

nello, nel, nella, nei [nay], nelle* [nel-lay] in the

nemmeno [nem-mayno] not even

neozelandese (m/f) [nay-o-dzaylandayzay] New Zealand (adj); New Zealander

neppure [nep-pooray] not even

nero (m) [nairo] black; (hair) dark

nervoso [nairvozo] nervous

nessun no; not any

nessun dubbio [doob-yo] no

doubt

nessuno, nessuna no; none; nobody; not any

da nessuna parte [partay] nowhere

netto clean

peso netto net weight

neve f [nayvay] snow

nevica [nayveeka] it is snowing

nevicata f snowfall

nevischio m [neveesk-yo] sleet

niente [n-yentay] nothing

di niente don't mention it

nient'altro? [n-yentaltro] anything else?

niente pesce oggi no fish today

non fa niente it doesn't matter

night m night club

nipote m/f [neepotay] nephew/niece; grandson/granddaughter

no no; not

nocivo [nocheevo] harmful

nodo m knot

noi* [noy] we; us

noioso [noy-ozo] boring

noleggiare [nolej-jaray] to rent; to hire out

noleggio barche [nolej-jo barkay] boat hire

noleggio biciclette [beecheeklet-tay] cycle hire

noleggio sci [shee] ski hire

nolo: a nolo for hire, to rent

nome m [nomay] name

nome da ragazza [ragatza]

maiden name

nome da sposata married name

nome di battesimo [bat-**tay**zeemo] Christian name

non not

non... affatto not ... at all

non bucare [book**a**ray] do not pierce

non capisco [kap**ee**sko] I don't understand

non esporre ai raggi solari do not expose to direct sunlight

non ferma a... does not stop at ...

non fumare no smoking

non fumatori nonsmokers

non lo so I don't know

non... mai [m**a**-ee] never, not ever

non... mica [m**ee**ka] not ... at all

nonna f grandmother

non... neanche [nay-**a**nkay] not even

non... nemmeno [nem-m**ay**no] not even

non... né... né [nay] neither ... nor ...

non... neppure [nep-p**oo**ray] not even

non... nessuno [nays-s**oo**no] no one; not anybody; nobody; not ... any; no

non... niente [n-y**e**ntay] nothing; not anything

nonno m grandfather

non... nulla nothing; not

anything

nono (m) ninth

non oltrepassare no trespassing

non oltrepassare la dose prescritta do not exceed the stated dose

nonostante [nonost**a**ntay] despite

non parlare al conducente do not speak to the driver

non... per niente [pair n-y**e**ntay] not ... at all

non... più [p-yoo] no more, no longer, not ... any more

non toccare do not touch

nord m north

nord-est m north-east

norma: a norma di legge in accordance with the law

normale [norm**a**lay] normal; (petrol/gas) 2- or 3-star, regular gas

norvegese (m/f) [norvayj**ay**zay] Norwegian

Norvegia f [norv**e**ja] Norway

nostro, nostra, nostri, nostre* [n**o**stray] our(s)

nota f note

notare [not**a**ray] to note

notificare [noteefeek**a**ray] to notify

notizie fpl [not**ee**tz-yay] news

noto well-known

notte f [n**o**t-tay] night
  la/di notte at night

novanta ninety

nove [n**o**-vay] nine

novellino m, **novellina** f

beginner
novello new
novembre m [novembray] November
nozze fpl [notz-zay] wedding
ns. (nostro) our(s)
nubile [noobeelay] (woman) unmarried
nudista m/f nudist
nudo naked
nulla nothing; anything
numeri di emergenza emergency phone numbers
numeri utili useful numbers
numero m [noomairo] number
numero di telefono phone number
numero di volo flight number
numeroso [noomairozo] numerous
nuocere [nwocheray] to harm
nuora f [nwora] daughter-in-law
nuotare [nwotaray] to swim
nuoto m [nwoto] swimming
Nuova Zelanda f [nwova dzaylanda] New Zealand
nuovo new
di nuovo again
nuvola f cloud
nuvoloso [noovolozo] cloudy

O

O (ovest) West
o or
o... o... either ... or ...
obbligare [ob-bleegaray] to oblige; to force
obbligatorio [ob-bleegator-yo] obligatory
obiettare [ob-yet-taray] to object
obiettivo m lens; objective
obiezione f [ob-yetz-yonay] objection
occasione f [ok-kas-yonay] chance; bargain
d'occasione secondhand; bargain (price)
occhiali mpl [ok-yalee] glasses, eyeglasses; goggles
occhiali da sole [solay] sunglasses
occhiata f [ok-yata] glance
occhio m [ok-yo] eye
occhio! watch out!
occidentale [ocheedentalay] western
occorrere [ok-kor-rairay] to be needed
occupare [ok-kooparay] to occupy
occuparsi di [dee] to take care of
occupato [ok-koopato] engaged, occupied; taken; busy
occupazione f [ok-koopatz-yonay] occupation
oculista m/f oculist
odiare [od-yaray] to hate
odierno [od-yairno] today's; present
odorare [odoraray] to smell
odore m [odoray] smell
offendere [of-fendairay] to

offend
offensivo offensive
offerta f [of-f**ai**rta] offer
offesa f [of-f**ay**za] offence; insult
officina (meccanica) f [of-feech**ee**na] garage (for car repairs)
offrire [of-fr**ee**ray] to offer
oggetti smarriti lost property, lost and found
oggetto m [oj-j**et**-to] object; thing
oggi [**oj**-jee] today
ogni [**on**-yee] each, every; all
ogni abuso sarà punito penalty for misuse
ognuno [on-y**oo**no], **ognuna** everyone
oliera f [ol-y**ai**ra] oil and vinegar cruet
olio m [**ol**-yo] oil
olio solare [sol**a**ray] suntan oil
oltre [**ol**tray] beyond
  oltre a in addition to
oltremare [oltray-m**a**ray] overseas
oltrepassare [oltray-pass**a**ray] to cross; to go beyond; to go past
ombra f shade
ombrello m umbrella
ombrellone m [ombrel-l**o**nay] sunshade
ombretto m eye shadow
ombroso [ombr**o**zo] shady
omosessuale (m/f) [omoses-sw**a**lay] homosexual
omosessualità f [omoses-

swal**ee**ta] homosexuality
On. (onorevole) MP
onda f wave
ondulato wavy
onestà f honesty
onesto honest
ONU f UN
opale m [**o**palay] opal
opera d'arte f [**d**artay] work of art
operare [opair**a**ray] to carry out; to operate; to act; to work
operatore m [opairat**o**ray] operator
operatrice f [opairatr**ee**chay] operator
operoso [opair**o**zo] hardworking
opposto opposite
oppure [op-p**oo**ray] or
opuscolo m brochure
opzionale [optz-yon**a**lay] optional
ora (f) hour; now; in a moment
  che ore sono? [kay **o**ray] what time is it?
ora di punta rush hour
ora locale [l**o**kalay] local time
orario m [or**a**r-yo] timetable, (US) schedule
orario degli spettacoli [d**ayl**-yee] times of performances
orario di apertura opening hours
orario di visita [v**ee**zeeta] visiting hours
orario di volo flight time

orario estivo summer timetable/schedule

orario ferroviario railway timetable/schedule

orario invernale [eenvairnalay] winter timetable/schedule

ordinare [ordeenaray] to order

ordinario [ordeenar-yo] ordinary, usual

ordinato tidy

ordine m [ordeenay] order

 mettere in ordine [met-tairay een] to tidy up; to put away

orecchini mpl [orek-keenee] earrings

orecchio m [orek-yo] ear

organizzare [organeetzaray] to organize

orgoglioso [orgol-yozo] proud

oriente m [or-yentay] east

orlo m edge

ormai [orma-ee] by now

oro m gold

orologeria f [orolojairee-ya] watchmaker

orologio m [oroloj-yo] clock; watch

orribile [or-reebeelay] horrible; awful

ortografia f spelling

ortolano m greengrocer

osare [ozaray] to dare

ospedale m [ospaydalay] hospital

ospitalità f hospitality

ospitare [ospeetaray] to put up (in accommodation)

ospite m/f [ospeetay] guest; host

osso m bone

ostello della gioventù m [joventoo] youth hostel

osteria f [ostairee-a] inn

otorinolaringoiatra m/f [otoreenolareengo-yatra] ear, nose and throat specialist

ottanta eighty

ottavo (m) eighth

ottenere [ot-tenairay] to obtain, to get

ottica f optician's

ottico m optician

ottimo excellent

otto eight

ottobre m [ot-tobray] October

otturatore m [ot-tooratoray] shutter (in camera)

otturazione f [ot-tooratz-yonay] filling (in tooth)

ovest m west

ovvio [ov-yo] obvious

ozioso [otz-yozo] lazy

P

pacchetto m [pak-ket-to] package, small parcel; packet (of cigarettes etc)

pacchi postali mpl parcels, packages

pacco m parcel, package

pace f [pachay] peace

padella f frying pan

padre m [padray] father

paesaggio m [pa-aysaj-jo] landscape

paese m [pa-ayzay] country;

town; village

pag. (pagina) p., pp.

pagamento m payment

pagare [pagaray] to pay

pagare alla cassa pay at the desk

pagare qui pay here

pagina f [pajeena] page

Pagine Gialle fpl [pajeenay jallay] Yellow Pages

paio m [pa-yo] pair

palazzo m [palatzo] palace

palazzo comunale [komoonalay] town hall

palco m box (in theatre)

paletta f spade (beach); dustpan

palla f ball

pallacanestro f basketball

pallamano f handball

pallavolo f volleyball

pallone m [pal-lonay] ball

palude f [palooday] marsh, swamp

panetteria f [panet-tairee-ya] baker's

paninoteca f [paneenotayka] bar selling sandwiches

panne: restare in panne [restaray een pan-nay] to break down

panno m cloth

pannolino m nappy, diaper

pantaloni mpl trousers, (US) pants

pantofole fpl [pantofolay] slippers

papà m dad

parabrezza m [parabretza] windscreen

paracadutismo m [parakadooteezmo] parachuting

paralume m [paraloomay] lampshade

paraurti m [para-oortee] bumper, fender

parcheggiare [parkej-jaray] to park

parcheggio m [parkej-jo] car park, parking lot; parking

parcheggio a giorni alterni parking on alternate days

parcheggio a pagamento paying car park/parking lot

parcheggio custodito car park/parking lot with attendant

parcheggio incustodito unattended car park/parking lot

parcheggio privato private parking

parcheggio riservato agli ospiti dell'albergo parking reserved for hotel guests only

parchimetro m parking meter

parco m park

parecchi [parek-kee], parecchie [parek-yay] several

parete f [paraytay] wall

Parigi f [pareejee] Paris

parità f [pareeta] equality

parlamento m parliament

parlare [parlaray] to talk; to speak

parola f word

parrucchiere m [par-rook-

yairay], parrucchiera f
hairdresser
parte f [partay] part
a parte except
d'altra parte however
da qualche altra parte
[kwalkay] elsewhere
da qualche parte
somewhere
una parte (di) a part (of), a
share of
partecipare (a) [partecheeparay]
to take part in
partenza f [partentza]
departure
partire [parteeray] to leave
partita f match (sport)
partito politico m political
party
Pasqua f [paskwa] Easter
passaggio a livello m [pas-saj-
jo a leevel-lo] level/grade
crossing
passaggio pedonale
[pedonalay] pedestrian
crossing
passante m/f [pas-santay]
passer-by
passaporto m passport
passatempo m pastime
passeggero m [pas-sej-jairo],
passeggera f passenger
passeggiata f [pas-sej-jata]
walk; stroll
passeggino m [pas-sej-jeeno]
pushchair
passo m pass; step
passo carrabile carraio
driveway

pasticceria f [pasteechairee-a]
cake shop
pastificio m [pasteefeecho]
fresh pasta shop
pastiglie per la gola fpl
[pasteel-yay pair] throat
pastilles
pastiglie per la tosse [tos-say]
cough sweets
pasto m meal
patatine [patateenay] crisps,
(US) potato chips
patente f [patentay] driving
licence
patria f [patr-ya] native land
pattinaggio su ghiaccio m
[pat-teenaj-jo soo g-yacho] ice
skating
pattinare [pat-teenaray] to
skate
pattini mpl skates
pattumiera f [pat-toom-yaira]
dustbin, trashcan
paura f [powra] fear
pavimento m floor
paziente (m/f) [patz-yentay]
patient
pazzia f [patz-ee-a] madness
pazzo [patzo] mad
sei pazzo? [say] you must
be crazy!
peccato: è un peccato it's a
pity
pecora f sheep
pedaggio m [pedaj-jo] toll
pedale m [pedalay] pedal
pedalò m pedal boat
pedata f kick
pedoni mpl pedestrians

peggio [**pe**j-jo] worse

peggiori [pej-j**o**ree], peggiore [pej-j**o**ray] worst; worse

pelle f [**pel**-lay] skin; leather

pelle scamosciata f [skamosh**a**ta] suede

pelletteria f [pel-let-tair**ee**-a] leather goods

pellicceria f [pel-leechair**ee**-a] furrier

pellicola (a colori) f (colour) film

pendolare m/f [pendol**a**ray] commuter

pendolino m [pendol**ee**no] special fast train, first class only

pene m [**pay**nay] penis

penicillina f [peneech**ee**l-leena] penicillin

penisola f [pen**ee**zola] peninsula

penna f [**pen**-na] pen

penna a sfera [sf**ai**ra] ballpoint pen

pennarello m [pen-nar**el**-lo] felt-tip pen

penna stilografica f fountain pen

pennello m paint brush

pensare [pens**a**ray] to think

pensilina f bus shelter

pensionato m [pens-yon**a**to], pensionata f pensioner

pensione f [pens-y**o**nay] guesthouse

pensione completa [kompl**ay**ta] full board

pentola f saucepan

pentolino f [pentol**ee**no] small saucepan

per [pair] for; by; through; in order to

per aprire svitare unscrew to open

per cento [**chen**to] per cent

perché [pairk**ay**] because

perché? why?

perciò [pair**cho**] therefore

percorso m [pairk**o**rso] route

perdere [pairda**i**ray] to lose

perdere un treno to miss a train

perdita f leak

per favore [pair fav**o**ray] please

perfetto perfect

perfino even

pericolo m danger

pericolo di valanghe [val**a**ngay] danger of avalanches

pericoloso: è pericoloso sporgersi it is dangerous to lean out of the window

periferia f [pairefair**ee**-a] suburbs, outskirts

periodo di validità:... valid for/until:...

permanente f [pairman**en**tay] perm

permesso (m) permit; allowed; excuse me

permettere [pairmet-tairay] to allow

però [pair**o**] but

per piacere [pair p-yach**ai**ray] please

persiane fpl [pairs-y**a**nay] shutters

persino even
perso lost
persona f person
persuadere [pairswadairay] to persuade
pertosse f [pairtos-say] whooping cough
per tutte le altre destinazioni all other destinations
per uso esterno for external use
per uso interno for internal use
per uso veterinario for veterinary use
p. es. (per esempio) e.g.
pesante [pezantay] heavy
pesare [pezaray] to weigh
pesca f [payska] fishing; peach
pesce m [peshay] fish
pescecane m [peshaykanay] shark
pescheria f [peskairee-a] fishmonger's
peso m [payzo] weight
peso netto net weight
peso netto sgocciolato dry net weight
pettegolare [pet-tegolaray] to gossip
pettinarsi to comb one's hair
pettine m [pet-teenay] comb
petto m chest; breast
pezzi di ricambio mpl [petzee dee reekamb-yo] spare parts
pezzo m [petzo] piece
piacere (m) [p-yachairay] pleasure; to like

per piacere [pair] please
piacere di conoscerla [konoshairla] pleased to meet you
piacevole [p-yachevolay] pleasant
pianerottolo m landing
pianeta m [p-yanayta] planet
piangere [p-yanjairay] to cry
piano (m) floor, storey; quietly; slowly
piano di sopra upstairs
piano di sotto downstairs
piano superiore [soopair-yoray] upper floor
pianoterra m ground floor, (US) first floor
pianta f plant; map
pianterreno m [p-yantair-rayno] ground floor, (US) first floor
pianura f plain
pianura padana Po valley
piastrella f tile
piatti: lavare i piatti to do the washing-up
piattino m saucer
piatto (m) plate; dish; flat (adj)
piatto di portata serving dish
piatto fondo soup plate
piatto piano plate
piazza f [p-yatza] square
piccante [peek-kantay] spicy
piccolo small
piede m [p-yayday] foot
  andare a piedi [p-yaydee] to walk
  a piedi on foot
  in piedi standing
Piemonte m [p-yaymontay]

Piedmont

pieno [p-**yay**no] full

pietra f stone

pigiama m [peej**a**ma] pyjamas

pigrizia f [peegr**eetz**-ya] laziness

pigro lazy

pila f torch

pillola f pill

pilota m pilot

pinacoteca f gallery

pinne fpl [**peen**-nay] flippers

pinze fpl [**peentzay**] pliers

pinzette fpl [peentz**et**-tay] tweezers

pioggia f [p-**yoj**-ja] rain

piove [p-**yo**vay] it's raining

piovere [p-**yo**vairay] to rain

pipa f pipe

piscina f [pee**sheen**a] swimming pool

piscina coperta indoor swimming pool

piscina per bambini paddling pool

piscina scoperta open-air swimming pool

pista f slope; rink; track; runway

pista ciclabile [cheekl**a**beelay] cycle path

pista da fondo cross-country ski track

pista da pattinaggio [pat-tee-**naj**-jo] ice rink

pista da sci [**shee**] ski slope

pista difficile [deef-f**ee**cheelay] difficult slope

pista facile [f**a**cheelay] easy slope

pista per slitte [sl**eet**-tay] toboggan run

pistola f gun

pittore m [peet-t**o**ray], **pittrice** f [peet-tr**ee**chay] painter

pittura f painting

più [p-**yoo**] more

non... più ... no more

più grande [gr**a**nday] bigger

più o meno [**may**no] more or less

piumino m [p-yoom**ee**no] duvet

piuttosto [p-yoot-t**o**sto] rather

pizzicheria f [peetzeekair**ee**-a] delicatessen

plastica f plastic

platea f [plat**ay**-a] stalls

p.le (piazzale) Sq., Square

pneumatico m [pnay-oomat**ee**ko] tyre

po': un po' (di) a little bit (of)

poca few

pochi [**po**kee], **poche** [**po**kay] few

pochino: un pochino [pok**ee**no] a little bit

poco few

fra poco in a little while

poesia f [po-ez**ee**-a] poetry; poem

poi [**poy**] then

politica f politics

politico m, **politica** f politician

politico political

polizia f [poleetz**ee**-a] police

polizia stradale [strad**a**lay] traffic police

poliziotta f [poletz-y**ot**-ta] policewoman

poliziotto m policeman
polleria f [pol-lair**ee**-a] butcher's specializing in poultry
pollice m [p**o**l-leechay] thumb
pollivendolo m butcher specializing in poultry
polmoni mpl lungs
polmonite f [polmon**ee**tay] pneumonia
polso m wrist
poltrona f seat in stalls; armchair
pomata f cream
pomata cicatrizzante [cheekatreetz**a**ntay] healing cream for cuts
pomeriggio m [pomair**ee**j-jo] afternoon
ponte m [p**o**ntay] bridge; deck
pontile m [pont**ee**lay] landing pier, jetty
popolazione f [popolatz-y**o**nay] population
popolo m the people
porca miseria! [meez**a**ir-ya] bloody hell!
porcellana f [porchel-l**a**na] porcelain; china
porta f door
portabagagli m [portabag**a**l-yee] porter (in station)
portacenere m [portach**e**nairay] ashtray(s)
porta d'ingresso f [deengr**e**s-so] front door
portafoglio m [portaf**o**l-yo] wallet
portamonete m [portamon**ay**tay] purse

portapacchi m [portap**a**k-kee] roof rack
portare [p**o**rt**a**ray] to carry; to take; to bring
portatile [port**a**teelay] portable
porte-enfant m [port-anf**a**n] carry-cot
portiere (di notte) m [port-y**a**iree dee n**o**t-tay] (night) porter, janitor
portinaio m [porteen**a**-yo], **portinaia** f caretaker
porto m harbour
porzione per bambini f [porz-y**o**nay pair] children's portion
posare [pos**a**ray] to put down
posate fpl [poz**a**tay] cutlery
possiamo* we can
posso* I can
possono they can
posta f mail
posta aerea [a-**a**iray-a] airmail
posta centrale [chentr**a**lay] main post office
postagiro m [postaj**ee**ro] postal giro
posteriore: sedile posteriore m [sayd**ee**lay postairee-**o**ray] back seat
posti a sedere mpl seats
posti in piedi standing room
postino m postman
posto m place; seat; space; job, post
posto di polizia [poleetz**ee**-a] police station
posto di telefono pubblico public telephone

PO

posto prenotato [prenotato] reserved seat

posto riservato a mutilati e invalidi seat reserved for disabled persons only

postumi della sbornia mpl [zborn-ya] hangover

potabile [potabeelay] drinkable**acqua potabile** [akwa] drinking water

potere* (m) [potairay] to be able, can; power

potete* [potaytay] you can

potuto* been able to

povero poor

povertà f poverty

PP.TT. (Poste e Telecomunicazioni) **fpl** Italian Post Office

pranzo m [prandzo] lunch

prato m lawn; meadow

prato all'inglese [al-leenglayzay] lawn

precedenza f [prechedentza] right of way

precipitarsi (in) [precheepeetarsee] to rush in

preferire [prefaireeray] to prefer

preferito favourite

prefisso m dialling code, area code

pregare [pregaray] to request
  si prega di (non)... please do (not) ...
  si prega di non fumare please refrain from smoking
  si prega di ritirare lo scontrino please get your receipt first

prego [praygo] please; pardon; you're welcome; after you
  prego? pardon?, pardon me?

prelevamenti withdrawals

prelevare dei soldi [prelevaray day] to withdraw money

prelievo m [prel-yayvo] withdrawal

premere [praymairay] to press

premio m [praym-yo] prize

prenda take

prendere* [prendairay] to take; to catch

prendere il sole [solay] to sunbathe

prendere in affitto to rent

prendersi: da prendersi a digiuno to be taken on an empty stomach
  da prendersi dopo/prima dei pasti to be taken after/before meals
  da prendersi secondo la prescrizione medica to be taken according to doctor's prescription
  da prendersi tre volte al giorno to be taken three times a day

prenotare [prenotaray] to book, to reserve

prenotato reserved

prenotazione f [prenotatz-yonay] reservation, booking

prenotazione obbligatoria [ob-bleegator-ya] reservation compulsory

preoccuparsi per [pray-okkooparsee pair] to worry about

prepare [prepararay] to prepare

prepararsi to get ready

prepararsi a scendere [shendairay] get ready to alight

presa f [praysa] socket

presa multipla adaptor

presentare [prezentaray] to introduce

presente [prezentay] present

preservativo m condom

preside m/f [prayseeday] headmaster; headmistress

preso* [prayzo] taken

pressione gomme f [pres-yonay gom-may] tyre pressure

prestare [prestaray] to lend

farsi prestare (da) to borrow (from)

prestito: prendere in prestito [presteeto] to borrow

presto soon; early

prete m [praytay] priest

pretendere [pretendairay] to claim; to demand

previsioni del tempo mpl [preveez-yonee] weather forecast

prezzo m [pretzo] price

prezzo intero full price

prezzo ridotto reduced price

prigione f [preejonay] prison

prima f first; first gear

prima di before

prima classe [klas-say] first class

prima colazione f [kolatz-yonay] breakfast

prima qualità high quality

primavera f spring

prima visione first release/showing

primo m first

primo piano m first floor, (US) second floor

primo tempo m first half

principale [preencheepalay] main

principe m [preencheepay] prince

principessa f [preencheepes-sa] princess

principiante m/f [preencheep-yantay] beginner

privato [preevato] private

probabilmente [probabeelmentay] probably

prodotto artigianalmente [arteejanalmentay] made by craftsmen

professore (Prof.) m teacher; professor

professoressa (Prof.essa) f teacher; professor

profondo deep

profumeria f [profoomairee-a] perfume shop

profumo m perfume

pro loco f tourist office in small town

prolunga f extension lead

promettere [promet-tairay] to promise

pronto ready; hello (on telephone)

pronto intervento m emergency service

pronto soccorso m first aid; casualty

pronunciare [pronooncharay] to pronounce

proprietario m [propr-yetar-yo], **proprietaria** f owner

proprio exactly; just; really; own

prosa f [proza] theatre drama **compagnia di prosa** theatre company

prossimo next

proteggere [protej-jairay] to protect

protestare [protestaray] to protest

provare [provaray] to try (on) **prova!** just try!

provincia f [proveencha] district

prudente [proodentay] cautious

prudenza f [proodentza] caution

prurito m itch

P.S. (Pubblica Sicurezza) f Police

P.T. (Poste e Telecomunicazioni) fpl Italian Post Office

pubblico (m) public; audience

pugilato m [poojeelato] boxing

pugno m [poon-yo] fist; punch **un pugno (di)** a handful (of)

pulire [pooleeray] to clean

pulito clean

pulitura f dry-cleaner's

pullman m coach, long-distance bus

pungere [poonjairay] to sting

punire [pooneeray] to punish

punteggio m [poontej-jo] score

punto di vista m point of view

puntuale [poontwalay] on time

puntura f [poontoora] bite; injection

può* [pwo] he/she/it can; you can

può darsi maybe, perhaps

puoi* [pwoy] you can

pura lana vergine pure virgin wool

pura seta pure silk

puro cotone pure cotton

puro lino pure linen

puzzle m jigsaw

puzzo m [pootzo] stink

p.zza (piazza) Square

Q

qua [kwa] here **di qua** (over) here, this way

quaderno m [kwadairno] exercise book

quadrato m [kwadrato] square

quadro m [kwadro] painting; picture

qualche [kwalkay] some, a few

qualcosa [kwalkoza] something; anything **qualcos'altro** [kwalkozaltro] something else

qualcuno [kwalkoono] somebody

quale [kwalay] which

qualità f [kwaleeta] quality

quando [kwando] when

quanta? [kwanta] how much?

quanti? [kwantee], **quante?** [kwantay] how many?

quantità f [kwanteeta] quantity

quanto? [kwanto] how much?

quaranta [kwaranta] forty

quarta f [kwarta] fourth (gear)

quartiere m [kwart-yairay] quarter, area

quarto (m) [kwarto] quarter, fourth

  tre quarti mpl three quarters

quasi [kwazee] almost, nearly

quattordici [kwat-tor-deechee] fourteen

quattro [kwat-tro] four

quello [kwel-lo] that (one)

  quello lì that (one)

questa [kwesta] this (one)

queste [kwestay] these

questi [kwestee] these

questo [kwesto] this (one)

  questo qui [kwee] this (one)

qui [kwee] here

quindi [kweendee] therefore

quindici [kween-deechee] fifteen

quinta f [kweenta] fifth (gear)

quinto (m) [kweento] fifth

R

racc. recorded delivery

racchetta (da tennis) f [rak-ket-ta] (tennis) racket

raccomandata f recorded delivery (mail)

raccomandata con ricevuta di ritorno [reechevoota] recorded-delivery mail with card sent back to sender on delivery

raccomandata espresso recorded-delivery express mail

raccordo autostradale m [owto-stradalay] motorway junction, highway intersection

radersi to shave

radiosveglia f [rad-yosvayl-ya] radio alarm

raffreddore m [raf-fred-doray] cold (illness)

ragazza f [ragatza] girl; girlfriend

ragazza alla pari au pair girl

ragazzo m [ragatzo] boy; boyfriend

raggio m [raj-jo] spoke

raggi X mpl [raj-jee eeks] X-ray

ragionevole [rajonayvolay] reasonable

ragno m [ran-yo] spider

RAI-TV (Radiotelevisione italiana) f [ra-eeteevoo] Italian radio and television

rallentare [ral-lentaray] reduce speed, slow down

rampe f [rampay] ramps

rappresentante m/f [rap-prezentantay] agent

raramente [raramentay] seldom

raro rare

rasoio m [razoy-o] razor;

shaver

ratto **m** rat

razza di idiota! [ratza] stupid idiot!

re **m** [ray] king

recinto **m** [recheento] fence

reclamare [reklamaray] to complain

reclamo **m** complaint

regalo **m** present

reggiseno **m** [rej-jeesayno] bra

regina **f** [rejeena] queen

regionale **m** [rejonalay] local train stopping at all stations

registratore (a cassette) **m** [rejeestratoray a kas-set-tay] tape/cassette recorder

Regno Unito **m** [ren-yo] United Kingdom

remare [remaray] to row

remo **m** [raymo] oar

rene **m** [raynay] kidney (in body)

Rep. (repubblica) **f** republic

reparto **m** department; ward

respirare [respeeraray] to breathe

respiratore (a tubo) **m** [respeeratoray a toobo] snorkel

responsabile [responsabeelay] responsible

restituire [resteetweeray] to give back

resto **m** rest; change (money)

il resto (di) **m** the rest (of)

rete **f** [raytay] net; goal; network

retromarcia **f** [retromarcha] reverse gear

riagganciare [ree-ag-gancharay] to hang up

ribassato reduced

ricambi **mpl** spare parts

ricamo **m** embroidery

ricco [reek-ko] rich

ricetta **f** [reechet-ta] recipe; prescription

ricevere [reechayvairay] to receive

ricevitore **m** [reecheveetoray] receiver

ricevuta **f** [reechevoota] receipt

ricevuta di ritorno acknowledgement of receipt

ricevuta fiscale [feeskalay] bill, (US) check (from a restaurant, bar etc)

ricominciare (da capo) [reekomeencharay] to start again

riconoscere [reekonoshairay] to recognize

ricordarsi (di) to remember

ridere [reedairay] to laugh

ridicolo ridiculous

ridiscendere [redeeshendairay] to go back down

ridotto reduced

ridurre [reedoor-ray] to reduce

riduttore **m** [reedoot-toray] adaptor

riduzione **f** [reedootz-yonay] reduction

riempire [r-yempeeray] to fill (in)

rientrare [r-yentraray] to go/come back (in/home)

rifiuti mpl [reef-**yoo**tee] rubbish

rilassarsi [reelas-**sa**rsee] to relax

rimandare [reemand**a**ray] to send back

rimanere [reeman**ai**ray] to stay, to remain

rimborsare [reembors**a**ray] to refund

rimorchio m [reem**or**k-yo] trailer

rimozione forzata illegally parked vehicles removed at owner's expense

rinfresco m reception

ringraziare [reengratz-y**a**ray] to thank

rione m [ree-**o**nay] neighbourhood

riparare [reepar**a**ray] to repair

riparazioni fpl [reeparatz-y**o**nee] repairs

riparo m shelter

ripartire [reepart**ee**ray] to set off again

ripetere [reep**ay**tairay] to repeat

ripido steep

riposarsi to have a rest

riposo m [reep**o**zo] rest

risata f [rees**a**ta] laugh

riscaldamento m heating

riscuotere un assegno [reeskw**o**tairay oon as-s**e**n-yo] to cash a cheque

riserva f [rees**ai**rva] reserve
di riserva spare

riservato [reesairv**a**to] reserved

riservato ai clienti dell'albergo for hotel guests only

riservato ai non fumatori non-smokers only

riservato carico loading only

riservato polizia police only

riservato scarico (merci) unloading (of goods) only

riservato tram, taxi, bus trams, taxis, buses only

riservato viacard for magnetic toll card holders only

risparmi mpl savings

rispedire [reesped**ee**ray] to send back

rispondere [reesp**o**ndairay] to reply

risposta f answer

ristorante m [reestor**a**ntay] restaurant

risultato m result

ritardo m delay
essere in ritardo to be late
in ritardo delayed

ritirata f toilet/rest room (on train)

ritiro bagagli m [bag**a**l-yee] baggage claim

ritornare [reetorn**a**ray] to return, to come/go back
ritorni go back

ritorno m return

riva f shore

rivista f magazine

rivoltante [reevolt**a**ntay] disgusting

roccia f [r**o**cha] rock; rock climbing

romano Roman

romanzo m [rom**a**ndzo] novel

rompere [**ro**mpairay] to break

rosa (**f**) rose; pink

rosolia f [rozol**ee**-a] German measles

rossetto m lipstick

rosso red

rosticceria f [rosteechair**ee**-a] take-away selling hot meat dishes

rotaie fpl [rot**a**-yay] tracks, rails

rotondo round

rotto broken

roulotte f [rool**ot**] caravan, (US) trailer

rovesciarsi [rovesharsee] to capsize

rovine fpl [rov**ee**nay] ruins

R.R. (ricevuta di ritorno) return receipt for registered mail

R.U. (Regno Unito) **m** UK

rubare [roob**a**ray] to steal

rubinetto m tap, faucet

rubrica f address book

rullino m film

rumore m [room**o**ray] noise

rumoroso [room**o**r**o**zo] noisy

ruota f [r**wo**ta] wheel

ruscello m [roosh**e**l-lo] stream

S

S. (santo/santa) St., Saint

sabato m Saturday

sabbia f [s**ab**-ya] sand

sacchetto (di plastica) m [sak-**ket**-to] (plastic) bag

sacco a pelo m [p**ay**lo] sleeping bag

sagra f feast; (open air) festival

sala f living room

sala da pranzo [pr**a**ndzo] dining room

sala d'aspetto waiting room

sala d'attesa [dat-t**ay**sa] waiting room

sala d'imbarco [deemb**a**rko] departure lounge

salato savoury; salty

saldi mpl sale

saldi di fine stagione [f**ee**nay staj**o**nay] end of season sales

sali da bagno mpl [b**an**-yo] bath salts

saliera f [sal-y**ai**ra] salt cellar

salire [sal**ee**ray] to go up; to get on/in

salita f slope; entry

in salita uphill

salone per uomo [w**o**mo] men's hairdresser

salotto m living room, lounge

saltare [salt**a**ray] to jump

salto m jump

salumaio m [saloom**a**-yo] delicatessen

salumeria f [saloomair**ee**-a] delicatessen

salumiere m [saloom-y**ai**ray] delicatessen

salute f [sal**oo**tay] health

(alla) salute! cheers!

in salute in good health

salute! bless you!

salvagente m [salvaj**e**ntay] rubber ring

salve! [**sal**vay] hi!

salvietta f [salv-**yet**-ta] napkin

sandali mpl [**san**dalee] sandals

sangue m [**san**gway] blood

sanguinare [sangween**a**ray] to bleed

sano healthy

sapere [sap**ai**ray] to know

sapone m [sap**o**nay] soap

sapore m [sap**o**ray] flavour

Sardegna f [sard**ayn**-ya] Sardinia

sartoria f [sartor**ee**-a] tailor's; dressmaker's

S.A.U.B. (Struttura Amministrativa Unificata di Base) f Italian national health service, Italian health care

sbagliato [zbal-**ya**to] wrong

sbaglio m [z**bal**-yo] mistake

sbarcare [zbark**a**ray] to disembark

sbrigarsi [zbreeg**a**rsee] to hurry

sbrigati! [zbr**ee**gatee] hurry up!

sbucciare [zbooch**a**ray] to peel

scacchi mpl [s**kak**-kee] chess

scadenza f [skad**en**tza] expiry date; deadline

scaffali mpl shelves

scala f ladder

scala mobile [m**o**beelay] escalator

scale fpl [s**ka**lay] stairs

scalo m stop-over

fare scalo to stop over

scandaloso [skandal**o**zo] shocking

scandinavo Scandinavian

scapolo m bachelor

scarpe fpl [s**kar**pay] shoes

scarpe da ginnastica [jeen-**na**steeka] trainers

scarponi da sci mpl [da **shee**] ski boots

scatola f box

la scatola priva del talloncino non può essere venduta without a coupon this box cannot be sold

scatola del cambio [**kamb**-yo] gearbox

scatto m unit

scavi mpl [s**ka**vee] excavations

scegliere [sh**ayl**-yairay] to choose

scendere [sh**en**dairay] to go down; to get off

scendere le scale [s**ka**lay] to go/come downstairs

scheda f [s**kay**da] card

scheda telefonica phonecard

scherzo m [s**ker**tzo] joke

schiaffo m [sk-**yaf**-fo] slap

schiena f [sk-**yay**na] back (of body)

schifo: che schifo! [kay sk**ee**fo] it's disgusting!

schifoso [skeef**o**zo] foul

schiuma da barba f [sk-**yoo**ma] shaving foam

schizzare [skeetz**a**ray] to splash

sci m [**shee**] ski; skiing

sciacquare [shak**wa**ray] to rinse

sci acquatico m [**shee**

akw**a**teeko] waterski; waterskiing

sciampo m [shamp**o**] shampoo

sciare [shee-**a**ray] to ski

 andare a sciare to go skiing

sciarpa f [sh**a**rpa] scarf

sciatore m [shee-at**o**ray] skier

sciatrice f [shee-atr**ee**chay] skier

sci d'acqua m [shee d**a**kwa] water-skiing

sci di fondo cross-country skiing

scienza f [shee-**e**ntza] science

sciocco (m) [sh**o**k-ko] silly; idiot

scivolare [sheevol**a**ray] to skid

scivoloso [sheevol**o**zo] slippery

scodella f bowl

scogliera f [skol-y**a**ira] cliff

scoglio m [sk**o**l-yo] rock

scolara f schoolgirl

scolaro m schoolboy

scommessa f bet

scommettere [skom-m**e**t-tairay] to bet; to stake

scomodo uncomfortable

scomparire [skompar**ee**ray] to disappear

scompartimento m compartment

scontento unhappy

sconto m discount

scontrino m receipt

scontro m crash

scopa f broom

scorciatoia f [skorchat**oy**-a] shortcut

scorso: l'anno scorso last year

scotch m Sellotape®, Scotch tape®

scottarsi to get sunburnt

scottatura f [skot-tat**oo**ra] sunburn; burn

Scozia f [sk**o**tzee-a] Scotland

scozzese (m/f) [skotz**ay**zay] Scottish; Scot

scrittura f [skreet-t**oo**ra] writing

scrivere [skr**ee**vairay] to write

scrivere a macchina [mak-k**ee**na] to type

scultura f sculpture

scuola f [skw**o**la] school

scuola di lingue [l**ee**ngway] language school

scuola di sci [shee] ski school

scuola elementare [elementaray] primary school

scuola media inferiore [m**ayd**-ya eenfair-y**o**ray] junior secondary school

scuola media superiore [soopair-y**o**ray] senior secondary school

scuotere [skw**o**tairay] to shake

scuro dark

scusa f [sk**oo**za] apology; excuse

 scusa! sorry!

scusarsi [skooz**a**rsee] to apologize

scusi! [sk**oo**zee] sorry!

 come, scusi? [k**o**may] pardon?, pardon me?

sdraiarsi [zdra-y**a**rsee] to lie down

se [say] if

sé [say] himself; herself; itself; oneself; themselves

sebbene [seb-baynay] although

sec. (secolo) century

seccante [sek-kantay] annoying

secchiello m [sek-yel-lo] bucket

secchio m [sek-yo] bucket

secco dry

secolo m [saykolo] century

seconda f second (gear)

seconda classe f [klas-say] second class

seconda visione f second release/showing

secondo (m) second

secondo tempo m second half

sedere m [saydairay] bottom (of person)

sedersi to sit down

sedia f [sayd-ya] chair

sedia a rotelle [rotel-lay] wheelchair

sedia a sdraio [zdra-yo] deck chair

sedici [say-deechee] sixteen

sedile m [saydeelay] seat; bench

seduto sitting, seated

seg. (seguente) following

sega f [sayga] saw

seggiola f [sej-jola] chair

seggiovia f [sej-jovee-a] chairlift

segnale m [sen-yalay] signal

segnale d'allarme [dal-larmay] alarm

segnaletica in rifacimento road signs being redone

segnaletica orizzontale in allestimento road signs being painted

segreteria telefonica f [segretairee-a] answering machine

segreto [segrayto] secret

seguire [segweeray] to follow

segua [saygwa] follow

sei* [say] you are

sei [say] six

selezionare il numero dial the number

sella f saddle

semaforo m traffic lights

sembrare [sembraray] to seem

semiasse m [semee-assay] axle; shaft

seminterrato m basement

semplice [sempleechay] simple

sempre [sempray] always

sempre d(i)ritto straight ahead, straight on

seno m [sayno] breast

sensato sensible

sensibile [senseebeelay] sensitive

senso: di buon senso [bwon] sensible

senso dell'umorismo m [del-loomoreezmo] (sense of) humour

senso unico one way

sentiero m [sent-yairo] path

sentire [senteeray] to feel; to hear; to smell

sentirsi (bene) [b**ay**nay] to feel (well)

sentirsi poco bene to feel unwell

senza [s**e**ntza] without

senza dubbio [d**oo**b-yo] undoubtedly

senza conservanti no preservatives

separatamente [separatam**e**ntay] separately

separato separate

sera f [s**ai**ra] evening

alle 8 di sera at 8 p.m.

la/di sera in the evening

serbatoio m [sairbat**oy**-o] tank

serio [s**ai**r-yo] serious

sul serio [s**oo**l] seriously; really

serpente m [sairp**e**ntay] snake

serratura f lock

servire [sairv**ee**ray] to serve

servitevi help yourselves

serviti help yourself

si serva help yourself

servire freddo serve chilled

servizi [sairv**ee**tzee] toilets, rest room

servizio m [sairv**ee**tz-yo] service

il servizio è gratuito free service

servizio a bordo in-flight service

servizio autotraghetto [**ow**totraget-to] car ferry

servizio compreso [kompr**ay**-zo] service charge included

servizio escluso not including service charge

servizio guasti faults service

servizio in camera room service

servizio traghetto [trag**e**t-to] passenger ferry

sessanta sixty

sessista sexist

sesso m sex

sesto (m) sixth

seta f [s**ay**ta] silk

sete: avere sete [av**ai**ray s**ay**tay] to be thirsty

settanta seventy

sette [s**e**t-tay] seven

settembre m [set-t**e**mbray] September

settimana f week

alla settimana per week

due settimane [d**oo**-ay set-teem**a**nay] fortnight

settimo (m) seventh

sfacciato [sfach**a**to] cheeky

sfinito exhausted

sfortunatamente [sfortoonatam**e**ntay] unfortunately

sgabello m [zgab**e**l-lo] stool

sgarbato [zgarb**a**to] rude

sgradevole [zgrad**ay**volay] unpleasant

si [see] himself; herself; itself; themselves

sì [see] yes

siamo* we are

siccome [seek-k**o**may] as, since

sicuro safe; sure

siete* [s-y**ay**tay] you are

sigaretta f cigarette

sigaro m cigar

Sigg. (signori) Messrs

sigillare [seejeel-la**ray**] to seal

significare [seen-yeefeeka**ray**] to mean

signor (Sig.) [seen-y**or**] Mr; Sir

signora (Sig.a) (f) [seen-y**or**a] lady; Mrs; madam

signore [seen-y**or**ay] gentleman

signore fpl ladies' toilet, rest room

signori mpl gents' toilet, rest room

signorina (Sig.na) [seen-yor**ee**na] Miss

silenzio m [seel**e**ntz-yo] silence

simile [s**ee**meelay] similar

simpatico nice

sinagoga f synagogue

sincero [seench**ai**ro] sincere, frank

singhiozzo m [seeng-y**o**tzo] hiccups

sinistra f [seen**ee**stra] left

a sinistra on/to the left

siringa f syringe

s.l.m. (sul livello del mare) above sea level

slogarsi [zloga**r**see] to sprain

smalto per le unghie m [zm**a**lto pair lay **oo**ng-yay] nail polish

smettere [zm**e**t-tairay] to stop

snello [zn**e**l-lo] slim

so: non (lo) so I don't know

sobborghi mpl [sob-b**or**gee] suburbs

soccorso m help; assistance

soccorso alpino mountain rescue

soccorso stradale [strad**a**lay] breakdown service

società f [soch**ay**ta] society; company

soffitta f loft

soffitto m ceiling

soggiorno m [soj-j**or**no] stay; lounge

sognare [son-ya**ray**] to dream

sogno m [s**on**-yo] dream

soldi mpl [s**o**ldee] money

sole m [s**o**lay] sun

soleggiato [solej-j**a**to] sunny (place)

solito [s**o**leeto] usual

di solito usually

sollevare [sol-leva**ray**] to lift

solo alone; only

solo il sabato/la domenica Saturdays/Sundays only

solo servizio cuccette e letti sleepers/sleeping cars only

soltanto only

soluzione salina per lenti a contatto f [solootz-y**o**nay – pair] soaking solution for contact lenses

somministrazione per via orale to be taken orally

sonnecchiare [son-nek-ya**ray**] to doze

sonnifero m sleeping pill

sonno: avere sonno to be sleepy

sono* I am; they are

sopra on; above

di sopra upstairs

sopracciglio m [soprach**ee**l-yo] eyebrow

soprammobile m [sopram-mobeelay] ornament

soprannome m [sopran-nomay] nickname

sordo deaf

sorella f sister

sorgente f [sorjentay] spring

sorpassare [sorpas-saray] to overtake

sorpasso fast lane, lane for overtaking

sorprendente [sorprendentay] surprising

sorpresa f [sorpraysa] surprise

sorridere [sor-reedairay] to smile

sorriso m smile

sosta autorizzata... parking permitted for ...

sosta vietata no parking

sostenere [sostenairay] to maintain; to uphold

sottile [sot-teelay] thin

sotto under; below

  di sotto downstairs

sottolineare [sot-toleenay-aray] to emphasize

sottopassaggio m [sot-topas-saj-jo] underpass

SP (strada provinciale) f secondary road

Spagna f [span-ya] Spain

spagnolo (m) [span-yolo], **spagnola** (f) Spanish; Spaniard

spago m string

spalla f shoulder

sparare [spararay] to shoot

sparire [spareeray] to disappear

sparisci! [spareeshee] get lost!

spartirsi to share

spaventoso [spaventozo] appalling, dreadful

spazzare [spatzaray] to sweep

spazzola f [spatzola] brush

spazzolino m [spatzoleeno] brush

specchietto retrovisore m [spek-yet-to retroveezoray] rearview mirror

specchio m [spek-yo] mirror

specialista m/f [spech-yaleesta] specialist

specialità f [spech-yaleeta] speciality, specialities

specialmente [spech-yalmentay] especially

spedire [spedeeray] to send; to post, to mail

spedire per posta to post, to mail

spegnere [spen-yairay] to switch off

spegnere il motore switch off engine

spendere [spendairay] to spend

sperare [speraray] to hope

spesa f [spaysa] shopping

spesso often

spettacolo m performance, show

spia f gauge

spiace: mi spiace [spee-achay] I'm sorry

spiaggia f [sp-yaj-ja] beach

spiccioli mpl [speecholee] (small) change

spiegare [sp-yaygaray] to explain

spilla f brooch

spilla di sicurezza [seekooretza] safety pin

spillo m pin

spina f plug (electrical); thorn

spingere [speenjairay] to push

spiritoso [speereetozo] witty

spogliarsi [spol-yarsee] to undress

spogliatoi mpl [spol-yatoy] changing rooms

spolverare [spolvairaray] to dust

sponda f shore; riverbank

sporco dirty

sporco maschilista m [maskeeleesta] male chauvinist pig

sporgersi (da) [sporjairsee] to lean (out)

sportello m counter; door (on train)

sportello automatico [owtomateeko] cash dispenser, automatic teller

sportello pacchi parcels counter

sport invernali mpl winter sports

sposato married

spugna f [spoon-ya] sponge

spuntata f trim

spuntino m snack

squadra f [skwadra] team

squalo m [skwalo] shark

SS (strada statale) f main road, national road

sta: come sta? [komay] how are you?

stadio m [stad-yo] stadium

stagione f [stajonay] season

stagno m [stan-yo] pond

stagnola f [stan-yola] silver foil

stai: come stai? [komay sta-ee] how are you?

stamattina this morning

stampa f Press

stampe printed matter

stampelle fpl [stampel-lay] crutches

stanco tired

stanotte [stanot-tay] tonight

stanza f [stantza] room

stare [staray] to be; to stand; to be located; to stay, to remain; to suit

stare bene [baynay] to be well

stare poco bene to be unwell

starter m choke

statale [statalay] national; state

state: come state? [komay statay] how are you?

Stati Uniti mpl [statee ooneetee] United States

stato* (m) been; state

statua f [statwa] statue

stazione f [statz-yonay] station

stazione degli autobus [dayl-yee owtoboos] bus station

stazione della metropolitana underground, (US) subway station

stazione delle corriere [del-lay

cor-y**ai**ray] coach station

stazione di servizio [sair**vee**tz-yo] petrol/gas station, service station

stazione ferroviaria railway station

steccato m fence

stella f star

stendersi to lie down

sterlina f pound (sterling)

sterzo m [s**ter**tzo] steering; steering wheel

stesso, stessa, stessi, stesse [st**es**-say] same

stile m [st**ee**lay] style

stirare [steer**a**ray] to iron

stirarsi [steer**ar**see] to stretch out

stitico [st**ee**teeko] constipated

stivali mpl [steev**a**lee] boots

stoffa f material, fabric

stomaco m stomach

storia f [st**o**r-ya] story; history

storia dell'arte f [del-l**ar**tay] history of art

stoviglie fpl [stov**ee**l-yay] crockery

straccio m [str**a**cho] rag; cloth; duster

strada f road

strada a fondo cieco blind alley

strada camionabile route for heavy vehicles

strada dissestata uneven road surface

strada ghiacciata ice on road

strada interrotta road blocked

strada privata private road

strada provinciale secondary road

strada sdrucciolevole slippery road

strada secondaria secondary road

strada senza uscita no thoroughfare, dead end

strada statale main road

straniero m [stran-y**ai**ro], **straniera f** foreigner

straniero foreign

strano strange

straordinario [stra-ordeen**a**r-yo] exceptional

stretto narrow

strillare [streel-l**a**ray] to scream

strisce pedonali fpl [str**ee**shay] pedestrian crossing

strofinaccio (da cucina) m [strofeen**a**cho (da kooch**ee**na)] tea towel

stronzo m bastard

studente m [stood**en**tay] student

studentessa f student

studiare [stood-y**a**ray] to study

studio m study

studioso [stood-y**o**zo] studious

stufa f heater

stupefacente [stoopayfach**en**tay] astonishing

stupefacenti mpl drugs

stupendo! brilliant!

stupro m rape

su [soo] on; up

sua* [s**oo**-a] his; her(s); its; your(s)

subito [s**oo**beeto] immediately

succedere [sooch**ay**dairay] to happen

sud m south

Sudafrica f South Africa

sudafricano (m), **sudafricana** (f) South African

sudare [sood**a**ray] to sweat

sud-ovest m [sood-**o**vest] south-west

sue* [**soo**-ay] his; her(s); its; your(s)

sul [sool], **sulla, sullo, sui** [**soo**-ee], **sugli** [**sool**-yee], **sulle*** [**sool**-lay] on the

suo* [**soo**-o] his; her(s); its; your(s)

suocera f [sw**o**chaira] mother-in-law

suocero m [sw**o**chairo] father-in-law

suoi* [swoy] his; her(s); its; your(s)

suola f [sw**o**la] sole (of shoe)

suonare [swon**a**ray] to play (instrument); to ring; please ring

superficie f [soopairf**ee**chay] surface; area

supermercato m supermarket

superstrada f motorway/highway without toll

supplementare [soop-plement**a**ray] extra

supplemento 3o letto third bed supplement payable

supplemento rapido [r**a**peedo] supplement for fast train

supporre [soop-p**o**r-ray] to assume

surf m surfboard; surfing

surgelati mpl [soorjel**a**tee] frozen food

surgelato frozen

sussurrare [soos-soor-r**a**ray] to whisper

svedese (m/f) [zved**ay**zay] Swedish; Swede

sveglia f [zv**a**yl-ya] alarm clock

svegliare [zvayl-y**a**ray] to wake

svegliarsi [zvayl-y**a**rsee] to wake up

sveglio [zv**a**yl-yo] alert; awake

svendita f [zv**e**ndeeta] sale

svenire [zven**ee**ray] to faint

Svezia f [zv**e**tzee-a] Sweden

sviluppare [zveeeloop-p**a**ray] to develop

svitato [zveet**a**to] cracked, nutty

Svizzera f [zv**ee**tzaira] Switzerland

svizzero (m), **svizzera** (f) Swiss

svuotare [zvwot**a**ray] to empty

T

T (tabaccheria) tobacconist's

tabaccaio m [tabak-k**a**-yo] tobacconist's

tabaccheria f [tabak-kair**ee**-a] tobacconist's

tabacchi mpl [tabak-kee] tobacco goods

tabacco m tobacco

tabellone m indicator board

taccuino m [tak-kweeno]
notebook

tachimetro m speedometer

taglia f [tal-ya] size

tagliando di controllo m [tal-yando] coupon guaranteeing quality; proof of purchase

tagliare [tal-yaray] to cut

tagliaunghie m [tal-ya-oong-yay] nail clippers

taglio m [tal-yo] cut

taglio di capelli haircut

taglio e cucito [ay koocheeto] dressmaking

talco m talcum powder

tallone m [tal-lonay] heel

tanta a lot; so much

tanti, tante [tantee, tantay] many, lots of

tanti auguri [owgooree] best wishes

tanto a lot; so much

tapparella f blind

tappeto m [tap-payto] carpet

tappezziere m [tap-petz-yairay] decorator; upholsterer

tappo m cap; plug; cork

tardi late

a più tardi [p-yoo] see you later

targa f number plate

tariffa f fare; charge

tariffa interna [eentairna] inland postage

tariffe postali internazionali fpl [tareef-fay – eentairnatz-yonalee] international postage rates

tariffe postali nazionali [natz-yonalee] national postage

rates

tasca f pocket

tassa f tax

tassista m/f taxi driver

tasso di cambio m [kamb-yo] exchange rate

tasso di interesse [eentairessay] interest rate

taverna f inn, tavern

tavola f [tavola] table

tavola a vela [vayla] sailboard

tavola calda snack bar

tavolino m coffee table

tavolo m table

tazza f [tatza] cup

tazzina da caffè f [tatzeena] espresso coffee cup

T.C.I. (Touring Club Italiano) m Italian touring club

te* [tay] you

tè m [tay] tea

teatro m [tay-atro] theatre

teatro lirico opera house

tedesco (m/f) [tedesko] German

TEE m Trans-Europe-Express train

tegame f [tegamay] pan

teglia f [tayl-ya] casserole dish

teiera f [tay-yaira] teapot

telefonare [telefonaray] to phone

telefonata f phone call

telefono m [telayfono] telephone

telefono a gettoni [jet-tonee] phone that takes tokens

telefono a scatti phone which counts time-units

used for which you pay at end of call

telefono a schede [sk**ay**day] cardphone

Telepass® electronic toll charge system on motorway

telo da bagno m [b**an**-yo] bath towel

temperino m penknife

tempesta f storm

tempo m time; weather

tempo libero free time, leisure

tempo limite di accettazione latest check-in time

temporale m [tempor**a**lay] thunderstorm

tenda f curtain; tent

tenere [ten**ay**ray] to hold; to keep

tenere lontano dalla portata dei bambini keep out of the reach of children

tenere rigorosamente la destra keep to the right

tergicristallo m [tairjeekreestal-lo] windscreen wiper

terminare [tairmeen**a**ray] to end

termometro m thermometer

termosifone m [termoseef**o**nay] radiator

terra f earth, soil

terrazzo m [tair-r**a**tzo] (large) balcony; patio

terza f [t**air**tza] third (gear)

terzo (m) third

tessera di abbonamento f season ticket

tesserino m travel card

tessuto m material, fabric

testa f head

testa del treno front of the train

tetto m roof

Tevere m [tev**ai**ray] Tiber

ti* [tee] you; yourself; to you

tiepido [t-y**ay**peedo] lukewarm

tifoso m, tifosa f fan (supporter)

timbro m rubber stamp; postmark

timido shy

tinello m small dining room

tintoria f [teentor**ee**-a] drycleaner's

tirare [teer**a**ray] to pull

tiro m shooting

titolo m title

tizio m [t**ee**tz-yo] bloke, guy

toccare [tok-k**a**ray] to touch

tocca a me [tok-ka a may] this round's on me; it's my turn

togliere [t**o**l-yairay] to take away; to remove

togliersi: togliti! [t**o**l-yeetee] get out of the way!

toilette f [twalet] toilet(s), rest room; dressing table(s)

tonnellata f [ton-nel-l**a**ta] tonne

tonsillite f [tonseel-l**ee**tay] tonsillitis

topo m mouse

torcia elettrica f [t**o**rcha] torch, flashlight

Torino f Turin

tornare [torn**a**ray] to return, to come back

tornare a casa to go home;

to come home

torneo m [tornay-o] tournament, competition

toro m bull

torre f [tor-ray] tower

torrefazione f [tor-refatz-yonay] shop selling coffee

Toscana f Tuscany

tosse f [tos-say] cough

tossire [tos-seeray] to cough

tostapane m [tostapanay] toaster

tostare [tostaray] to toast

tovagliolo m [toval-yolo] serviette

tra among; between

tradizionale [tradeetz-yonalay] traditional

tradurre [tradoor-ray] to translate

traduzione f [tradootz-yonay] translation

traffico m traffic

traghetto m [traget-to] ferry

tragitto m [trajeet-to] route; journey

tramonto m sunset

trampolino m diving board; ski jump; trampoline

tranne [tran-nay] except

tranquillo [trankweel-lo] quiet

transito con catene o pneumatici da neve chains or snow tyres compulsory

tranviere m [tranv-yairay] tram driver

trapano m drill

trapunta f quilt

trascinare [trasheenaray] to

drag

trasferimento bancario m [bankar-yo] bank transfer

trasmissione f [trasmees-yonay] transmission; TV/radio programme

trattoria f [trat-toree-a] restaurant

traversata f crossing (sea)

tre [tray] three

tredici [tray-deechee] thirteen

treni feriali/festivi trains on weekdays/holidays

treno m [trayno] train

treno diretto through train

treno espresso long-distance express train

treno interregionale long-distance, stopping train

treno merci freight train

treno metropolitano city/suburban train

treno regionale local train, stopping at all stations

trenta thirty

tribunale m [treeboonalay] law courts

tricolore m [treekoloray] Italian flag

trimestre m [treemestray] term

triplo triple, treble

triste [treestay] sad

tritatutto m food processor

troppo too; too much

trovare [trovaray] to find

truccarsi to put on one's make-up

trucco m make-up

tu* [too] you

tua* [**too**-a] your(s)

tubo m [**too**bo] pipe

tubo di scappamento exhaust pipe

tue* [**too**-ay] your(s)

tuffarsi to dive

tuffo m dive

tuo [**too**-o], tuoi* [**twoy**] your(s)

tuono m [**two**no] thunder

turismo m [too**ree**zmo] tourism

turista m/f tourist

tuta da ginnastica f [jeen-na**stee**ka] tracksuit

tutta all; everything

  tutta la... all the ...; the whole ...

tuttavia however

tutte [**too**t-tay] all; every; everybody

  tutte le direzioni all routes

  tutte le/tutti i... all the ... every ...

tutti all; every; everybody

  tutti e due [ay d**oo**-ay] both of them

tutto all; everything

  in tutto altogether

  tutto il... all the ...; the whole ...

tutto compreso all inclusive

U

ubriaco drunk

uccello m [oo**chel**-lo] bird

uccidere [oo**chee**dairay] to kill

UE (Unione Europea) f [00-ay] EU (European Union)

ufficio m [oof-**fee**cho] office

ufficio cambi [**kam**bee] bureau de change

ufficio del turismo [too**ree**zmo] tourist office

ufficio di informazioni turistiche [eenformatz-y**o**nee too**ree**steekay] tourist information centre

ufficio informazioni tourist information

ufficio postale [po**sta**lay] post office

ufficio prenotazioni [prenotatz-y**o**nee] reservations

ufficio prenotazioni merci reservations office for goods

ufficio prenotazioni passeggeri reservations office for passengers

ufficio turistico tourist office

uguaglianza f [oogwal-y**a**ntza] equality

uguale [oogw**a**lay] equal, same

ultimo [**oo**lteemo] last

umido [**oo**meedo] wet

umore m [oom**o**ray] mood

umorismo m [oomor**ee**zmo] humour

un, una* [**oo**na] a; one

undici [**oo**n-deechee] eleven

Ungheria f [oongair**ee**-a] Hungary

unghia f [**oo**ng-ya] fingernail

unguento m [oong**wen**to] ointment

unico single

Unione Europea f [oon-y**o**nay ay-

ooro**pay**-a] European Union
unità socio-sanitaria locale f local health centre(s)
università f [ooneevairseeta] university, universities
uno* [**oo**no] a; one
uomini mpl [**wo**meenee] men; gents' (toilet), mens' rest room
uomo m [**wo**mo] man
urlare [oorl**a**ray] to yell
urtare [oort**a**ray] to hit, to knock
usare [ooz**a**ray] to use
uscire [oosh**ee**ray] to go out
  uscire di casa to leave the house
  uscire di nuovo [n**wo**vo] to go/come back out
uscita f [oosh**ee**ta] exit, way out; gate (airport)
uscita automezzi vehicle exit
uscita camion works exit
uscita d'emergenza emergency exit
uscita di sicurezza emergency exit
uscita operai workers' exit
uso e dosi use and dosage
U.S.S.L. (Unità Socio-Sanitaria Locale) f local health centre(s)
utensili da cucina mpl [kooch**ee**na] cooking utensils
utile [**oo**teelay] useful

V

v. (vedi) see
va he/she/it goes; you go
  come va? [**ko**may] how are things?
  va bene! [**bay**nay] that's fine!, it's OK!; that's right
  va' a farti friggere! [free**j**-jairay] go to hell!
  va' a quel paese! [kwel pa-**ay**zay] get lost!
vacanze fpl [vak**a**nzay] holidays, vacation
vacanze di Natale [nat**a**lay] Christmas holidays/vacation
vacanze di Pasqua [**pa**skwa] Easter holidays/vacation
vacanze estive [est**ee**vay] summer holidays/vacation
vaccinazione f [vacheenatz-**yo**nay] vaccination
vaccino m [vach**ee**no] vaccination
vada oltre... [**o**ltray] go past the ...
vado* I go
vaffanculo! fuck off!
vaglia internazionale m [**val**-ya eentairnatz-**yo**nalay] international money order(s)
vaglia postale [post**a**lay] money order(s)
vaglia telegrafico telegram money order(s)
vagone m [vag**o**nay] carriage,

car

vagone bagagliaio [bagal-ya-yo] luggage/baggage van

vagone letto sleeper, sleeping car

vagone ristorante [reestorantay] restaurant car

vai* [va-ee] you go

valanghe [valangay] avalanches

validità f validity

valigia f [valeeja] suitcase
disfare le valigie [deesfaray lay valeejay] to unpack

valle f [val-lay] valley

valore: di valore [dee valoray] valuable

valuta f currency

valvola f [valvola] valve

vanga f spade

vanitoso [vaneetozo] vain

vanno* they go

vaporetto m passenger ferry

varechina f [varaykeena] bleach

variabile [varee-abeelay] changeable

vasca da bagno f [ban-yo] bathtub

vasellame m [vazel-lamay] crockery

vaso m [vazo] vase; pot

vassoio m [vas-soy-o] tray

vattene! [vat-tenay] go away!

vecchia (f) [vek-ya] old; old woman

vecchio (m) old; old man

vedere [vedairay] to see
fare vedere to show
vedere data sul coperchio/sul retro see date on lid/back

vedi foglio illustrativo see illustrated instructions leaflet

vedova f [vaydova] widow

vedovo m widower

vegetariano (m) [vejetar-yano], **vegetariana** (f) vegetarian

veicoli lenti crawler lane

veicolo m [vay-eekolo] vehicle

vela f [vayla] sail; sailing

veleno m [velayno] poison

veliero m [vel-yairo] sailing ship

veloce [velochay] fast

velocemente [velochaymentay] quickly

velocità f [velocheeta] speed

vendere [vendairay] to sell

vendesi for sale

vendita f sale

venerdì m Friday

Venezia f [venetzee-a] Venice

veneziane fpl [venetz-yanay] Venetian blinds

veneziano [venetz-yano] Venetian

vengo* I come

vengono* they come

veniamo* we come

venire* [veneeray] to come

venite* [veneetay] you come

venti twenty

ventilatore m [venteelatoray] fan (electrical)

vento m wind

venuto* come

veramente [vairamentay] really

verde [vairday] green
al verde broke

vernice f [vairn**ee**chay] paint
  vernice fresca wet paint
vero [v**ai**ro] true
vero cuoio [k**wo**-yo] real
  leather
versamenti deposits
versamento (bancario) m
  payment; (bank) giro
versare dei soldi [vairs**a**ray day]
  to pay in money
vescica f [vaysh**ee**ka] bladder;
  blister
vespa f wasp
vestaglia f [vestal-ya] dressing
  gown
vestire [vest**ee**ray] to dress
vestirsi to get dressed
vestito m dress
vetro m glass (material)
vetta f summit, peak
vettura f coach, carriage
VF (Vigili del Fuoco) mpl fire
  brigade
vi* [vee] you; yourselves; to
  you; each other
via (f) [**vee**-a] road, street;
  way; away
via aerea f [a-**ai**ray-a] airmail
viacard® f motorway/
  highway magnetic card
viaggiare [v-yaj-j**a**ray] to travel
viaggio m [v-y**a**j-jo] journey,
  trip; tour
  fare un viaggio to go on a
  journey
viaggio d'affari business trip
viaggio organizzato
  [organeedz**a**to] package tour
viale m [vee-**a**lay] avenue,

boulevard
vialetto m [v-yal**e**t-to] path
vicino m [veech**ee**no], **vicina** f
  neighbour
vicino (a) near; nearby
vicolo m alleyway
vicolo cieco [ch**ay**ko] cul-de-
  sac; dead end
videoregistratore m [veeday-o-
  rejeestrat**o**ray] video recorder
viene* [v-y**ay**nay] he/she/it
  comes; you come
vieni* [v-y**ay**nee] you come
vietato [v-yayt**a**to] forbidden
vietato accendere fuochi no
  campfires
vietato ai minori di 14 anni no
  admittance to children
  under 14
vietato attraversare i binari do
  not cross the tracks
vietato bagnarsi no bathing
vietato campeggiare no
  camping
vietato entrare no entry
vietato fumare no smoking
**vietato gettare oggetti dal
  finestrino** do not throw
  objects out of the window
vietato l'ingresso no entry;
  no admittance
**vietato l'uso dell'ascensore ai
  minori di anni 12 non
  accompagnati**
  unaccompanied children
  under 12 must not use the
  lift/elevator
vietato pescare no fishing
vietato sporgersi dal finestrino

Vi

do not lean out of the
window
vietato sputare no spitting
vietato tuffarsi no diving
**vietato usare la toilette
durante le fermate e nelle
stazioni** do not use the
toilet/rest room when the
train has stopped or is in
the station
vigili del fuoco mpl [veejeelee
del f**wo**ko] fire brigade
vigili urbani mpl traffic police
vigna f [veen-ya] vineyard
villaggio m [veel-laj-jo] village
villetta f small detached
house
vincere [veenchairay] to win
vincitore m [veencheeto**ray]
winner
vincitrice f [veencheetree**chay]**
winner
viola [v-yo**la]** purple
violenza f [v-yole**ntza]** violence
visita f [veezeeta] visit
visita guidata [gweed**a**ta]
guided tour
visitare [veezeeta**ray]** to visit
vista f view
visto m visa
vita f life; waist
vitamine fpl vitamins
vitaminico vitamin
(-enriched)
vite f [veetay] screw
vivere [veevairay] to live
vivo alive
v.le (viale) m avenue
voce f [vochay] voice

voglia: ho voglia di... [o v**o**l-ya]
I feel like ...
vogliamo* [vol-ya**mo]** we want
voglio* [vol-yo] I want
vogliono* [vol-yono] they want
voi* [voy] you
volante m [vola**ntay]** steering
wheel
volare [vola**ray]** to fly
voler dire [deeray] to mean
volere* (m) [vola**iray]** to want;
will, wish
volete* [vola**ytay]** you want
volgare [volga**ray]** coarse
voli internazionali mpl
[eentairnatz-yon**a**lee]
international flights
voli nazionali [natz-yona**lee]**
domestic flights
volo m flight
volo a vela [va**yla]** gliding
volo di linea [leenay-a]
scheduled flight
volo diretto direct flight
volta f time
qualche volta [kw**a**lkay]
sometimes
una volta once
una volta scongelato il
prodotto non deve essere
ricongelato do not refreeze
once thawed
voltarsi to turn round
volutamente [voloota**mentay]**
deliberately
voluto* wanted
vomitare [vomeeta**ray]** to
vomit, to be sick
vorrei [vor-ray] I would like

vostro, vostra, vostri, vostre* [**vo**stray] your(s)

vs. (vostro) your(s)

vulcano m [voolk**a**no] volcano

vuoi* [vwoy] you want

vuole* [vw**o**lay] he/she/it wants; you want

  vuole...? [vw**o**lay] do you want ...?

vuotare [vwot**a**ray] to empty

vuoto [vw**o**to] empty

vuoto a perdere no deposit (on bottle)

vuoto a rendere returnable (bottle)

W

W (viva...!) long live ...!

water m [vat**air**] W.C.

windsurf m windsurfing; windsurfing board

Z

zaino m [dz**a**-eeno] rucksack

zanzara f [dzandz**a**ra] mosquito

zerbino m [dzairb**ee**no] doormat

zia f [t**zee**-a] aunt

zio m uncle

zitto [t**zee**t-to] quiet; silent

  zitto! shut up!

zona f [dz**o**na] area

zona a traffico limitato restricted traffic area

zona disco parking discs only

zona pedonale pedestrian precinct

Menu
Reader
Food

abbacchio alla romana [ab-**bak**-yo] spring lamb

acciughe [ach**oo**gay] anchovies

acciughe sott'olio [sot-t**ol**-yo] anchovies in oil

aceto [ach**e**to] vinegar

affettato misto variety of cold, sliced meats such as salami, ham etc

affogato al caffè [kaf-**fay**] ice cream with hot espresso poured over it

affumicato smoked

aglio [**al**-yo] garlic

agnello [an-**yel**-lo] lamb

agnello al forno roast lamb

agnolotti al burro e salvia [an-yol**ot**-tee – ay **salv**-ya] meat-filled pasta shapes served with butter and sage

agoni alla graticola grilled long, narrow fish from Lake Como

albicocca apricot

alloro laurel

anacardi cashew nuts

ananas pineapple

ananas al maraschino [marask**ee**no] pineapple with sweet liqueur

anatra duck

anatra all'arancia [ar**anch**a] duck à l'orange

anello di riso e piselli rice and peas cooked in a ring-shaped mould

anguilla al forno [ang**wee**l-la] baked eel

anguria water melon

antipasti starters, hors d'oeuvres

antipasti caldi hot starters

antipasti freddi cold starters

antipasti misti variety of starters

antipasti misti toscani croutons with liver pâté, salami and cured ham

antipasto di pesce assortito [**pe**shay] mixed seafood starter

arachidi [ar**a**keedee] peanuts

aragosta spiny lobster

arancia [ar**anch**a] orange

arancini [aranch**ee**nee] fried rice balls

aringa herring

arista di maiale al forno [my-**a**lay] roast chine of pork

arrosto roast

asiago [az-**ya**go] full-fat white cheese

asparagi [aspara**jee**] asparagus

astice [**a**steechay] lobster

avocado all'agro avocado pears with oil, lemon and vinegar dressing

baccalà dried cod

baccalà alla vicentina [veechent**ee**na] dried salted cod cooked with onions, olive oil, milk, anchovies, parsley and parmesan and served with polenta

bagnacauda [ban-yak**ow**da] vegetables, usually raw in an oil, garlic and anchovy sauce

barbabietole [barbab-**ay**tolay] beetroot

basilico [baz**ee**leeko] basil

bastoncini di pesce [bastonch**ee**nee dee p**e**shay] fish fingers

bavarese [bavar**ay**zay] (ice-cream) cake with cream

Bel Paese [pa-**ay**zay] soft, full-fat white cheese

besciamella [besham**e**l-la] béchamel sauce, white sauce

bignè [been-y**ay**] cream puff

biscotti e verduzzo [ay vaird**oo**tzo] home-made biscuits served with a glass of dry white wine

biscotto biscuit

bistecca steak

bistecca alla fiorentina [f-yorent**ee**na] large charcoal-grilled beef steak

bistecca di manzo [m**a**ndzo] beef steak

bistecca di cavallo horsemeat steak

bocconcini di manzo e vitello [bok-konch**ee**nee dee m**a**ndzo ay] chopped beef and veal

bollito boiled

bollito misto assorted boiled meats with vegetables

bomba ice cream bombe; doughnut

bombolone [bombol**o**nay] doughnut

bra full-fat white cheese

braciola di maiale [brach**o**la dee my-**a**lay] pork chop

branzino al forno [brantz**ee**no] baked sea bass

brasato [braz**a**to] braised; braised beef with herbs

brasato al Barolo braised beef cooked in Barolo wine

bresaola [br**e**za-ola] dried, salted beef sliced thinly and eaten cold

brioche [bree-**o**sh] croissant

broccoletti all'aglio [al-lal-yo] broccoli cooked in garlic

brodetto fish casserole

brodo clear broth

brodo di pollo chicken broth

brodo vegetale [vejayt**a**lay] clear, vegetable broth

bruschetta alla romana [broosk**e**t-ta] toasted bread rubbed with garlic and sprinkled with olive oil

bucatini al pomodoro pasta similar to spaghetti (only thicker and with a hole through it) with tomato sauce

budino pudding

burro butter

caciotta [kach**o**t-ta] type of creamy, white, medium-soft cheese

caciotta toscana slightly mature, medium-soft cheese from Tuscany

caciucco alla livornese [kach**oo**k-ko **a**l-la leevorn**ay**zay] soup made from seafood, tomato and wine served with home-made bread

calamari fritti fried squid

calamari in umido stewed squid

calamaro squid

calzone [kaltz**o**nay] folded pizza with tomato and mozzarella or ricotta and ham, or other fillings inside

calzone all'amalfitana calzone with cottage cheese, egg, ham and grana cheese

canestrato hard ewes milk cheese

cannella cinnamon

cannelloni al forno rolls of pasta filled with meat and baked in a sauce

cannoli alla siciliana [seecheel-**y**ana] cylindrical pastries filled with ricotta and candied fruit

cannoncini alla crema [kan-non**ch**e**e**nee] cylindrical pastries filled with custard

cantuccini [kantooch**ee**nee] almond biscuits

caponata di melanzane [melandz**a**nay] fried aubergines/eggplants and celery cooked with tomato, capers and olives

cappelle di funghi porcini alla griglia [kap-p**e**l-lay dee f**oo**ngee porch**ee**nee **a**l-la gr**ee**l-ya] grilled boletus mushroom tops

cappelletti small, filled pasta parcels

capperi capers

cappone lesso [kap-p**o**nay]

boiled capon

capretto al forno roast kid

caprino fresh, soft goat's cheese

capriolo in salmi roe deer venison in game sauce

caramella sweet

carciofi [karch**o**fee] artichokes

carciofini sott'olio [karcho-**fee**nee sot-t**o**l-yo] baby artichokes preserved in oil

carne [**ka**rnay] meat

carne macinata [macheen**a**ta] minced meat

carote [kar**o**tay] carrots

carpaccio [karp**a**cho] finely sliced raw beef fillets with oil, lemon and grated Parmesan

carré di maiale al forno [kar-r**ay** dee my-**a**lay] roast loin of pork

carrello dei dolci [dolch**ee**] dessert trolley

cassata siciliana [seecheel-**y**ana] Sicilian ice-cream cake with candied fruit, chocolate and ricotta

castagnaccio alla toscana [kastan-y**a**cho] tart from Tuscany made with chestnut flour

castagne [kastan-**y**ay] chestnuts

catalogna [katal**o**n-ya] type of chicory with large leaves

cavoletti di Bruxelles [br**oo**ks**e**l] Brussels sprouts

cavolfiore [kavolf-**yo**ray] cauliflower

cavolo cabbage

cavolo rosso red cabbage

cazzuola alla milanese [katzwola al-la meelanayzay] spicy pork sausage, pork and beans stewed in gravy

ceci [chaychee] chickpeas

cefalo [chefalo] mullet

cernia [chairn-ya] grouper (fish)

cervella al burro [chairvel-la] brains cooked in butter

cetriolo [chetree-olo] cucumber

charlotte [sharlot] ice-cream cake with cream, biscuits and fruit

chiacchiere [k-yak-yairay] sweet pastries fried in lard and sprinkled with fine sugar

chiodi di garofano [k-yodee] cloves

ciambella [chambel-la] ring-shaped cake

cicoria [cheekoree-a] chicory

cicorino [cheekoreeno] small chicory plants

ciliege [cheel-yay-jay] cherries

cima alla piemontese [cheema al-la p-yaymontayzay] baked veal stuffed with chicken and chopped vegetables, served cold

cime di rapa [cheemay] young leaves of turnip plant

cinghiale in salmì [cheeng-yalay] wild boar in game sauce

cioccolata [chok-kolata] chocolate

cioccolata al latte [lat-tay] milk chocolate

cioccolata fondente [fondentay] plain chocolate

cioccolato [chok-kolato] chocolate

cipolle [cheepol-lay] onions

cocktail di gamberetti prawn cocktail

coda alla vaccinara [vacheenara] oxtail diced and stewed with vegetables

colomba pasquale [paskwalay] dove-shaped cake with candied fruit eaten at Easter

conchiglie alla marchigiana [konkeel-yay al-la markeejana] pasta shells in tomato sauce with celery, carrot, parsley and ham

condimento per l'insalata salad dressing

coniglio [koneel-yo] rabbit

coniglio in salmì rabbit in game sauce

cono gelato [jelato] ice-cream cone

contorni vegetable side dishes

coperto cover charge (usually includes bread)

coperto pane e grissini cover charge includes bread and breadsticks

coppa cured neck of pork, finely sliced and eaten cold

cornetto croissant

cosciotto di agnello al forno [koshot-to dee an-yel-lo] baked leg of lamb

costata alla fiorentina [f-yorenteena] Florentine

entrecôte

costata (di manzo) [mandzo] beef entrecôte

costoletta chop

costoletta di vitello alla griglia [greel-ya] grilled veal chop

cotechino [kotekeeno] spiced pork sausage, usually boiled

cotoletta veal cutlet

cotoletta alla milanese [meelanayzay] veal escalope in breadcrumbs

cotoletta alla valdostana veal chop with ham and cheese cooked in breadcrumbs

cotolette di agnello [an-yel-lo] lamb chops

cotolette di maiale [kotolet-tay dee my-alay] pork chops

cotto cooked

cozze [kotzay] mussels

cozze alla marinara mussels in marinade sauce

crauti [krowtee] white cabbage cut in strips, cooked in vinegar and white wine

crema [krayma] custard

crema al caffè [kaf-fay] coffee custard pudding

crema al cioccolato [chok-kolato] chocolate custard pudding

crema alla vaniglia [vaneel-ya] vanilla-flavoured custard pudding

crema di ... cream of ... soup

crema pasticciera [pasteechaira] confectioner's custard

crêpe [krep] pancake

crêpe suzette flambéed pancake with orange sauce

crescente [kreshentay] type of flat, fried Emilian bread

crescenza [kreshentza] soft, creamy white cheese

crescione [kreshonay] watercress

crespelle [krespel-lay] savoury pancakes

crocchette di patate [krok-kettay dee patatay] potato croquettes

crocchette di pesce [peshay] fish croquettes

crocchette di riso rice croquettes

crostata casalinga [cazaleenga] home-made lattice pie with jam or custard

crostata di frutta fruit tart

crostata di mele [maylay] apple pie

crostini ai funghi [a-ee foongee] croutons with mushrooms cooked in oil with garlic and parsley

crostini toscani croutons with liver pâté

crostoni di mozzarella [dee motzarel-la] mozzarella and tomato sauce served hot on home-made bread

crudo raw

dadi stock cubes

datteri dates

dentice al forno [denteechay] baked dentex (type of sea bream) dolce [do**l**chay] dessert

dolci [do**l**chee] cakes, gâteaux, desserts etc

dolci della casa home-made cakes

endivia belga [end**ee**v-ya] Belgian endive

entrecôte (di manzo) [ma**n**dzo] beef entrecôte

erbe aromatiche [**ai**rbay aroma**te**ekay] herbs

fagiano [fa**j**ano] pheasant

fagioli [fa**j**olee] beans

fagioli alla messicana type of chili con carne

fagioli all'olio [al-lo**l**-yo] beans with salt, pepper, oil and vinegar

fagioli borlotti in umido fresh borlotti beans cooked in vegetables, herbs and tomato sauce

fagiolini [fajol**ee**nee] green beans

fagiolini lessi [**l**es-see] boiled French beans

faraona [fara-**o**na] guinea fowl

farina flour

fatto in casa [**k**aza] home-made

fegatini di pollo chicken livers

fegato [**f**aygato] liver

fegato alla veneta [ven**ay**ta] liver cooked in butter with onions

ferri: ai ferri [**a**-ee] grilled

fetta biscottata slices of crispy toast-like bread

fettuccine [fet-tooch**ee**nay] ribbon-shaped pasta

fichi [**fee**kee] figs

filetti di merluzzo [mairl**oo**tzo] fillets of cod

filetti di pesce persico [**p**eshay **p**airseeko] fillets of perch

filetto fillet

filetto ai ferri [**a**-ee] grilled fillet of beef

filetto al cognac fillet of beef in cognac

filetto al pepe verde [**pay**pay **v**airday] fillet of beef with green pepper

filetto al sangue [**s**angway] rare fillet of beef

filetto a media cottura [**may**d-ya] medium-done fillet beef

filetto ben cotto well-done fillet of beef

filetto di manzo [ma**n**dzo] fillet of beef

filone (di pane) [feel**o**nay dee **p**anay] large French stick

finocchi gratinati [feen**o**k-kee] fennel with melted grated cheese

finocchio [feen**o**k-yo] fennel

fiori di zucca fritti [f-y**o**ree dee tz**oo**k-ka] fried pumpkin flowers

flan di spinaci [speen**a**chee] spinach flan

focaccia [fok**a**cha] flat bread sprinkled with olive oil and baked or grilled

foglie di vite alla greca [fol-yay dee v**ee**tay] Greek-style vine leaves

fondue Bourguignonne
[boorgeen-**yon**] cubes of fillet
steak fried in oil and dipped
in various sauces

fonduta fondue made with
cheese, milk and eggs

fontina soft, mature cheese
often used in cooking

formaggi misti [form**a**j-jee]
selection of cheeses

formaggio [form**a**j-jo] cheese

forno: al forno roast

fragole [fr**a**golay] strawberries

fricassea di coniglio [freekas-
say-a dee kon**ee**l-yo] chopped
rabbit cooked in butter and
aromatic herbs

frico e polenta [ay] fried
latteria cheese with polenta

frittata type of omelette

frittelle di banane [freet**e**l-lay dee
ban**a**nay] banana fritters

frittelle di mele [m**a**ylay] apple
fritters

fritto fried

fritto misto mixed seafood in
batter

frittura di pesce [p**e**shay]
variety of fried fish

frutta fruit

frutta alla fiamma [f-y**a**m-ma]
flambéd fruit

frutta fresca di stagione
[staj**o**nay] seasonal fruit

frutta secca dried fruit; nuts

frutti di bosco mixture of
forest fruits

frutti di mare [m**a**ray] seafood

frutti di mare gratinati seafood

au gratin

funghi [f**oo**ngee] mushrooms

funghi porcini [porch**ee**nee]
boletus mushrooms

funghi trifolati mushrooms
fried in garlic and parsley

fusilli al pomodoro [fooz**ee**l-lee]
pasta twirls with tomato
sauce

galantina di pollo chicken
with spices and herbs served
in gelatine

gallina chicken

gamberetti shrimps

gamberetti in salsa rosa [r**o**za]
shrimps in mayonnaise and
ketchup sauce

gamberi crayfish; prawns

gamberoni king prawns

gelatina [jelat**ee**na] gelatine

gelato [jel**a**to] ice cream

gelato di crema vanilla ice
cream

gelato di frutta fruit-flavoured
ice cream

ghiacciolo [g-yach**o**lo] ice lolly

giardiniera di verdure [jardeen-
yaira dee vaird**oo**ray] diced,
mixed vegetables, cooked
and pickled

gnocchetti verdi [n-yok-k**e**t-tee
v**ai**rdee] small flour, potato
and spinach dumplings
sometimes served with
melted gorgonzola

gnocchi [n-yok-kee] small flour
and potato dumplings

gnocchi ai formaggi [a-ee
form**a**j-jee] potato dumplings

with gorgonzola, fontina, mascarpone and Parmesan

gnocchi alla romana small semolina dumplings baked in butter

gnocchi al ragù dumplings with minced meat and tomato sauce

gorgonzola strong, soft blue cheese from Lombardy or Piedmont

grana generic name of cheeses similar to Parmesan

grana padano cheese similar to Parmesan

grancevola [granchayvola] spiny spider crab

granchio [grank-yo] crab

grasso fat

gratin di patate [grateen dee patatay] potatoes with grated cheese

griglia: alla griglia [al-la greel-ya] grilled

grigliata di pesce [greel-yata di peshay] grilled fish

grigliata mista mixed grill (meat or fish)

grissini breadsticks

gruviera [groov-yaira] Gruyère cheese

gulash ungherese [oongarayzay] Hungarian goulash

impanato breaded, in breadcrumbs

indivia [eendeev-ya] endive

insalata salad

insalata caprese [kaprayzay] sliced tomatoes, mozzarella

and oregano

insalata di carne [karnay] meat salad

insalata di mare [maray] seafood salad

insalata di nervetti sinewy, chopped boiled beef or veal, served cold with beans and pickles

insalata mista mixed salad

insalata russa Russian salad

insalata verde [vairday] green salad

involtini small beef olives

involtini di prosciutto [pro-shoot-to] small rolls of sliced ham filled with Russian salad

krapfen doughnut

lamponi raspberries

lardo al pepe [paypay] fatty ham with pepper

lasagne al forno [lazan-yay] lasagne

latteria [lat-tairee-a] full-fat white cheese

lattuga lettuce

legumi pulses

lenticchie [lenteek-yay] lentils

lepre [lepray] hare

lesso boiled

limone [leemonay] lemon

lingua [leengwa] tongue

lingua salmistrata ox tongue marinaded in brine and then cooked

linguine al pesto [leengweenay] kind of flat spaghetti with crushed basil, garlic, oil and

Parmesan dressing
lombatina di vitella ai ferri
[**a**-ee] grilled loin of veal
lonza di maiale al latte [l**o**ntza
dee my-**a**lay al l**a**t-tay] pork loin
cooked in milk
maccheroni alla siciliana [mak-
kair**o**nee **a**l-la seecheel-y**a**na]
macaroni with tomato sauce
and grated Sicilian ricotta
cheese
maccheroni al ragù macaroni
in a minced beef and
tomato sauce
macedonia di frutta [mached**o**n-
ya] fruit salad
macedonia di frutta al
maraschino [mara-sk**ee**no]
fruit salad in Maraschino
liqueur
maggiorana [maj-jor**a**na]
marjoram
maiale [my-**a**lay] pork
maionese [my-on**ay**zay]
mayonnaise
mandarancio [mandar**a**ncho]
clementine
mandorle [m**a**ndorlay] almonds
mantovana almond cake
from Prato
manzo [m**a**ndzo] beef
marinato marinated, soused,
pickled
marmellata jam
marmellata d'arance
[dar**a**nchay] marmalade
marroni chestnuts
marzapane [martzap**a**nay]
marzipan

mascarpone [maskarp**o**nay]
full-fat, cream cheese, often
used in desserts
medaglioni di vitello [medal-
y**o**nee] round pieces of veal
mela [m**a**yla] apple
mela flambé flambéd apple
melanzane [melandz**a**nay]
aubergines/eggplants
melanzane alla piastra [p-
y**a**stra] grilled
aubergines/eggplants
melanzane alla siciliana
[seecheel-y**a**na] baked
aubergine/eggplant slices
with parmesan, tomato
sauce and egg
melone [mel**o**nay] melon
melone al porto melon with
port
menta mint
menu fisso set menu
menu turistico tourist menu
meringata meringue pie
meringhe con panna
[mair**ee**ngay] meringues with
cream
merluzzo [mairl**oo**tzo] cod
merluzzo alla pizzaiola [peetza-
y**o**la] cod in tomato sauce
with anchovies, capers and
parsley
merluzzo in bianco [b-y**a**nko]
boiled cod with oil and
lemon
messicani in gelatina
[jelat**ee**na] rolls of veal in
gelatine
miele [m-y**ay**lay] honey

millefoglie [meel-lefol-yay] custard slice

minestra di orzo [ortzo] barley soup

minestra di riso e prezzemolo (in brodo) [pretzaymolo] parsley and rice soup

minestra di verdure [vairdooray] vegetable soup

minestra in brodo soup with vegetables and pasta or rice

minestre [meenestray] soups

minestrone [meenestronay] thick vegetable broth with rice or thin pasta

mirtilli [meerteel-lee] bilberries

montasio [montaz-yo] full-fat white cheese

Montebianco [monteb-yanko] pureed chestnut and whipped cream pudding

more [moray] mulberries, blackberries

mortadella large, mild-flavoured cured sausage, usually served in thin slices

mostarda di Cremona preserve made from candied fruit in grape must or sugar with mustard

mousse al cioccolato [chok-kolato] chocolate mousse

mozzarella [motzarel-la] white, mild, slightly rubbery buffalo milk cheese

mozzarella in carrozza [een kar-rotza] slices of bread and mozzarella coated in flour and fried

nasello [nazel-lo] hake

naturale: al naturale [natooralay] plain, natural

nervetti con cipolla [cheepol-la] chopped, sinewy beef and veal with onions

nocciole [nocholay] hazelnuts

noccioline [nocholeenay] peanuts

noce di cocco [nochay] coconut

noce di vitello ai funghi [a-ee foongee] veal with mushrooms

noce moscata nutmeg

noci [nochee] walnuts

nodino veal chop

oca goose

olio [ol-yo] oil

olio di semi [saymee] vegetable oil

olio d'oliva olive oil

oliva olive

omelette omelette

orata al forno baked gilthead (fish)

orecchiette al sugo (di pomodoro) [orek-yet-tay] small pasta shells with tomato sauce

orecchiette con cime di rapa [cheemay] orecchiette with turnip tops

origano oregano

orzo [ordzo] barley

ossobuco stewed shin of veal

ostriche [ostreekay] oysters

paglia e fieno [pal-ya ay f-yayno] mixture of ordinary and

green tagliatelle

pagnotta [pan-**y**ot-ta] round loaf

paillard di manzo [pa-**ya**r dee m**a**ndzo] slices of grilled beef

paillard di vitello slices of grilled veal

pancetta [panch**e**t-ta] bacon

pancotto stale bread cooked with tomatoes etc

pan di Spagna [sp**a**n-ya] sponge cake

pandoro kind of sponge cake eaten at Christmas

pane [p**a**nay] bread

pane bianco [b-**ya**nko] white bread

pane integrale [eentegr**a**lay] wholemeal bread

pane tostato toast

pane casereccio [kazair**e**cho] home-made bread

pane di segale [**sa**ygalay] rye bread

pane e coperto cover charge including bread

pane in cassetta sliced bread

pane nero [n**a**iro] wholemeal bread

panettone [panet-t**o**nay] dome-shaped cake with sultanas and candied fruit eaten at Christmas

panforte [panf**o**rtay] nougat-type spiced delicacy from Siena

panini sandwiches; filled rolls

panna cream

panna cotta kind of pudding

typical of Tuscany

panna montata whipped cream

panna per cucinare [pair koocheen**a**ray] cream for cooking

panzanella [pantzan**e**l-la] Tuscan dish of bread with fresh tomatoes, onions basil and olive oil

papaia [pap**a**-ya] papaw, papaya

pappa col pomodoro tomato soup with toasted home-made bread typical of Tuscany

parmigiana di melanzane [parmeej**a**na dee meland**za**nay] baked dish of layers of aubergines/eggplants, tomato sauce, mozzarella and Parmesan

parmigiano reggiano [parmeej**a**no rej-j**a**no] Parmesan cheese

passato di patate [pat**a**tay] cream of potato soup

passato di verdure [vaird**oo**ray] cream of vegetable soup

pasta pasta; cake; pastry

pasta al forno pasta baked in white sauce with grated cheese

pasta alla frutta fruit pastry

pasta e fagioli [ay faj**o**lee] very thick soup with blended borlotti beans and small pasta

pasta e piselli pasta with peas

pasticcino [pasteecheeno] small cake

pasticcio di fegato d'oca [pasteecho dee faygato] baked, pasta-covered dish with goose liver

pasticcio di lepre [lepray] baked, pasta-covered dish with hare

pasticcio di maccheroni [makkaironee] baked macaroni

pastiera napoletana [past-yaira] flaky pastry with wheat, ricotta and candied fruit

pastina in brodo noodle soup

patate [patatay] potatoes

patate al forno baked potatoes

patate arrosto roast potatoes

patate fritte [freet-tay] chips, French fries

patate in insalata potato salad

patate prezzemolate [pretzemolatay] boiled potatoes with oil and parsley

patate saltate [saltatay] sautéed potatoes

patatine [patateenay] crisps, (US) potato chips

patatine fritte [freet-tay] chips, French fries

pâté di carne [karnay] pâté

pâté di fegato [faygato] liver pâté

pâté di pesce [peshay] fish pâté

pecorino strong, hard ewe's milk cheese

pecorino sardo hard, mature Sardinian ewes cheese

pelati peeled tinned tomatoes

penne [pen-nay] pasta quills

penne ai quattro formaggi [a-ee kwat-tro formaj-jee] penne with sauce made from four cheeses

penne all'arrabbiata [ar-rabyata] penne with tomato and chili pepper sauce

penne rigate [reegatay] penne with ridges

pepe [paypay] pepper (spice)

peperonata peppers cooked in olive oil with onion, tomato and garlic

peperoncino [pepaironcheeno] chilli pepper

peperone [pepaironay] pepper (vegetable)

peperoni ripieni (di carne) [reep-yaynee dee karnay] stuffed peppers (filled with meat)

peperoni sott'olio [sot-tol-yo] peppers in oil

pera [paira] pear

pernice [pairneechay] partridge

pernice alla cacciatora [kachatora] stewed spiced partridge

pesca [peska] peach

pesce [peshay] fish

pesce al cartoccio [kartocho] fish baked in foil with herbs

pesce in carpione [karp-yonay] soused fish

pesce spada swordfish

pesche sciroppate [peskay sheerop-patay] peaches in

syrup

petti di pollo alla bolognese [bolon-**yay**zay] chicken breasts in breadcrumbs with tomato sauce

petti di pollo impanati chicken breasts in breadcrumbs

piatti di carne [p-**yat**-tee dee **ka**rnay] meat dishes

piatti di pesce [**pe**shay] fish dishes

piatto unico freddo [p-**yat**-to] cold sliced meat with pickles

piccata di vitello al limone [**lee**monay] veal in sour lemon sauce

piccione [peech**o**nay] pigeon

piccione arrosto roast pigeon

piedini di maiale [p-yayd**ee**nee dee my-**a**lay] pigs' trotters

pinoli pine nuts

pinzimonio [peentzeem**o**n-yo] selection of whole, raw vegetables eaten with oil and vinegar dressing

piselli peas

piselli al prosciutto [prosh**oo**t-to] fresh peas cooked in clear broth, with butter, ham and basil

pistacchi [peest**a**k-kee] pistachios

pizza ai porcini [porch**ee**nee] pizza with boletus mushrooms

pizza ai quattro formaggi [**kwa**t-tro form**a**j-jee] pizza with four cheeses – mozzarella,

gorgonzola, latteria, grana

pizza agli asparagi [**a**l-yee asp**a**rajee] asparagus pizza

pizza alla diavola [d-**ya**vola] pizza with spicy salami

pizza alla marinara pizza with tomato, oregano, garlic and anchovies

pizza alla zingara [tz**ee**ngara] pizza with aubergines/ eggplants, peppers, mushrooms and olives

pizza al S. Daniele [san dan-**yay**lay] pizza with cured ham

pizza campagnola [kampan-**yo**la] pizza with mushrooms and peppers

pizza capricciosa [kapreech**o**sa] pizza with tomato, ham, mushrooms and artichokes

pizzaiola [peetza-ee-**o**la] slices of cooked beef in tomato sauce, oregano and anchovies

pizza Margherita [margair**ee**ta] pizza with tomato and mozzarella

pizza napoletana pizza with tomato, mozzarella and anchovies

pizza nordica pizza with chopped salami and frankfurters

pizza orchidea [orkeed**ay**-a] pizza with peppers and egg

pizza pugliese [pool-**ya**zay] tomato and onion pizza

pizza quattro stagioni [staj**o**nee] pizza with ham,

mushrooms, artichokes and anchovies

pizza romana pizza with tomato, mozzarella, anchovies and oregano

pizza siciliana [seecheel-yana] pizza with anchovies, capers, olives and oregano

pizzetta [peetzet-ta] small pizza

pizzoccheri alla Valtellinese [peetzok-kairee al-la valtelleenayzay] thin, pasta strips with green vegetables, melted butter and cheese

polenta yellow cornmeal porridge, left to set and cut in slices, can be fried or baked

polenta concia [koncha] sliced polenta baked with garlic, cheese and butter

polenta e osei [ozay-ee] small birds served with polenta

polenta e uccellini [oo-chelleenee] small birds served with polenta

polenta fritta fried polenta

polenta pasticciata [pasteechata] layers of polenta, tomato sauce and cheese

pollame [pol-lamay] poultry

pollo chicken

pollo alla cacciatora [kachatora] chicken chasseur – pieces of fried chicken in a white wine and mushroom sauce

pollo alla diavola [dee-avola] chicken pieces pressed and

fried

polpette [polpet-tay] meatballs

polpettone [polpet-tonay] meatloaf

polpi alla veneziana [venetzyana] chopped boiled octopus, seasoned with garlic, lemon juice and parsley

polpo octopus

pomodori tomatoes

pomodori alla maionese [my-onay-zay] tomatoes with mayonnaise

pomodori pelati peeled tinned tomatoes

pomodori ripieni di riso [reep-yaynee] tomatoes stuffed with rice

pomodoro tomato

pompelmo grapefruit

porchetta [porket-ta] roast sucking pig

porchetta allo spiedo [sp-yaydo] sucking pig on the spit

porro leek

portata course (of meal)

prezzemolo [pretzaymolo] parsley

primi piatti [p-yat-tee] first courses

prosciutto [proshoot-to] ham

prosciutto al madera ham with madeira

prosciutto cotto cooked ham

prosciutto crudo dry-cured ham

prosciutto crudo di S. Daniele

[san dan-yaylay] finest quality prosciutto crudo from S. Daniele

prosciutto di Praga type of dry-cured ham

provolone [provolonay] oval-shaped cheese, with a slight smoked and spicy flavour

prugne [proon-yay] plums

punte di asparagi all'agro [poontay dee asparajee] asparagus tips in oil and lemon dressing

purè di patate [pooray dee patatay] creamed potatoes

quaglie [kwal-yay] quails

radicchio [radeek-yo] chicory

ragù sauce made with minced beef and tomatoes

rapa type of white turnip with flavour similar to radish

ravanelli radishes

ravioli egg pasta filled with meat or cheese

ravioli al pomodoro ravioli in tomato sauce

razza [ratza] skate

resta di Como speciality of Como, pastry rolled around a stick and baked

ribollita vegetable soup with toasted home-made bread, typical of Tuscany

ricotta soft white cheese, similar to cottage cheese

ricotta piemontese [p-yay-montayzay] similar to ricotta romana

ricotta romana soft, white cheese often used in desserts

ricotta siciliana [seecheel-yana] slightly mature and salty ricotta

rigatoni al pomodoro short, ridged pasta shapes with tomato sauce

ripieno [reep-yayno] stuffed

risi e bisi risotto with peas and small pieces of ham

riso rice

riso alla greca boiled rice with olives, cheese and tomato

riso in brodo rice in clear broth

riso pilaf rice cooked slowly in the oven with butter and onion

risotto rice simmered slowly in clear broth

risotto al Barolo risotto with Barolo wine

risotto alla castellana risotto with mushroom, ham, cream and cheese sauce

risotto alla marinara seafood risotto

risotto alla milanese (allo zafferano) [meelanayzay al-lo tzaf-fairano] risotto with saffron

risotto al nero di seppia [nairo dee sep-ya] risotto with cuttlefish ink

risotto al salto sautéed saffron risotto

risotto con la salsiccia

[salseecha] risotto with pork sausage

roast-beef all'inglese [eenglayzay] thin slices of roast beef served cold with lemon

robiola [rob-yola] soft cheese from Lombardy

rognone trifolato [ron-yonaÿ] small pieces of kidney in garlic, oil and parsley

rombo turbot

rosetta kind of roll

rosmarino rosemary

rucola rocket

Saint-Honoré [santonoray] tart with soft, pastry base and small cream éclairs

salame [salamay] salami

salame di cioccolato [dee chok-kolato] mixture of broken biscuits and chocolate in the shape of a salami

salatini [salateenee] tiny salted crackers, crisps and peanuts (eaten with aperitifs)

sale [salay] salt

salmone [salmonay] salmon

salsa sauce

salsa cocktail mayonnaise and ketchup sauce, served with fish and seafood

salsa di pomodoro tomato sauce

salsa tartara tartar sauce

salsa vellutata white sauce made with clear broth instead of milk

salsa verde [vairday] sauce made from chopped parsley, anchovies and oil, served with meat

salsiccia [salseecha] sausage

saltimbocca alla romana slices of veal rolled up with ham and sage and fried

salvia [salv-ya] sage

sangue: al sangue [sangway] rare

sarago [sarago] white bream

sarde ai ferri [sarday a-ee] grilled sardines

scaloppine [skalop-peenay] veal escalopes

scaloppine al Marsala veal escalopes in Marsala

scamorza affumicata [skamortza] smoked, soft, oval-shaped cheese

scamorza alla griglia [greel-ya] grilled soft cheese

scampi crayfish, scampi

scarola type of endive

schiacciata toscana [skee-achata] bread with fresh oil and rosemary

scorfano scorpion fish

scorpena [skorpayna] scorpion fish

scorzonera al burro [skortzonaira] type of root cooked in butter

secondi (piatti) [p-yat-tee] main courses, second courses

sedano [saydano] celery

sedano di Verona Veronese celery

sella di cervo [chairvo] rump

of venison

selvaggina [selvaj-**jee**na] game

semifreddo ice cream and sponge dessert

senape [**se**napay] mustard

seppie in umido [**sep**-yay] stewed cuttlefish

sfogliata agli spinaci [sfol-**y**ata a-yee speen**a**chee] flaky pastry with spinach filling

sfogliata al salmone [sal-**mo**nay] flaky pastry with salmon filling

sofficini al formaggio [sof-feech**ee**nee al form**a**j-jo] Findus® crispy pancakes with cheese filling

sogliola [**sol**-yola] sole

sogliola alla mugnaia [moon-**y**a-ya] sole cooked in flour and butter

sorbetto sorbet; soft ice cream

sottaceti [sot-tach**ay**tee] pickles

soufflé al formaggio [form**a**j-jo] cheese soufflé

soufflé al prosciutto [pro-**sh**oot-to] ham soufflé

spaghetti alla carbonara spaghetti with egg, cheese and diced bacon sauce

spaghetti alla marinara spaghetti with seafood

spaghetti all'amatriciana [amatree-**cha**na] spaghetti with bacon, onions and tomato sauce

spaghetti alla puttanesca spaghetti with anchovies, capers and black olives in tomato sauce

spaghetti all'arrabbiata [al-lar-rab-**y**ata] spaghetti with tomato and chilli sauce

spaghetti alle noci [**no**chee] spaghetti with fresh cream, grated nuts and cheese

spaghetti alle vongole [**vo**ngolay] spaghetti with clams

spaghetti al nero di seppia [**na**iro dee **sep**-ya] black spaghetti flavoured with cuttlefish ink

spaghetti al pesto spaghetti in crushed basil, garlic, oil and Parmesan dressing

spaghetti al ragù spaghetti with minced beef and tomato sauce

spalla di maiale al forno [my-**a**lay] shoulder of roast pork

speck type of dry-cured, smoked ham

spezie [spa**y**tz-yay] spices

spezzatino di vitello [spetzat**ee**no] veal stew

spiedini [sp-yayd**ee**nee] small pieces of a variety of meat or fish roasted on a spit

spiedo: allo spiedo [sp-y**ay**do] on a spit

spigola sea bass

spinaci [speen**a**chee] spinach

spinaci all'agro spinach with oil and lemon

spuma di salmone [sp**oo**ma dee

salmonay] salmon mousse

spuntino snack

stoccafisso dried cod

stracchino [strak-**kee**no] soft cheese from Lombardy

stracchino alle fragole [al-lay **fra**golay] dessert of strawberries and whipped cream liquidized and frozen

stracciatella [stracha-**tel**-la] vanilla ice cream with chocolate chips; beaten eggs cooked in boiling, clear broth

strangolapreti [strangolap**ray**tee] little spinach and potato balls

strozzapreti al basilico e pomodoro [strotzap**ray**tee al ba**zee**leeko ay] small dumplings with tomato and basil

strudel di mele [**may**lay] apple strudel

stufato stewed

stufato con verdure [vaird**oo**ray] meat stewed with vegetables and herbs

sugo al tonno tomato sauce with garlic, tuna and parsley

svizzera [zv**eet**zaira] hamburger

tacchino [tak-**kee**no] turkey

tagliata [tal-**ya**ta] finely-cut beef fillet

tagliatelle [tal-yat**el**-lay] thin, flat strips of egg pasta

tagliatelle alla bolognese [bolon-**yay**zay] tagliatelle with

minced beef and tomato sauce

tagliatelle al ragù tagliatelle with minced beef and tomato sauce

tagliatelle rosse [**ros**-say] tagliatelle with chopped red peppers

tagliatelle verdi [**vair**dee] tagliatelle with chopped spinach

taglierini al tartufo [tal-yair**ee**nee] very thin pasta strips with truffles

taglierini gratinati thin pasta strips au gratin

tagliolini [tal-yol**ee**nee] thin, soup noodles

tagliolini verdi panna e prosciutto [**vair**dee – ay prosh**oo**t-to] thin green noodles with cream and ham sauce

taleggio [tal**ej**-jo] full-fat, semi-mature, mild, soft cheese from Northern Italy

tartine [tart**ee**nay] canapés

tartufo round ice cream sprinkled with cocoa and chocolate powder; truffle (edible fungi)

tavola calda snack bar serving hot dishes

testina di vitello head of small calf

timballo di riso alla finanziera [fee-nantz-**yai**ra] type of rice pie filled with chicken entrails and crests

timo thyme

tiramisù dessert made of coffee-soaked sponge, eggs, Marsala wine, mascarpone cheese and cocoa powder

toast [tost] toasted sandwich

tomini sott'olio [sot-tol-yo] cheese with pepper marinated in oil and herbs

tonno tuna fish

torrone [tor-ronay] nougat

torta cake; tart; flan

torta della nonna tart with cream and pine nuts

torta di mele [maylay] apple tart

torta di noci [nochee] walnut tart

torta di ricotta type of cheesecake

torta gelato [jelato] ice-cream tart

torta lorenese [lorenayzay] quiche lorraine

torta pasqualina [paskwaleena] flaky pastry with spinach, cheese, ham and hard-boiled eggs

tortelli home-made ravioli filled with ricotta and spinach

tortelli di patate [patatay] home-made ravioli filled with mashed potato and nutmeg

tortellini small pasta filled with pork loin, ham, Parmesan and nutmeg

tortellini al ragù tortellini with minced beef and tomato sauce

tortelloni di magro pasta filled with cheese, parsley and vegetables

tortelloni di ricotta pasta filled with cheese, parsley and vegetables

tortino di asparagi [asparajee] asparagus pie

tortino di patate [patatay] potato pie

tournedos [toornaydo] round, thick slice of beef fillet

tramezzino [tramedzeeno] sandwich

trancio di coda di rospo [trancho] angler fish cutlet

trancio di palombo smooth hound slice (fish)

trancio di pesce spada [peshay] swordfish steak

trenette col pesto [trenet-tay] type of flat spaghetti with crushed basil, garlic, oil and cheese sauce

triglia [treel-ya] mullet

trippa tripe

trota trout

uccelletti [oochel-let-tee] small birds wrapped in bacon on cocktail sticks

umido stewed

uova [wova] eggs

uova affogate [af-fogatay] poached eggs

uova all'occhio di bue [ok-yo dee boo-ay] fried eggs

uova al tegamino con

pancetta [panch**e**t-ta] eggs and bacon

uova farcite [farch**ee**tay] eggs stuffed with tuna, capers and mayonnaise

uova in camicia [kam**ee**cha] poached eggs

uova in cocotte [kok**o**t] eggs cooked in a cast-iron pan

uova strapazzate [strapatz**a**tay] scrambled eggs

uovo [**wo**vo] egg

uovo alla coque [kok] boiled egg

uovo sodo hard-boiled egg

uva grapes

uva bianca white grapes

uva nera [n**ai**ra] black grapes

valigette verdi al gorgonzola [valeej**e**t-tay v**ai**rdee] large green ravioli filled with gorgonzola cheese

vaniglia [van**ee**l-ya] vanilla

vellutata di piselli creamed peas with egg yolks

vellutata al pomodoro cream of tomato soup with fresh cream

vellutata di asparagi [asp**a**rajee] creamed asparagus with egg yolks .

veneziana [venetz-y**a**na] type of small panettone cake sprinkled with sugar

verdura [vaird**oo**ra] vegetables

verdura di stagione [staj**o**nay] seasonal vegetables

verdure fresche di stagione [vaird**oo**ray fr**e**skay] seasonal vegetables

vermicelli [vairmeech**e**l-lee] pasta thinner than spaghetti

vitello veal

vitello tonnato sliced veal in blended tuna, anchovy, oil and lemon sauce

vol-au-vent alla crema di formaggio [kr**ay**ma dee form**a**j-jo] cream cheese vol-au-vent

vongole [**vo**ngolay] clams

würstel [**voo**rstel] frankfurter

zabaglione/zabaione [tzabal-y**o**nay] dessert made from beaten eggs, sugar and Marsala

zafferano [tzaf-fair**a**no] saffron

zampone con lenticchie [tzamp**o**nay kon lent**ee**k-yay] stuffed pig's trotters with lentils

zucca [tz**oo**k-ka] pumpkin

zucchero [tz**oo**k-kairo] sugar

zucchine [tzook-k**ee**nay] courgettes

zucchine al pomodoro chopped courgettes in tomato, garlic and parsley sauce

zuccotto [tzook-k**o**t-to] ice-cream cake with sponge, fresh cream and chocolate

zuppa [tz**oo**p-pa] soup

zuppa inglese [eengl**ay**zay] trifle

zuppa pavese [pav**ay**zay] soup with home-made bread, grated cheese and an egg

Menu Reader
Drink

acqua [akwa] water

acqua minerale [meenairalay] mineral water

acqua minerale gassata sparkling mineral water

acqua minerale non gassata still mineral water

acqua naturale [natooralay] still mineral water

acqua tonica tonic water

alcol alcohol

alcolici [alkoleechee] alcoholic drinks

Amaretto liqueur made from apricot kernels, giving it a strong almond-type flavour

amaro dark, bitter, herbal digestive liqueur

analcolici [analkoleechee] non-alcoholic drinks

aperitivo aperitif

aranciata [aranchata] orangeade

Asti Spumante [spoomantay] sparkling sweet white wine from Asti in Piedmont

Barbaresco dry red wine, typical of the Piedmont region

Barbera [barbaira] dark dry red wine from Piedmont

Bardolino dry red wine from area around Verona

Bardolino secco dry red wine from the Veneto region

Barolo dark dry red wine from Piedmont

bevande drinks

bianco [b-yanko] white

Bianco dei Castelli secco dry white wine from Lazio

bibita analcolica soft drink

birra [beer-ra] beer

birra alla spina draught beer

birra chiara [k-yara] amber-coloured light beer, lager

birra grande [granday] large beer (40 cl, approx. 1 pint)

birra in bottiglia [bot-teel-ya] bottled beer

birra media [mayd-ya] medium beer (30 cl)

birra piccola small beer (20cl, approx. 1/2 pint)

birra rossa darker, maltier beer

birra scura [skoora] beer similar to bitter, darker than birra rossa

bitter bitter-tasting red or orange alcoholic aperitif

Brachetto [braket-to] sweet sparkling red wine from Marche or Acqui, Piedmont

Brunello di Montalcino [montalcheeno] expensive dry red wine, from Montalcino, Tuscany

Cabernet [kabairnay] dry red wine from Veneto

cacao [kaka-o] cocoa

caffè [kaf-fay] coffee(s); café(s)

caffè corretto espresso coffee with a dash of liqueur or spirit

caffellatte [kaf-fel-lat-tay] half espresso, half milk

caffè lungo weak black coffee

caffè macchiato [mak-yato]
espresso coffee with a dash
of milk

caffè ristretto extra-strong
espresso coffee

caffè solubile [soloobeelay]
instant coffee

camomilla camomile tea

cappuccino [kap-poocheeno]
espresso coffee with
foaming milk, sprinkled
with cocoa/chocolate
powder

Cartizze [karteetz-zay] sparkling
dry white wine from Veneto

Chianti [k-yantee] dark red
Tuscan wine

china [keena] liqueur made
from chinchona bark

chinotto [keenot-to] sparkling,
dark soft drink

cioccolata calda [chok-kolata]
hot chocolate

Cirò [cheero] slightly sweet,
delicate red, rosé or white
wine

Coca Cola® Coke®

Cortese [kortayzay] dry
Piedmontese wine

Corvo di Salaparuta dry
Sicilian red wine

cubetto di ghiaccio [g-yacho]
ice cube

degustazione (di vini)
[degoostatz-yonay] wine tasting

denominazione di origine
controllata mark
guaranteeing the quality of
a wine

digestivo [deejesteevo]
digestive liqueur

D.O.C. (Denominazione di
Origine Controllata) certifies
the origin of a wine

D.O.C.G. (Denominazione di
Origine Controllata e
Garantita) guarantees the
quality of a wine

Dolcetto [dolchet-to] dry red
wine from Piedmont area

espresso strong black coffee

Est-Est-Est dry or sweet
white wine from around
Montefiascone area in Lazio

frappé [frap-pay] whisked
milkshake or fruit drink
with crushed ice

frappé al cioccolato [chok-
kolato] chocolate milkshake
with crushed ice

frappé alla banana banana
milkshake with crushed ice

frappé alla fragola strawberry
milkshake with crushed ice

Frascati dry white wine from
area around Rome

Freisa [frayza] dry red wine
from Piedmont region

frizzante [freedzantay] fizzy

frullato di frutta milkshake
with fruit and crushed ice

gazzosa [gatz-zoza] clear
lemonade

ghiaccio [g-yacho] ice

granita drink with crushed
ice

granita di caffè [kaf-fay] coffee
granita

granita di caffè con panna coffee and fresh cream granita

granita di limone [leem**o**nay] lemon granita

grappa very strong, clear spirit distilled from grape husks

Grignolino [green-yol**ee**no] dry red wine, light in colour

Grumello dry, red wine with slight strawberry flavour

Inferno dry red wine from Lombardy

Lambrusco sweet red or white sparkling wine from Emilia Romagna area

latte [**lat**-tay] milk

latte macchiato con cioccolato [mak-y**a**to kon chok-kol**a**to] foaming milk with a sprinkling of cocoa or chocolate powder

Lemonsoda® sparkling lemon drink

limonata lemonade; lemon juice

liquore [leekw**o**ray] liqueur

lista dei vini [day] wine list

Malvasia [malvaz**ee**-a] dry white wine, sometimes slightly sparkling, from Sardinia or Friuli

Marsala thick, very sweet wine similar to sherry

Merlot [mairl**o**] very dark red wine with slightly herby flavour, of French origin

Moscato sweet, sparkling

fruity wine

Nebbiolo [neb-y**o**lo] dry red wine from Piedmont region

Oransoda® sparkling orange drink

Orvieto [orvee-**ay**to] crisp white wine, usually dry

Pinot [p**ee**no] light, dry white wine from the north

Pinot bianco [b-y**a**nko] dry slightly sparkling white wine from the north

Pinot grigio [gr**ee**jo] dry white wine from the north

Pinot nero [**nai**ro] dry red wine from the north

porto port

prodotto e imbottigliato da... produced and bottled by ...

Prosecco sparkling or still white wine from Veneto, can be either sweet or dry

Recioto [rech**o**to] sweet sparkling red wine from Veneto

Refosco dry red wine from Friuli

Riesling [**ree**zling] dry white wine form various Northern regions

rosatello [rozat**el**-lo] dry rosé wine

rosato [roz**a**to] dry rosé wine

rosé [roz**ay**] rosé wine

rosso red

Sambuca (con la mosca) aniseed-flavoured liqueur (served with a coffee bean in the glass)

Sangiovese [sanjov**ay**zay] heavy, dry red wine

Sassella dry, delicate red wine from Vatellina area

Sauvignon [soveen-**yon**] dry white wine from Veneto

sidro cider

Soave [so-**a**vay] light, dry white wine from region around Lake Garda

spremuta d'arancia [d**aran**cha] freshly squeezed orange juice

spremuta di limone [leem**o**nay] freshly squeezed lemon juice

spumante [spoom**a**ntay] sparkling wine, like champagne

Strega® [str**ay**ga] sweet liqueur made from a secret recipe

succo [s**oo**k-ko] juice

succo d'arancia [d**aran**cha] orange juice

succo di albicocca apricot juice

succo di pera pear juice

succo di pesca peach juice

succo di pompelmo grapefruit juice

tè [tay] tea

tè al latte [**lat**-tay] tea with milk

tè al limone [leem**o**nay] lemon tea

Terlano dry white wine from area around Bolzano

Tocai [tok-**a**-ee] dry white wine from Veneto and Friuli

Valpolicella [valpoleech**el**-la] dry red wine from Veneto region

Verdicchio [vaird**ee**k-yo] dry white fruity wine from Marche

Vermentino dry wine from Liguria and Sardinia

Vernaccia di S. Gimignano [vairn**a**cha dee san jeemeen-**ya**no] dry white wine from Tuscany

vino wine

vino bianco [b-**ya**nko] white wine

vino da dessert [des-**sair**] dessert wine

vino da pasto table wine

vino da tavola table wine

vino della casa house wine

Vino Nobile di Montepulciano [n**o**beelay dee montepoolch**a**no] high-class Tuscan red wine

vino rosato [roz**a**to] rosé wine

vino rosé [roz**ay**] rosé wine

vino rosso red wine

Vin Santo type of dessert wine from Tuscany